To Karley,
See you at The
Premiere!
Love from Your Gran.

# THE
# RIVERKEEPERS

*Two Activists Fight
to Reclaim Our Environment
as a Basic Human Right*

JOHN CRONIN
AND
ROBERT F. KENNEDY, JR.

A Touchstone Book
*Published by Simon & Schuster*

*We dedicate this book with love and respect to our wives,*
*Constance Hough and Mary Richardson,*
*and our children,*
*Sasha, John Donald, Bobby, Kick, Conor, Kyra, and Finbar*

🐦

TOUCHSTONE
Rockefeller Center
1230 Avenue of the Americas
New York, NY 10020

First Touchstone Edition 1999

TOUCHSTONE and colophon are registered trademarks of Simon & Schuster Inc.
Riverkeeper is a registered trademark of Riverkeeper, Inc.
Designed by Erich Hobbing
Set in Bembo

Manufactured in the United States of America

3   5   7   9   10   8   6   4

The Library of Congress has cataloged the Scribner edition as follows:
Cronin, John, date.
The riverkeepers: two activists fight to reclaim our
environment as a basic human right / John Cronin
and Robert F. Kennedy, Jr.
p.   cm.
Includes index.
1. Environmentalism—United States. 2. Environmental
policy—United States. 3. Hudson River Valley
(N.Y. and N.J.)—Environmental conditions.
4. Environmentalists—United States.
I. Kennedy, Robert Francis, date. II. Title.
GE197.C76   1997
363.7'00973—dc21   97-13371
CIP

ISBN 0-684-83908-3
0-684-84625-X (Pbk)

# Acknowledgments

We are grateful to an extraordinary group of people whose inspiration, leadership, and labor have guided us for far longer than the many months spent writing this book.

It is our good fortune to have the daily counsel of two environmental pioneers whose surrogate wisdom and experience are too often mistaken for our own: John Adams, executive director of the Natural Resources Defense Council and founding board member of Riverkeeper, Inc., who understands that community activism is the foundation of the environmental movement and that the benefits of global battles are best measured at home; and Robert H. Boyle, author and founding president of Riverkeeper, Inc., who believes that you can change the world from your own backyard.

We have enjoyed the advice and partnership of Karl Coplan of the Pace Environmental Litigation Clinic, Greg Wetstone of the NRDC, Michael Oppenheimer of the Environmental Defense Fund, Chris Meyer of the New York Public Interest Group, and David Gordon and Theresa Hanczor of Riverkeeper, Inc.—all working advocates who deserve more public recognition than we can provide.

This book would not have been possible without the keen investigative skills of our chief researcher Kevin Madonna, whose efforts on our behalf knew neither clock nor calendar. We are thankful for the research assistance of Mark Naud and Lori Caramanian, the keyboard wizardry of Lori Morash, and the dedication and talent of Connie Hough, Mary Beth Postman, and Deborah Vargulick.

Some individuals and organizations went beyond the call of duty to provide us with invaluable information and assistance—in particular: Allison Daly and Daniel Barry of Clearinghouse on Environmental

Advocacy and Research; the Center for Responsible Politics; the Institute for First Amendment Studies; Tarso Ramos of the Western States Center; and John C. Stauber of PR Watch.

For steadfast faith and support during even the strangest of our cases, we thank Richard Ottinger, dean of the Pace University School of Law; Steve Solow, former codirector of the Pace Environmental Litigation Clinic; Nicholas Robinson of the Pace Center for Environmental Legal Studies; Faith Colangelo, criminal defense attorney extraordinaire; Dr. Bruce Bell, Matt Carter, Ralph Huddleston, and Patrick O'Malley of Carpenter Environmental Associates; and the staff and interns of Riverkeeper, Inc., the Pace Clinic, and the NRDC.

There should be a special place in heaven for our editors, Nan Graham and Gillian Blake, whose patience and editing skills we tested regularly. Kris Dahl at ICM has been more than our agent, she has been the glue that has held this project together from the start.

Perhaps the greatest contribution to this book was made by our families, who endured our physical and mental absences with love and grace.

Bobby owes special thanks to Augustine and Kateri Tekakwitha for inspiration and guidance.

Finally, each day we are reminded of the personal sacrifice and courage of those who blazed the trails we are now privileged to walk. We will always be indebted to Tom Whyatt, the first Hudson Riverkeeper, Pete Seeger, Fred Danback, and the late Dr. R. Ian Fletcher, whose single-minded dedication to truth was an environmentalist's best friend.

# Contents

# Preface

The title of this book refers to many people: the handful of fishermen who used a seventy-year-old navigation law to fight some of the nation's most notorious polluters in the 1960s, the millions of everyday people who took to the streets on Earth Day 1970 to demand protection of the nation's water, air, and land, the thousands of grassroots groups who stopped the 104th Congress from eviscerating the Clean Water Act and the rest of the nation's environmental laws. They shared a common belief in their fundamental right to protect themselves and their communities from the threat of pollution and environmental abuse. This book is about that right. Every polluting factory, landfill, and toxic dump is located in someone's neighborhood. Those who live nearby pay with their health, their property values, their jobs, and their quality of life. If you are concerned about the water that your family drinks, or whether your children can swim and fish where you once did, or what may be buried in your local landfill, you are like tens of millions in thousands of communities who have the same concerns.

The front line in the battle to save the American environment is occupied by ordinary people taking on extraordinary odds to defend those communities. Our community is New York's Hudson River Valley. Its story is like the story of waterways all across America where local people became sick and tired of the condition of their local environment. But what distinguishes the Hudson River is that the people here began their fight more than thirty years ago. At first they were spurred on by anger—at the sewage, oil, and chemicals ravaging the river that was a source of their recreation, livelihood, even peace of mind. Soon their anger gave way to an understanding that they had to fight for their river as if it were part of their neighborhood, as if it were home. On behalf of their community they challenged a status quo that said all was expendable in the name of business and profit. And they changed the destiny of a major American river.

What they accomplished through sheer will and perseverance is now a legacy for a new generation of activists throughout the nation. What they believed intuitively about their right to defend their community has proven to be upheld by ancient legal doctrines, dating back to the Code of Justinian, that are the foundation of modern American democracy.

Every locale has stories to tell the world. The story we have chosen to tell here is how-to. How to use these ancient rights to fight your local polluter and make it pay for abusing your community. How to spot the phony organizations, greenwashing, and junk science that anti-environmental forces are foisting on an unwitting public. How to fight the members of Congress who with their hired guns in public relations firms and ad agencies are trying to convince you that saving your local river is anti-American.

We will introduce you to heroes who could have come from your hometown and issues that could happen in your own backyard, if they are not happening there already. Though much of this book is taken from where we live, it is not about a particular river. It is about a people defending the place in which they live. It is about how they did it and your right to do the same.

We welcome you to join the battle.

—JOHN CRONIN and ROBERT F. KENNEDY, JR.

# Foreword

America's waterways have always been a vital force providing opportunities for commerce, routes for exploration, inspiration of ideas, means of recreation, sources of drinking water and creating much of the natural beauty that helps define our national identity. Perhaps most importantly, our waters seamlessly connect our citizens, our land, and our communities to one another.

Throughout our history, the path to prosperity has been plied down America's waterways. Rivers carried explorers West; powered the nation's first industrial mills in New England; and fed America's early major ports on the East Coast, the Ohio River, and the great Mississippi.

But as our nation grew and our economy became industrialized, we began to turn our backs on our waterways, in many cases treating them more as dumping grounds than as national treasures. Nowhere was this more prevalent than on the Hudson River, which by the 1960s had become severely polluted—so polluted that some considered it to be dead.

Determined not to leave a legacy of pollution and abandonment, a small group of citizens living on the Hudson developed a strategy to clean up the river. They embraced an environmentalism that said that we are each invested in our local environment. They fought to protect the Hudson not only for nature's sake but for the values that nature represented to them—its ability to enrich them and their communities economically, spiritually, and culturally.

This early activism was epitomized by a group of commercial and recreational fishermen known as the Hudson River Fishermen's Association. The group worked to dramatize the plight of the Hudson, pro-

11

viding fellow citizens with a firsthand look at the neglect and pollution of the river, spurring the community to act. Through vigilance and aggressive application of our national environmental laws, the HRFA's effort began to succeed, with the river steadily improving and their work producing seminal case law that communities across America have used to protect their own local ecosystems.

Citizens on the Hudson issued a clarion call that waterways across the nation were in jeopardy. Americans responded, as we always do to a national crisis, with strong determination to make things right. The country rallied around its natural heritage and Congress enacted a comprehensive body of law to protect our waters, highlighted by passage of the National Environmental Policy Act (NEPA) in 1970, the Clean Water Act in 1972, and the Safe Drinking Water Act in 1974. Through a combination of community activism and federal environmental law, Americans began to reconnect to their waterways and reengage in their communities.

Today, after years of court cases and community activism and with the cooperation and support from a broader coalition of proud neighbors of the river, the Hudson is beginning to recover. The water is cleaner, the fish are returning, and those responsible for polluting the river are being held accountable for their actions and occasionally joining efforts to restore the river. The Hudson has shown a remarkable resilience in bouncing back from the years of neglect, and the citizens living in the watershed have found that in their efforts to restore the river they are improving their overall quality of life as well.

*The Riverkeepers* is the kind of personal account America needs to hear more often. It is a firsthand look by two accomplished environmental veterans, Robert F. Kennedy, Jr., and John Cronin, at the tragedy and elation that average citizens experience every day as they engage in the struggle to protect their waterways. It is as much about the environmental ties that bind communities together as it is about the battles they engage in.

Those whose object is a sustainable future will recognize the importance of rivers to our environment, economy, heritage, culture, and communities. The example set by the citizens living on the Hudson River and the thousands of Americans who cherish their own waterways will be a continuing inspiration.

In a profound sense, our rivers are a part of our national commons—a meeting ground where Americans from all walks of life gather to trade, reflect, rejoice, and restore. As we move into the twenty-first century with a renewed sense of stewardship and appreciation for our rivers, we must carry that spirit with us.

—VICE PRESIDENT AL GORE

# THE
# RIVERKEEPERS

# CHAPTER 1

# Battleground

*In the field, Hastings-on-Hudson, March 1994:* The thick odor of rot and decay filled our nostrils as we entered the dim light of Building 15. To our left, a load-bearing wall was buckling. Forty feet above, the roof was in a state of collapse. We trod lightly, fearing our footfalls could send the entire sixty-thousand-square-foot brick-and-steel structure crashing into a heap.

We were investigating a complaint by local residents that Building 15 was polluting the Hudson, that foul liquid and smells were emanating from it and garbage was flying out the windows. Once the operations center of the wire and cable division of the Anaconda Company, a notorious international polluter, Building 15 was part of the company's turn-of-the-century factory compound located on the Hudson River, one of twenty similarly dilapidated structures that marked the industry's graveyard like giant tombstones.

We climbed through an opening and found nearly 180,000 cubic yards of garbage filling the structure, reaching a height of three stories and covering an area the size of two football fields.

Hundreds of tons of garbage were pushing down walls and pouring through the ten-foot-high windows into the Hudson River—oil drums, car parts, roof shingles, insulation, tons of broken asphalt and concrete, thousands of tires, and all kinds of domestic wastes. At the bottom of the pile a putrid ooze leaked through floor drains that emptied directly into the river.

Back outside we examined the north side of the building. Plastic tarpaulins that had been fastened to window frames in an attempt to stem the spill of garbage gave the structure the appearance of an inflated cartoon building ready to pop. On the west side, facing the river, the sun's ultraviolet rays had broken down the polyethylene of the tarps. Tattered shreds fluttered in the breeze while landslides of garbage cascaded from the glassless window like icebergs breaking off a slow-moving glacier. Where the base of the building met the water, the river's shallows were littered with metal, plastic, tires, and other trash.

The property around Building 15 resembled London after the blitz. We walked through rubble-strewn factory yards, past tumble-down buildings, and around the rusting skeletons of trucks and automobiles and rotting fifty-five-gallon drums. Everywhere, heaped mounds of rotting refuse provided forage for rats, raccoons, stray cats, and dogs. Four twenty-foot-high tanks of questionable durability and long-forgotten contents made a foreboding silhouette against the sky.

But the site's invisible wastes were our greatest concern. We had already learned from recent studies that beneath our feet the ground and water were contaminated with petrochemicals, heavy metals, solvents, polychlorinated biphenyls (PCBs), and asbestos—the result of decades of spills, discharges, and on-site disposal of wastes by the Anaconda Company.

Promising Hastings' city fathers that their factory would "help maintain a high standard of living in the community," Anaconda had delivered three decades of pollution-based prosperity and turned twenty-six acres of prime river real estate into a toxic Armageddon. Land that should have been the centerpiece of community life and economic vitality was transformed by avarice and short-term thinking into a stinking, oozing dump, fenced from the public, mired in tax arrears, a pillaged battlescape reaping silent revenge on the community that had believed Anaconda's promises. Clouds of toxic particles rained from spontaneous landfill fires; subterranean waves of leaching poisons threatened community groundwater; and gaping holes in the fencing enclosure beckoned Hastings' children to play in the deadly structures. Disgusted, we walked toward the river's edge to occupy our senses otherwise.

Toxic landmarks like the Anaconda dump are not unique to the Hudson Valley. Every American community boasts its own monuments to short-term planning. While the Hudson is cursed with more that its share, it was blessed since the early 1960s with an activist community that engaged polluters with an intensity and ingenuity that made the Hudson the most critical legal battleground of the modern environmental era. Its brand of aggressive and litigious environmentalism saved the river, and its victories generated a wealth of environmental jurisprudence that communities across America now use to protect their own public resources.

The organization for which we work, Riverkeeper, played an important role in that history. The organization appointed John Cronin as its Hudson Riverkeeper in 1983 and Robert F. Kennedy, Jr., began working as its chief prosecuting attorney a year later.

Riverkeeper was created by a blue-collar association of commercial and recreational fishermen that first coalesced in 1966 to track down Hudson River polluters and bring them to justice. From the outset, the organization's philosophy was rooted in a sense of public ownership of local water bodies. Its approach was to use law and science to confront polluters and reassert community control over waters that were injured by pollution or coveted by developers.

In the decade that preceded our tour of the Anaconda site, the two of us had investigated and prosecuted environmental abuses and abusers of every stripe—midnight dumpers, hazardous-waste sites, landfills, oil tankers, sewage treatment plants, factories, prisons, and power plants. We scaled fences, reconnoitered underground tunnels, and slogged through mud and sludge amassing evidence; videotaping, collecting, and analyzing samples. We had filed close to one hundred lawsuits and brought over one hundred polluters to justice, forcing them to spend close to half a billion dollars on the Hudson.

We created a law clinic at Pace University Law School, where ten students and two professors did nothing but prosecute Hudson River polluters—as many as forty at a time. From small-claims court to the federal court of appeals we challenged oil companies, power utilities, factories, towns, cities, and government agencies that threatened drinking water, commercial and recreational fisheries, endangered species, fish and wildlife habitats, and property values. We tried cases in every court in New York and helped orchestrate a watershed agreement that garnered $1.5 billion from New York City to buy land and otherwise restore and protect the Catskill and Westchester streams that feed the Hudson.

Because of the work of Riverkeeper and other Hudson River groups, the Hudson, condemned as an open sewer in the 1960s, today is regarded as one of the richest water bodies on earth, producing more fish per acre and more biomass per gallon than any of the other major estuaries in the North Atlantic. In the Hudson River Estuary Management Act of 1985, the New York State legislature declared that the Hudson had become one of the only estuaries on the east coast of the United States to "still retain strong spawning stocks of its historical fish species." Everett Nack, a commercial fisherman from Claverack, New York, says that American shad seeking out their spawning grounds in the freshwater reaches of the river are virtually bumping their heads on the federal dam at Troy, the headwaters of the 154-mile tidal portion of the river. That was not always the case. Twenty miles below the dam the river was once so badly polluted that oxygen levels dropped to zero.

Hudson River environmentalism has become a national model for ecosystem protection. Twenty other Keepers are working on waterways from Cook Inlet in Alaska to Casco Bay in Maine—from the Chattahoochee and Cape Fear to Santa Monica and San Francisco Bays, from Puget Sound to Long Island Sound.

We hope that *The Riverkeepers* will serve as a manual for new members of the Keeper movement—a primer for the philosophy and methods that have made the Riverkeepers' brand of environmentalism so successful. We hope that Keepers will patrol each river, stream, sound, bay, inlet, and estuary in America, protecting them from injury and abuse on behalf of the local community.

Like every locale, the Hudson Valley has stories to tell the world. Its landscapes record great tales of victory and defeat, abuse and recovery—and smaller tales too. But this book is not about a particular river. It is about a people defending the place in which they live. It is about their, and your, right to do so.

The decaying waterfront at our backs stood in sharp contrast to the natural beauty of the estuary before us. Across the river, the Palisades' red cliffs rose from the western shore. To our south the river ran the last leg of a long journey that began in a two-acre wilderness pond on the highest peak in New York and ended in the Atlantic Ocean in the shadow of New York City's spectacular skyscrapers.

The Hudson is small compared to the other great American rivers, only 315 miles from its source at Lake Tear of the Clouds in the Adirondacks to the Battery at the southern tip of Manhattan, but its geological diversity is unmatched in North America. It drains precipitation from three mountain ranges, the Berkshires, the Adirondacks, and the Catskills. Forty miles north of the city, its path through the fairy-tale peaks of the Hudson Highlands forms what *Life* magazine called "one of the grandest passages of river scenery in the world." The great German traveler Baedeker swore that the river views in the stretch between Storm King and Dundenberg Peak were "finer than the Rhine."

Eighteen miles south from where we stood, the Atlantic Ocean sloshed in and out of the Hudson's mouth driving the tide north past Albany, along the vertically undulating river bottom, which lies below sea level. The lower 150 miles of the Hudson from the federal lock and dam at Troy is not a river but a tidal estuary where freshwater fishes such as trout, pike, and bass mix with seals, dolphins, sea horses, bluefish, sharks, and occasionally even whales. For vast schools of migratory shad, sturgeon, herring, alewives, blue crab, mackerel, menhaden, and striped bass, the Hudson is an unimpeded corridor from the Atlantic to their ancestral spawning grounds. Tidal action stirs the brackish broth and traps the rich stock of nutrients and minerals drained from the Hudson's 13,500-square-mile watershed, feeding the young migratory fishes and making the Hudson one of the two principal spawning grounds on the East Coast. These fishes support recreational and commercial fisheries along the Atlantic coast worth hundreds of millions of dollars and a 350-year-old commercial fishery within the Hudson.

The lofty mountains and scenic grandeur of the Hudson's tidal stem have inspired writers as diverse as Washington Irving, James Fenimore Cooper, and Herman Melville. The ranges that feed it freshwater gave birth to America's landscape architecture movement led by A. J. Downing and to the nation's defining school of art—the nineteenth-century Hudson River School. The river's mouth forms the greatest natural port in the world. Its waters and scenery are a lodestar of American invention, from James Fulton's steamboat to the Erie Canal to the engineering miracle of the New York City aqueduct system.

The Hudson is the only river that cuts through the Appalachian chain at sea level, making it the most strategic point on the East Coast of North America—economically and militarily. After construction of the Erie Canal in 1825, it became the transit route between bountiful midwestern farms and the East Coast and European markets. That commerce helped grow the city at its mouth into the greatest on earth. During the American Revolution, the Hudson was the topographical centerpiece of the British strategy to drive a wedge between the armies of New England and Virginia. The Patriots fortified the Hudson Highlands and stretched great chains across the river to foil British plans. Innumerable battles were fought on the Hudson's shores. Throughout the war, the Hudson Highlands was America's natural citadel, from which the Patriots protected the river against northward thrusts by the British Navy trying to link with Canadian-based redcoat forces on Lake Champlain and the upper Mohawk. West Point, fortified by General Washington in 1777 to foil British grand strategy, became the object of the first great scandal in American history when our best general and hero, Benedict Arnold, tried to hand the fort— and the Hudson—to the British spy Major Andre before fleeing downriver on the British warship *Vulture*.

Nearly two hundred years later, the Hudson Valley would emerge as the central battleground of the American environmental movement. Its incomparable scenery helped inspire the first wave of the American conservation movement at the turn of the century. It became the most fertile breeding ground for environmental activists in the nation— including Teddy Roosevelt, Frederick Law Olmsted, John Burroughs, E. H. Harriman, Bob Marshal, and Frederick and Fairfield Osborn— and the locus for the most heated environmental skirmishes, including the early struggles to preserve the Adirondacks and the Catskills from the lumbermen in 1892, and the Palisades and Highlands from the quarrymen in 1901. Years later, during the second wave of American environmentalism in the 1960s and 1970s, the Hudson emerged as the Mount Vernon of environmental law.

One of the central figures in that latter movement was a sportswriter and fisherman named Robert H. Boyle. Boyle is the founder of the Hudson River Fishermen's Association and the chairman of the Hudson Riverkeeper, Inc. Boyle championed a brand of environmentalism that put people first and that recognized that the value of nature is its ability to enrich humanity. His was a bare-knuckled advocacy that used science and law as weapons and pitted people directly against polluters for control of our natural resources. The Riverkeeper was Boyle's conception. The organization reflects his philosophy and personality, and he was mentor to both of us.

Boyle's 1969 book, *The Hudson River: A Natural and Unnatural His-*

*tory,* is a definitive account of the geology, biology, and human history of the river. Regarded by many as the best book ever written about a river, it quickly became a classic among nature and history readers and has gone through nearly a dozen printings. It is taught next to Rachel Carson's *Silent Spring* and alongside Aldo Leopold, John Muir, and Henry David Thoreau in college courses on America's great nature writers. Boyle is universally acknowledged to know more about the Hudson than anyone alive.

His achievements as an advocate are often overshadowed by his reputation as a writer, sports authority, fly-fisherman, and naturalist. He is revered by anglers as one of the gurus of dry-fly tying. He has written or coauthored over a dozen books on topics ranging from sports heroes to largemouth bass, fly tying to acid rain, and on cancer, global warming, and water.

Boyle is an extraordinary storyteller with a bawdy wit and a contagious laugh that has enchanted even his opponents. His encyclopedic recall allows him to speak for hours in intricate detail and gives him instant access to the Latin names of hundreds of species of Hudson River fish and crustaceans. He also remembers the names of everyone who's ever insulted the river—and most of them bear the scars of his slings.

Boyle's short neck, round bald head, compressed features, and pugnacious jaw lend him the aspect of a bulldog. When angered by a foolish bureaucrat or unrepentant polluter, he looks like Jimmy Cagney—the corners of his mouth turn down, his bottom lip pushes up, his eyes squint, and an index finger emerges from his fist as he delivers a lethal verbal blow. His Catholic-school education and journalistic training give him an absolute reverence for the truth and an intolerance for all affronts to the public trust.

From the outset, Boyle's style was combative. He provoked Consolidated Edison to cancel its advertising in a Hudson Valley paper when he compared the company in an editorial to Genghis Khan. He once slapped a giant striped bass on a congressman's desk during a hearing on the Indian Point fish kills, and he dismissed Lyndon and Lady Bird Johnson's popular American Beautification program as "rouge on a cancer patient."

The intensity of his indignation is tolerable because it is born not of cynicism but of a faith that the system is supposed to work. The immensity of his disappointment when government officials don't do as they're supposed to is commensurate with the immensity of his faith that most of them do. The contagious nature of his outrage and his sense of humor are the source of Boyle's power as a crusader. Even jaded old Republican Henry Luce was reluctantly infused with Boyle's rage. Commenting on Boyle's 1964 *Sports Illustrated* article on the declining American environment, Luce admitted that "as Boyle got madder and madder, I got madder and madder."

Boyle's gift as a writer is his burning curiosity about people. And as one might expect from an ex-marine and journalist who spent forty-two years at *Sports Illustrated,* Boyle's environmentalism is grounded in his vision that working Americans should be the centerpiece of the movement. His most crucial influence has been in conceiving the link between the environment and ordinary people. He broke the conservation tradition that saw protecting the environment as a pursuit of the wealthy, and made it a blue-collar issue of protecting ecology, communities, and livelihoods.

As early as 1964, Boyle complained in a landmark *Sports Illustrated* article that traditional conservationists were ignoring and alienating their natural allies in the "hook and bullet" groups by focusing their best energies on preserving thousands of acres of empty lands in places like Wyoming while ignoring community battles in Teaneck, Ossining, and New York City. He argued that environmentalism ought to be about enriching communities and that everyone should be involved. He spent the next three decades fighting to ensure that hunters and commercial and recreational fishermen had a space in the growing environmental movement.

Boyle himself became interested in fishing—and the fate of the Hudson—when he moved to New York in the early '60s under the auspices of *Sports Illustrated*. The first people he met on the Hudson who knew anything about it were the rivermen in Verplanck, a working-class fishing village on Haverstraw Bay forty-five miles upriver from Manhattan. Even New Yorkers are sometimes surprised to learn that the Hudson still hosts a commercial fishery, but fishing families still work the river from the George Washington Bridge north past Albany. The Hudson's commercial fishery is one of the oldest in the nation and one of the last traditional gear fisheries.

The first rivermen Bob befriended were Ace Lent and Charlie

White, partners from Verplanck Point, who together tipped the scales at five hundred pounds. With them at that time was Ace's cousin, Spitz, a sturgeon fisherman whose even wider girth and jolly red face guaranteed him winter employment as Santa Claus at the Sears Roebuck in Peekskill when the fishing was slow. Ace and Spitz Lent had left the Point only once—when they went to fight in World War II—and were happy never to leave again. They wove their giant gill nets out of tug hawsers they recovered from the river and furnished their homes with flotsam and jetsam that washed ashore on Verplanck Point. Bob's trip to the point began a friendship with the rivermen that would last their lifetimes and enrich all of them. They would teach him what they knew about the river, fish with him, and assist him in collecting specimens for aquariums and museums. During the years Boyle was inventorying the Hudson's species, the rivermen regularly brought him unusual specimens they found in their nets. Ace Lent alone uncovered three species never before reported in the Hudson.

Boyle also managed to seek out and enlist the Hudson's tiny handful of sports anglers and motley collection of aquarium enthusiasts for their information on the river. One of these was Seth Rosenbaum, a computer engineer at New York University, who had the largest private collection of fishing plugs in the world and a pet octopus that would climb to the top of its fish tank and squirt most visitors to Seth's Queens apartment. Seth usually fished the East River where he'd caught Spanish mackerel and bonita along with the usual assortment of striped bass and bluefish. During the winter he was part of a club of oddball anglers in Manhattan who fished the warm-water fishery over the Fifty-ninth Street sewer. They would drop bloodworms or plugs through the grates and, when they got lucky, pull a giant striped bass up to the metal bars for the others to admire before cutting the leader and releasing the fish. In warmer weather they would move up to Seventy-second Street where a richer blend of raw sewage brought in the large schools. Seth still speaks nostalgically about the big striper runs at Seventy-second Street that would attract up to forty anglers.

In late 1963, Boyle decided he wanted to do a piece on the river, and he began researching seriously. He learned that a game fish laboratory had just opened up near the Hudson's mouth at Sandy Hook in New Jersey, and he began spending time with its scientists. Boyle's Hudson River article ran in the August 17, 1964, issue of *Sports Illustrated*. He did a second major bonus piece on the Sandy Hook lab. While researching these pieces Boyle made discoveries about ecological mechanics that surprised most Americans at that time. Wetlands, to most Americans, were mosquito-infested swamps that ought to be reclaimed. Boyle told his readers that swamps and tidelands were valuable.

Boyle had the utmost reverence for scientists. Here was a group of people whose curiosity about the world and obsession with truth and detail was as intense and blithe as his own. Their credentials would roll off his tongue the way an epicure recites a menu. He formed lasting relationships with the nation's top aquatic and marine scientists. When he became an activist they would form an invaluable stable of experts for litigation.

It was through researching these articles for *Sports Illustrated* that Boyle's love affair with the Hudson began. Years later he had fished most of the streams that flow into the Hudson and most of the river's main stem. He has waded and seined dozens of the river's twelve hundred feeder ponds and lakes. But the reach of the Hudson that attracted him most then and today was Haverstraw Bay, the giant expanse of water that is north of Croton Point and one of the richest pieces of water on earth.

Haverstraw is the Hudson's widest stretch and the heart of its productivity. Thirty miles north of the city, the bay is three miles wide and six miles long and shallow enough to allow sunlight to reach the rooted aquatic vegetation that carpets its bottom, giving food and shelter to an extraordinary two hundred marine, aquatic, and estuarine fish species and dozens of species of invertebrates. "If I have a personal wish about the Hudson," Boyle once wrote, "it is to know [Haverstraw] bay in its entirety, to know every fish, every crab and shrimp, every bird and every plant and to mark their shifts and movements with the ebb and flow of the tide and change of season." He made the bay his Walden Pond, studying the algal blooms, seining its beaches, measuring its temperature and the depths of its channels, and fishing for stripers, bluefish, white perch, and yellow perch.

Boyle has sampled, fished, and collected on every acre of the bay from the rocky shores at the base of High Tor and the Palisades to the mudflats and Indian middens off Croton Point. He seines with a custom-made sixty-foot net that can be pulled, with effort, by two people parallel to the beach and then, after the ends are closed, dragged up the beach, funneling the catch into a bag at its center. Seining with Bob is always a blast. It's one of those magical experiences that helped hook both of us on the Hudson. Each week and day and tide yields some unexpected treasure—thousands of silver-sided minnows that Bob will gingerly gather for the sautéing pan, fifty-pound carp that will stop traffic on riverfront highways, some tiny flounder called hogchokers that tile the Hudson's muddy bottom, Johnny darters that make enchanting aquarium fish walking on the bottom, and jack crevalle and ladyfish from the Caribbean, not to mention smelt, mummichogs, blueback herring, yellow perch, crappies, common suckers, American sole, catfish, eels, tomcod, grass shrimp, prawns, sand sharks, blue crabs, goldfish, anchovies, and pipefish. Bob has become one of the primary sources for cataloging Hudson River fish, and his specimens, live or preserved, are in public aquariums and museums throughout the country.

Since the early 1960s, Bob has kept a mock-up of Haverstraw Bay in a six-foot aquarium in his living room, complete with bricks and oyster shells to faithfully reproduce the river bottom off Senasqua beach. He is perpetually experimenting with new fish that he obtains on collecting expeditions. He studies their behavior and has a story for every fish that has shared his living room. In the evening, after a few drinks, he often lies on the floor of his living room and looks up at his aquarium and pretends he's on the bottom of Haverstraw Bay.

After publishing his first Hudson River piece, Boyle filed a rapid succession of articles on the American environment and America's waterways. At one point in 1964, his editor Andre LaGere commented to Boyle, "I brought you back here to cover the Green Bay Packers but you have disappeared under the water." Boyle said, "Andre, it's much more important under water. Much more important than the Green Bay Packers."

In 1963, Bob heard that a small group of environmentalists calling themselves the Scenic Hudson Preservation Conference was mobilizing to fight a proposal by New York's principal electric utility, Consolidated Edison, to construct a pump storage facility on Storm King Mountain in the Hudson Highlands. A sugarloaf mountain that rises 1,355 feet out of the banks of the river, Storm King presents a sight so stunning that it became practically an obligatory subject for Thomas Cole and other painters of the Hudson River School.

Con Ed threatened to transform the mountain into a giant electric battery by blasting a six-billion-gallon reservoir from the rock at the summit of Storm King and dropping a forty-foot-wide pipe down its face. In the evening, as most New Yorkers slept, Con Ed would use surplus electricity to suck a million cubic feet per minute of Hudson River water through its giant pipe to fill the reservoir. In the morning, when New Yorkers turned on their lights and took their electricity-driven commuter trains, Con Ed would release the stored water back down the pipe, driving turbines and generating power that the utility could sell at peak rates. Storm King would be the largest pump storage facility in the world, costing in excess of $162 million in 1962 dollars. The company planned to desecrate the mountain by building a 240-acre storage reservoir, despoil the riverfront with an eight-hundred-foot-long powerhouse, and string ugly power lines across Westchester and Putnam Counties.

On September 26, 1962, Harland Forbes, chairman of Consolidated Edison, held a press conference to announce the project. The following day, the *New York Times* quoted Forbes as saying, "No difficulties are anticipated." Little did he know that he was picking a fight that would last seventeen years and mark the beginning of the era of modern environmental law in America.

In late 1963, Con Ed applied to the Federal Power Commission (FPC) for a license to construct Storm King. Carl Carmen, the New York State Historian, and attorney Leo Rothchild, chairman of the New York–New Jersey Trail Conference, complained about the project to Governor Nelson Rockefeller. Rockefeller suggested that if they were so concerned, they should buy the mountain. Undeterred, Carmen and Rothchild joined with Walter Boardman, president of the Nature Conservancy, and organized the Scenic Hudson Preservation Conference to oppose the project. The committee quickly found support among the well-heeled residents of the Hudson Highlands. Many of its founding members were the children and grandchildren of the Osborns, Stillmans, and Harrimans, the robber barons who had laid out great estates amid the Highlands' spectacular scenery and whose descendants had fought fiercely since the turn of the century to preserve the views for themselves and the public.

Scenic Hudson retained a lawyer, Dale Doty, and quickly intervened in Con Ed's license application hearing. Their principal objections were to the defacing of Storm King and the aesthetic injuries to Westchester and Putnam Counties from the erection of power lines.

Although witnesses for Scenic Hudson spoke eloquently about the cultural and spiritual significance of the Hudson, hearing examiner Edward Marsh recommended on July 31, 1964, to the FPC commissioners that the plant be approved, implicitly accepting Con Ed's assessment that Scenic Hudson's case was no more than "self-centered complaints" of a "few local dreamers." But the commissioners' final decision was still pending.

Three weeks later, Boyle walked into Scenic Hudson's temporary headquarters in the National Audubon Society's building on Fifth Avenue and Eighty-eighth Street to introduce himself. Boyle's article on the Hudson was running in that week's issue of *Sports Illustrated.* Boyle met with two Scenic Hudson leaders, Ben Frazier and Smokey Duggan, and congratulated them for their defense of the scenic issues. But he wanted them to know that the Hudson River in the vicinity of the Storm King plant was one of two principal spawning grounds for America's Atlantic Coast striped bass population. Boyle told them that during the course of his research he had come across a 1957 *New York Fish and Game Journal* containing a report by two state biologists named Rathjen and Miller that proved that close to 90 percent of striped bass eggs in the entire Hudson were collected in the seven-and-a-half-mile stretch between Highland Falls and Dennings Point where Storm King is situated. "The striped bass spawn here," Boyle said, "and it's a very important area for larvae and plankton, and the pump storage plant will suck up the eggs and young." Duggan recognized that this was the issue that could win the case. She rose with a gleeful smile and proclaimed, "They're going to kill the fish! They're going to kill the fish!" She was so excited, recalls Boyle, "It was like Churchill hearing Pearl Harbor had been bombed."

However, when Scenic Hudson petitioned the commission to reopen the record to include Boyle's information, the request was denied. During the initial hearing the only testimony about fish life had been made by Con Ed's witness, Dr. Alfred Perlmutter, a marine biology professor at New York University and former employee of the New York State Conservation Department, who swore that he could "almost guarantee" that the Storm King project would have "little effect" on fish life. He testified that "the last study on the Hudson River was made in 1938" and "it hadn't been done since." This study, Perlmutter said, proved that the premier spawning grounds for striped bass were "much farther upriver."

Boyle was aghast at Perlmutter's testimony, since it conflicted directly with virtually all the important conclusions of Rathjen and Miller's 1957 report. Boyle noted that their study had been commissioned by the New York State Conservation Department *while* Perlmutter had also been employed there. Boyle tracked down first Rathjen in Alaska and then Miller, who both assured him that Perlmutter was not only fully aware of their study, but had in fact hired them to conduct it. Bob did a *Sports Illustrated* piece on Perlmutter entitled "Hardly a Memory Expert," which was the first of many articles Boyle would publish on the Storm King battle.

Boyle then came across two Long Island Sound fishermen with hard evidence on the potential hazards of the Storm King project. One was Art Glowka, an Eastern Airlines pilot who had published an article on striped bass fishing in the Hudson for *Outdoor Life*. The other was Dominick Pirone, consulting biologist for the Long Island League of Salt Water Sportsmen. On June 12, 1963, Pirone and Glowka had visited Con Ed's Indian Point power plant a few miles downstream of Storm King. Indian Point's daily withdrawal of hundreds of millions of gallons of Hudson River water to cool its reactors made it an excellent laboratory for predicting the impact that the proposed Storm King withdrawals would impose on the Hudson's fish. Pirone and Glowka found ten thousand dead fish killed on screens erected to keep debris from fouling the intake pipes. Other fishermen had complained about Indian Point fish kills. Pirone himself had been shown photos in which dead stripers were piled twelve feet high at a Con Ed dump. When Boyle went to look for the photos, they were gone. He learned that the photos had all been gathered and suppressed by government officials. The Conservation Department's official position was that the kills didn't exist. Despite the state's denials, Boyle felt that Con Ed's fish kills at Indian Point raised even graver doubts about the vast water withdrawals the company was now proposing at Storm King.

Bob was intent on making the dead fish stench at Indian Point stick to Storm King. He prepared to testify at the upcoming state legislative hearings convened by Senator R. Watson Pomeroy. Boyle firmly believed that once the truth about Con Ed's fraudulent science was exposed, the government agencies that had previously supported the utility would shun it. Bob recalls thinking as he penned his testimony in the wee morning hours, "How could they possibly go forward after they know the truth?"

Opponents to the project packed the hearing room at the Bear Mountain Inn, cowing badly outnumbered Con Ed officials who had arrogantly appeared wearing their "Dig We Must" buttons. Boyle called Perlmutter's testimony into serious question and cited the Rathjen and Miller study that showed that the Highlands was one of the two principal spawning grounds of Atlantic Coast striped bass. Storm King's intakes, he said, would suck in the bass, their eggs, and larvae and fingerlings. The plunge down the mountain would kill them by the millions. Boyle also testified about the Indian Point carnage and that Storm King's project, twice the size of Indian Point's, would turn the fishery into a slaughterhouse.

The coup de grâce was administered by John Clark, a fisheries biologist from the U.S. Marine Gamefish Laboratory at Sandy Hook, whom Boyle had lured to the hearing. Clark recalls, "In '63, I made the mistake of talking to Bob Boyle. By '64, he had me in court." Clark attacked Perlmutter's calculations and testified that the Storm King reach was a critical bass spawning ground. As a biologist from the Fish and Wildlife Service, Clark's testimony had a special substance. By breaking ranks with the government position, Clark showed extraordinary personal courage, though not for the first time. After he finished testifying at Bear Mountain, Clark turned to Bob. "Boyle," he said, "you're gonna have me counting seals in the Pribiloff Islands."

The fishery testimony was not the only painful moment for Con Ed. Scenic Hudson's witness, a former chief engineer for the New York City Bureau of Gas and Electric and senior engineer for the New York City Transit Authority, showed conclusively that Con Ed could meet peaking capacity more effectively and save ratepayers tens of millions by using nonpolluting gas turbines instead of the Storm King alternative.

On February 16, 1965, the Pomeroy committee voted unanimously to reject the Storm King project. However, environmentalists feared that the FPC commissioners would nevertheless exercise their discretion to ignore the legislative committee's recommendation.

Meanwhile Boyle's and Clark's testimony at the Pomeroy hearings alerted a whole new constituency to the Storm King controversy, including boat owner and sport fishermen associations, commercial fishing groups, and dozens of Connecticut and Long Island Sound townships and counties. They flooded the FPC with petitions to reopen the proceedings and to admit them as parties.

But the FPC was little more than a lapdog to the industry it was charged with regulating. It denied all petitions, agreeing with Con Ed that the "allegations" about potential fishery impacts were "irrelevant." On March 9, 1965, the FPC, citing Dr. Perlmutter as an "outstanding ichthyologist," granted Con Ed a license to build Storm King.

But the battle had only begun. Boyle continued searching for the "missing" photographs. It took him about half a year to find them. The photos Pirone saw had been confiscated by Conservation Department officials. But conservation officer Bob Mahon told Boyle that a bank officer in Peekskill named George Yellot had copies of the pictures. Yellot, who died in 1968, was also a deputy game warden for the department and had actually taken the photographs. Boyle visited Yellot at his bank office in Peekskill. Yellot explained that soon after he took the pictures a Conservation Department official ordered him to turn them over. "So I gave him the pictures," he said. Two weeks later the official returned asking for any duplicates. "So I gave him the duplicates." And then Yellot took a sheaf of photos out of his desk drawer and, smiling, handed them to Boyle and said, "But they never asked about triplicates."

On April 26, 1965, Boyle published "A Stink of Dead Stripers" in *Sports Illustrated.* Shortly after his article appeared, the Department of Environmental Conservation investigated private home telephone records for dozens of its employees "to see who squealed to Boyle."

In August 1965 Scenic Hudson sued to reverse the FPC decision in the Federal Circuit Court of Appeals in New York. Con Ed's principal argument was jurisdictional; Scenic Hudson had no "standing" to sue under the U.S. Constitution, since its members had not suffered any personal economic injury from the FPC action. Prior cases held that the Constitution required plaintiffs to demonstrate tangible economic harm to maintain a case in federal courts. That requirement had always prevented environmentalists whose only objection was scenic, aesthetic, or recreational from claiming the protection of the courts.

On December 29, the Court of Appeals handed down its decision. For the first time in history, the court reversed an FPC decision to license a power plant, holding that injury to aesthetic or recreational values was sufficient to provide an aggrieved party with constitutional "standing." The court ordered the FPC to begin its hearing process from scratch and ruled that "The Commission's renewed proceedings must include as a basic concern the preservation of natural beauty and of national historic shrines, keeping in mind that, in our affluent society, the cost of the project is only one of several key factors to be considered." The court also criticized the commission for "seemingly placing great reliance on the testimony of Dr. Perlmutter" and for "inexplicably" excluding evidence offered by the fishermen. The court specifically ordered the commission "to consider the fisheries question before deciding whether Storm King is to be licensed." The Supreme Court refused to hear Con Ed's appeal, allowing the "Storm King Doctrine" to stand as the law of the land.

By the end of 1965, Storm King had become a cause célèbre across the nation. The Hudson Valley public had long been furious at Con Ed's proposal to deface a local monument that, along with Niagara Falls, was considered to be the most spectacular natural site east of the Mississippi. Now, thousands of Americans joined the battle. Over twenty-two thousand people from forty-eight states sent contributions to Scenic Hudson, including many Con Ed stockholders who sent their dividend checks. *Fortune* magazine called Con Ed "the company you love to hate." Interior Secretary Stewart Udall held hearings on the project and condemned Con Ed. In an extraordinary departure from judicial restraint, Supreme Court Justice William O. Douglas sent a letter supporting efforts to stop the project. Congressman Richard Ottinger, who had been elected in the fall of 1964 directly as a result of his opposition to Storm King, held congressional hearings. In November 1967, Scenic Hudson chartered a Circle Line Tour boat for its annual fund-raiser. Ottinger and Senator Robert Kennedy, who had defeated Con Ed supporter Kenneth Keating, rode from Manhattan to Storm King with two dozen news reporters and three hundred New York community leaders to celebrate efforts to stop the project.

The Storm King decision, however, did not mean that the mountain was protected. It merely required the FPC to hold new hearings and consider the nonmonetary issues. The FPC's utter servility to the power industry virtually guaranteed a decision in favor of the project no matter what the evidence showed. The hearings opened in

November 1966. In this round, a new group, the Hudson River Fishermen's Association, joined Scenic Hudson as an intervener. Boyle and a coalition of commercial and recreational fishermen had founded the Fishermen's Association earlier in the year. "The Fishermen," as they came to be called, would become the principal voice for the Hudson's ecology and, in later years, would evolve into Riverkeeper, the organization for which we work. During the Storm King hearings, the Fishermen were the primary advocates on the fishery issues.

Even though thousands of pages of compelling evidence against the project had accumulated when those hearings closed two years later, the FPC hearing examiner in August 1968 once again recommended to the commissioners that the Storm King plant be licensed. But then New York City intervened with a new concern; the blasting might damage the New York City aqueduct, which crossed beneath the Hudson near Storm King. It would take two additional years for Con Ed and New York City to work out an agreement. The FPC commissioners withheld their decision pending the resolution of that dispute.

In the interim, Congress passed the 1970 Clean Water Act, which required state water quality certification for any federally licensed facility that discharged into a state water body. Con Ed would have to leap this new bureaucratic hurdle before commencing construction. The State Conservation Department scheduled hearings in July 1971 to allow public comment on the certification, giving environmentalists another opportunity to stop the project.

Con Ed submitted a fisheries study it had commissioned pursuant to the federal court order. Referred to as the Carlson/McCann Fish Study, it supposedly "proved" that Storm King would have minimal impact on fish. To counter this study, Boyle once again draged Dr. John Clark into the fray. Upon reading the Carlson/McCann report, Clark realized that Con Ed's scientists had failed to incorporate the Hudson's tidal fluctuations into their mathematical formulae for measuring fish kills. Thus Carlson and McCann's study had assumed the giant populations of migratory fish eggs and larvae would pass by Storm King's proposed intake only once, imposing mortalities of less than 3 percent. Clark knew that, in reality, each fish would pass by the intake ten times before reaching the safety of the lower river. When the error was corrected, Clark would write that "the removal rate from the project increases by more than 10 times, to approximately 35 percent."

Clark was unable to testify in the state proceedings but the Fishermen's lawyer Al Butzel figured that Boyle could testify that the river was tidal at Storm King. After all, this was a fact known to virtually every human in the Hudson Valley. Once this was on the record, the defendant's study—and the entire case—would fall to pieces.

But the state hearings examiner, the Honorable Emanuel Bund, refused to allow Bob to testify, declaring that Boyle was not an expert in tides. As he left the stand in disbelief, Boyle pleaded to Bund, "Ask the Coast Guard, ask the Corps of Engineers," but Bund ordered silence. Both Bund and the smirking Con Ed attorneys understood that Boyle's removal would allow the industry estimates of striped bass mortality to stand unchallenged in the judicial record.

After the final day of hearings, Scenic Hudson board member Pierre LeDoux hosted a cocktail party for all participants at his Cornwall home. Bund got tipsy and played the ukulele and confided to Boyle's attorney, Al Butzel, that he regretted what he had done to Boyle but that he had got his "marching orders in Albany."

During another construction delay caused by the environmentalists' appeal of the Bund decision, Con Ed's second reactor unit at the Indian Point nuclear power plant came up for licensing before the Atomic Energy Commission. Boyle and the Hudson River Fishermen succeeded in persuading the AEC to include Indian Point's fish kills as an issue for consideration. Although years of litigation would follow, that concession by the Atomic Energy Commission in the licensing proceedings at Indian Point II was the beginning of the end for the Storm King project.

This time Dr. John Clark was able to testify. At hearings conducted by the AEC and the newly created federal Environmental Protection Agency, Clark's testimony helped persuade the agencies to reject the Carlson/McCann report and to conlude that massive fish kills would occur if Indian Point was permitted to withdraw cooling water from the river as proposed. Therefore, the AEC conditioned its grant of a license upon the installation of a closed-cycle cooling system. Fishermen had long fought to require closed-cycle cooling because such a system would reduce the use of Hudson River water, and fish kills, by 95 percent. Under the AEC order, the plant would either have to shut down completely or construct expensive closed-cycle cooling towers.

With the decision in hand, the Hudson River Fishermen's Association and Scenic Hudson, now represented by attorneys from the Natural Resources Defense Council, a newly created environmental law firm, filed a petition to the FPC on February 2, 1973, to reopen the hearings on Storm King. The FPC refused, and the environmentalists appealed to the Second Circuit Court of Appeals. In May 1974, the court ordered the FPC to hold further hearings on the fishery issue.

Criticizing the Carlson/McCann report for its failure to recognize the tidal impacts on their fish mortality predictions, the court scolded the commissioners for denying the HRFA/Scenic Hudson petitions. The court ordered the FPC to hold new hearings to determine the danger posed to the fisheries, and to consider reopening licensing proceedings completely.

The fishery issue became a nightmare for Con Ed. It was now public knowledge that the combined impacts of Indian Point and Storm King would pose catastrophic consequences for both the Hudson and the Atlantic Coast fisheries. The cooling towers that the EPA and the AEC had ordered Con Ed to install at Indian Point would cost the company $240 million. Using enough concrete to build a football stadium, the towers would stand five hundred feet over the riverbanks and would dramatically impede the scenic beauty of the Hudson Valley.

The EPA provided Con Ed with a small glint of hope that it might escape cooling towers with a license provision that read that the agency might "consent to the substitution of other suitable methods for fish protection." But the company recognized that it would not escape building cooling towers without the agreement of the environmental groups. The Storm King battle had already changed the legal landscape dramatically. The appellate court's decision required that environmentalists and their concerns now had a place at the table.

Con Ed's new chairman, Charles Luce, reaching for a way to disengage from the legal and public relations nightmares at Indian Point and Storm King, asked for a powwow. The environmental groups had their own incentives to negotiate. After nearly two decades of fighting, they still faced long years of litigation during which the Indian Point plants would continue to kill fish. In all probability, an obedient FPC would again relicense Storm King as soon as the new fishery hearings were completed. There was also the prospect of opening dangerous rifts within their own ranks, which would quickly be exploited by the utilities if the Fishermen insisted on cooling towers that might offend

Scenic Hudson's members. Russell Train, a former EPA administrator, was selected to mediate settlement discussions among eleven interested parties, which included the federal government, five utilities, two state agencies, and three environmental groups: Scenic Hudson, the Fishermen, and the Natural Resources Defense Council.

In December 1980, the Hudson River Peace Treaty was announced. The agreement required that the Storm King pump storage facility be abandoned and the land donated as a park. At Indian Point, Con Ed would have to design and install devices to prevent entrapment of larger fish on its intake screens and schedule plant shutdowns during the spawning season to protect the eggs and larvae from being sucked into the intakes. In return, Con Ed and the other utilities would be temporarily spared the costs of constructing cooling towers while they investigated new technologies for reducing fish kills. At Boyle's insistence, the utility was forced to pay $12 million to endow a Hudson River Foundation whose mission would be to conduct research on the Hudson fisheries so as to better manage the resource in the future. The foundation now has a $37 million capital fund.

The peace treaty ended seventeen years of litigation and closed the most important lawsuit in the history of environmental jurisprudence. The Storm King case opened up the courts to environmentalists for the first time in history. By enlarging constitutional "standing" to embrace aesthetic, recreational, and cultural injuries, the decision radically expanded the jurisdiction of federal courts, allowing them to hear cases by plaintiffs who wanted to protect public resources from polluters or developers.

The decision required the FPC to perform a full environmental review of the Storm King project, the first full environmental impact statement ever. In 1969, Congress codified the Storm King decision in the most important piece of environmental legislation in history. The National Environmental Policy Act forced federal agencies to assess the full environmental impacts of every major decision. Since then, sixteen states have adopted "little NEPAs" requiring environmental reviews of state projects. Over 125 nations have also passed their own versions of NEPA—all derived from the original Storm King rationale.

The Storm King decision also laid the constitutional groundwork for "citizen suits," the critical enforcement provisions that make environmental law—from the Clean Water Act to the Endangered Species

Act—function. The term "environmental law" began appearing in the American lexicon for the first time about three years after the Storm King decision as environmentalists on the Hudson and across the country began exploiting the opening it had provided them to the courthouse.

Of course, the catastrophic blackouts that Con Ed had predicted if the Storm King Plant wasn't built never materialized. Today, New York is a net exporter of energy, despite the absence of Storm King and the seven Hudson River nuclear plants that the utilities at one time swore were absolutely critical to New York's economic survival.

After one of the victories in the long battle against Con Ed, Bob Boyle received a call from the Hudson Valley papers. "How do you feel about your victory?" the reporter asked him. "How do I feel?" Boyle answered. "How do I feel? If this were a war, a real war, I'd be out on the battlefield slaying the wounded!"

Boyle had been radicalized. Fifteen years before the final settlement, he prepared testimony for the Pomeroy hearing believing that once everyone knew the truth, government would step in and stop the robber barons. When he realized they were all in cahoots, he helped start a war that would change the history of the Hudson Valley and create a new environmental movement that would become a national model.

Boyle discovered that instead of protecting the public interest, the federal agencies, the Army Corps, and the FPC were often the authors of the worst injuries to the river. The state agencies were indentured servants to the industries they were charged with regulating. In Boyle's view, they weren't just destroying the environment, they were corrupting democracy in the process. Moreover, Boyle discovered, to his dismay, that both industry and government were involved in suborning science to deceive the public and the courts into accepting unworthy projects. Even the agency judges were disgusted. Judge Yost, an EPA hearing officer who presided over the fishery hearings, summarized utility lawyer Peter Bergen's "recipe" for winning in court: "Combine one large grain of salt with two cups of self-interest, stir vigorously with tame scientists until slightly thick, adjust seasoning to taste."

The long Storm King battle helped make the Hudson home to one of the most vigilant, sophisticated, and aggressive environmental communities in the world. Con Ed, in trying to steamroll the public interest, created an army of battle-hardened environmental warriors that would, over the next decade, reclaim the river from the polluters. Citizens' groups emerged at every bend, on both banks, to take a stand against any odds. Their victories were impressive and unprecedented. In addition to Storm King, a short list of derailed projects includes: seven nuclear power plants, an oil refinery, a coal terminal, a pump project to remove a billion gallons a day of the river's freshwater flow for New York City, an expressway that would have buried river nursery grounds along Westchester County, a high-rise complex in the midst of the Highlands, an oil tanker rinsing operation at Hyde Park, a highway on the West Side of Manhattan that would have destroyed wintering grounds for striped bass, and scores of actions by lawless polluters and developers. The river battles of the 1960s would create black-letter jurisprudence that would be used by communities across the country to protect their own natural resources. Those cases trained a generation of young environmental lawyers who would go on to argue many of the seminal cases in American environmental law. Among Storm King's legacies to the Hudson are four environmental groups: Clearwater, cofounded in 1969 by folksinger Pete Seeger; Scenic Hudson; the Hudson River Fishermen's Association; and the Natural Resources Defense Council (NRDC).

The largest of these Hudson River groups and the only one with a national outlook was the NRDC. Founded in 1970 by a group of litigators from the U.S. Attorney's office in Manhattan and crucial to the Storm King victory, the NRDC was modeled on the NAACP Legal Defense Fund to pose the kind of direct, face-to-face legal challenges to polluters that was emerging as the modus operandi of the Hudson River groups. One of these young attorneys, John Adams, would push the Natural Resources Defense Council into the forefront of the many groups that would write and lobby the dozens of environmental statutes passed after Earth Day 1970. But its heart was in litigation. The NRDC was all bristles and spears, and despite its successes on Capitol Hill over the next twenty-five years, the Hudson would remain one of its premier causes.

But the hardest-edged of all the Hudson River groups was the Fishermen. Its character reflected the personality and values of its principal founder, Bob Boyle, his faith in science and in the law, his devotion to angling, his alliance with the commercial fishermen, and his conviction that government could not be trusted to protect the environment. The

Fishermen espoused a blue-collar environmentalism that regarded the river as public property and equated its protection with the protection of fundamental democratic values. Its members were largely working people with American flags on their houses, who lived near the river because it was their livelihood or their place of recreation. These were people who couldn't fly off to Yosemite. The Hudson was their national park, or, as one of the fishermen called it, "our Monte Carlo, our Riviera." It was the fishermen's community, the reason they lived where they lived.

Boyle first saw the need for a group like the Fishermen in the spring of 1964, a few months before he made his first visit to Smokey Duggan at Scenic Hudson, when he was fishing for trout in the Croton and the water suddenly turned the color and consistency of coffee grounds. He followed the muck upstream to its source and found that a New York State Department of Transportation highway contractor by the name of Buddy Ottaviano was stripping the Croton of its vital gravel beds. When the Croton turned brown, Boyle didn't consider turning to Scenic Hudson, whose primary focus was Storm King. He intensely admired their cultural refinement and devotion to the Hudson's viewshed. But to him, the Croton's greatest beauty was its biological productivity. At the same time he was preparing with Scenic Hudson for the Pomeroy hearings and writing about Storm King, Boyle was organizing a small group of Croton hunters and anglers, who, for a full year, pressed the state Conservation Department for justice on the Croton. In the end, the state Conservation Department fined Ottaviano a mere $100.

In February 1966, after the Second Circuit Court's Storm King decision ordered Con Ed to consider its impacts on fish, Boyle held a small meeting in his living room in Croton. A motley crew sat around his six-foot-long aquarium. Boyle had summoned them with a letter proposing to form a group called the Hudson River Fishermen's Association "for the ecological betterment of the watershed." The group included entomologist Dom Pirone; oceanographer Jim Alexander and his wife, Betty, a marine biologist; Eastern Airlines pilot Art Glowka, the Long Island Sound fisherman who, along with Dom Pirone, had first exposed the fish kills at Indian Point (a few years later, during the height of the Storm King case, Glowka would execute a historic slide landing on no foam and no wheels at LaGuardia and then help the passengers evacuate, including Con Ed's CEO Charles Luce); photographer Bob Hoeberman; Augie Berg, a prison guard at nearby Sing Sing; Richie Garrett, a grave digger; Ronald Dagon, ecologist and assistant to the curator of conservation at the New York Botanical Garden; and Danny Salzberg, a Croton orthodontist and member of the Croton Rod and Gun Club who had helped Bob in his fight against Ottaviano's dredging in the Croton River. They decided the dues would be three dollars per year and that Richie Garrett should be president.

Since he was a boy, Richie had spent every free moment on the Croton's salt marshes, trapping eels and minnows, crabbing, and seine-netting alewives and herring for bait for the commercial fishermen. He fished for smallmouth bass on the Croton reservoir all summer, and cast plugs and bloodworms for stripers in the lower Croton during the spring run. As a child he also rode a fifty-pound snapping turtle with a wire bridle. His fishing partner since high school was Augie Berg. They had co-owned six car-toppers and two outboards. Richie and Augie sometimes sneaked fishing rods into Sing Sing so inmates could fish while unloading the coal barges. Garrett, who dug graves and superintended St. Augustine's Cemetery in Ossining, liked to joke to his new followers that "I'll be the last to let you down."

Seated around Boyle's aquarium, the group talked about the decline of the Hudson—fish kills at Indian Point, the paint from Tarrytown's GM plant that dyed the river, the oil from the Penn Central pipe that blackened the banks of the Croton and made the fish taste of diesel. They spoke about how New York State was trying to fill ten miles of near-shore shallows to build an expressway from Tarrytown to Crotonville and pave an eighteen-mile stretch of the Beaverkill and Willowmac Creeks—two of America's finest trout streams and the birthplace of American fly-fishing—for a four-lane superhighway. Boyle related how he had phoned the American Geographical Society to complain that the society's recently published map slated the entire lower river as an industrial waste conveyance. Boyle demanded to know who had made the designation; they told him with finality, "It's been set aside for industrial purposes. That's just the way it is."

There was a deep sense of impotent rage in the room. These were the days before the environmental statutes, before the Clean Water Act, Superfund, and the National Environmental Policy Act, before citizen suits and freedom-of-information laws and environmental impact statements. The government was on the side of the polluter, in a partnership that was stealing the local people's livelihoods and recreation, their vacations and childhoods. The discussion began to turn desperate. Somebody even suggested floating a raft of dynamite beneath the Con Ed piers where it would be sucked into the intake; someone else said Penn Central's pipe could be plugged with a mattress, or ignited with a match.

Then Boyle offered another strategy. He told the group that in researching his article on the Hudson, he had come across the Federal Refuse Act of 1899, and the New York Rivers and Harbors Act of 1888. These statutes banned the discharge of pollutants into America's navigable waters, including the Hudson and its tributaries. Equally interesting, both statutes contained a bounty provision allowing the person who reported the violator to keep half of the penalty charged! Boyle had asked Time Inc.'s libel lawyers to research, and they confirmed that those laws were still on the books, though the bounty provision had never been enforced. After listening to Boyle with escalating excitement, they all agreed to organize themselves to target and attack polluters one at a time until they were all eliminated.

The Fishermen's board of directors was composed of the attendees of Boyle's meeting and Ric Riccardi, a Citibank loan officer who hunted the Hudson's giant carp with bow and arrow and fed them to his basenji. Among the first members were commercial fishermen Ace Lent and Charlie White from Verplanck; Henry Gourdine, a black man with striking blue eyes who ran shad crews of twenty men during the big shad runs of the 1930s and 1940s; and Everett Nack, a commercial fisherman from Claverack who still smokes some of the finest shad in the Hudson Valley and for a long time supplemented his income by capturing the Hudson's giant goldfish for sale to collectors. In three years the membership grew to 300 sports fishermen, commercial fishermen, bait-and-tackle shop owners, biologists, and others.

The day after St. Patrick's Day 1966, Richie, an ex-marine with four nephews in Vietnam, opened the first public meeting of the Hudson River Fishermen's Association at Crotonville's Parker-Bale American Legion Hall. The meeting drew a standing-room-only crowd, with people seated on wooden folding chairs, leaning against rifle racks, and hanging from rafters. At least fifty of the new members were Richie's Crotonville neighbors—the roofers, lathers, factory workers, masons, carpenters, and commercial fishermen.

Crotonville was an Irish and German shantytown on the steep slopes of Croton Gorge near where the Croton flows into the Hudson. Many men made their living as commercial fishermen, with the younger boys assisting them in hauling the nets. One of these was Richie's uncle Joe, who had collapsed one day on a bait cage in Croton marsh and was found floating facedown on a box of live killifish. Garrett told the story to Boyle one day as they slogged through the reeds in Croton Marsh and then remarked, half to himself, "God almighty, what a beautiful way to die."

The Croton River—its beaches, swimming holes, and the diving cliffs of Croton Gorge—was the centerpiece of life for Crotonville residents. On summer weekends most villagers would carry picnic baskets down the steep slopes on a railroad-tie staircase hacked in the cliff by Crotonville men early in the century.

Boyle gave a short lecture on the Harbors and Refuse Acts, and Pirone presented a slide show on Hudson River ecology. Congressman Dick Ottinger appeared at the meeting to update the group on the federal legislation he was writing. A dark horse Democratic congressional candidate in 1964, Richard Ottinger had made pollution of the river and the Indian Point fish kills the centerpiece of his campaign in the mid-Hudson Republican strongholds of Westchester and Putnam Counties. He hired Scenic Hudson's public relations director, Mike Kitzmiller, to run his campaign, and won handily. He acknowledged, "I swam to office on the waters of the Hudson River."

Ottinger recognized that the environmental issue appealed to liberals who regarded pollution, like racism and sexism, as another form of social inequality as well as to moderate conservatives who, in the tradition of Teddy Roosevelt, acknowledged a trusteeship obligation to preserve natural resource assets for future generations. But in following his instincts, he made a shrewd political discovery. As Samuel Freedman wrote in his 1996 book, *The Inheritance: How Three Families and America Moved from Roosevelt to Reagan and Beyond,* "What stunned him as a candidate was learning how deeply working-class voters, people he associated with factories, taverns, and wakes, cared for the outdoors." That evening, surrounded by the blue-collar environmentalists who formed his core support, Ottinger canceled his other scheduled stops to stay and listen and argue until 1:00 A.M.

When the discussion moved to the floor, fishermen complained that

Hudson River fish were anathema in the marketplace. Buyers at the Fulton Fish Market would underpay them and quickly mark the fish boxes with tags falsely identifying the stripers as having been caught in Chesapeake Bay. Many of the people present worked in the factories that still lined the Hudson. Risking their jobs, they rose one by one to report dumping and discharging and pollution by their employers. A construction worker on a Riverdale apartment building reported a pipe discharging crud into the Harlem River. "I see it during lunch and I want to throw up," he said. "What can we do to stop it?"

The association decided that night that its first target would be Penn Central Railroad, whose diesel yards at Croton Harmon had been vomiting oil waste from a three-foot-wide pipe into the mouth of the Croton for years. Ducks would drown in the discharges that sometimes turned the river into a fire hazard. For Boyle and Garrett, this pipe became a symbol of government corruption and the triumph of corporate power over the public trust. The Fishermen began a campaign of repeated and persistent letters and calls to the federal agencies with jurisdiction over the discharges: the Army Corps of Engineers, the Coast Guard, and the U.S. Attorney. Boyle personally called the Corps over fifty times. He finally visited the Corps headquarters in Manhattan in June 1967 and asked a Corps official why the agency refused to enforce the law. The officer told Boyle, "We're dealing with top officials in industry. You just don't go around treating those kinds of people like that."

Nor could the fishermen get the U.S. Attorney interested in the case. Once an assistant U.S. Attorney who had grown increasingly irate at Boyle's daily calls threatened him if the badgering didn't stop, "I'll have you in front of the grand jury." Replied Boyle, "I'll be there in twenty minutes."

In June 1968, the HRFA, the Fishermen, and Congressman Dick Ottinger joined in suing Penn Central, the Secretary of the Army, and the Corps of Engineers. Motivated partially by this lawsuit and largely by Art Glowka's persistent complaints, the U.S. Attorney in 1969 finally took action on Penn Central, suing the railroad under the federal Refuse Act of 1899. When the dust settled, the railroad paid $4,000 and the HRFA got a $2,000 bounty. It was the first time a private organization had ever received the bounty on polluters that Congress had provided for seventy years before.

Following their victory against Penn Central, the HRFA printed and distributed ten thousand copies of the Refuse Act on "Bag a Polluter" postcards that people could fill in with polluters' names and mail pre-paid to the Fishermen's address in Ossining. In quick succession, the Fishermen initiated successful actions against Ciba Geigy, Standard Brands, Philmont Finishing, and American Cyanamid, collecting bounties with each victory. Using the Refuse Act, the HRFA forced the National Guard to restore a two-acre tidal wetland it had filled at Camp Smith near Peekskill. "No one in this country had ever gone against the polluters," recalls Boyle. "We did."

Richie Garrett's involvement in the new organization transformed his life. Suddenly, the grave digger's quiet existence was over. He found himself writing letters to editors and dragging a slide show of oil slicks and fish kills around the Hudson Valley to bingo parlors, Knights of Columbus halls, garden club meetings, and Scout gatherings. His mail was filled with reports from fishermen and others of illegal dumping and he was regularly awakened by midnight calls. He was profiled in the *Daily News, Field and Stream,* and *Reader's Digest.* He was even asked to appear on Johnny Carson's *Tonight Show* (he declined, fearing the sin of pride). In June 1969 he made his first airplane trip— to Washington, D.C., to testify before the House Subcommittee on Fisheries, Wildlife and Conservation on Governor Nelson Rocke-feller's proposed Hudson River expressway.

In his testimony, Richie described himself to the committee as "simply just a citizen who grew up along the Hudson," and who, like others who loved the river, was "supposed to take the count." He begged Congress to protect people like him from "what Governor Rockefeller and his highwaymen are planning to do to this wonderful river." He closed his stirring depiction of pollution and corruption threatening the Hudson by saying, "I am not a radical in asking for this, I am simply an American."

On April 22, 1970, Earth Day, Richie spoke alongside Leonard Bernstein to a crowd of 100,000 in Union Square in New York City. It was a revelation for the Fishermen. For almost five years they'd been fighting lonely battles to save isolated communities from powerful industries and indifferent government officials. They were often treated as kooks or malcontents. Now on Earth Day twenty million Americans joined them and stood behind them. Richie describes it as "a movie where the skinny kid going up against the brawny town bully, with no chance of winning, is suddenly joined by a whole army of kids behind him, and the bully turns and runs."

"The Hudson is my life," he announced to the crowd. "The country has problems with drugs and crimes and racial hatred. But the way I figure it, clean water and clean air and a clean earth is the most important issue of all. If we lose our rivers, the other social problems will be dwarfed. Black or white, hawk or dove, we'll all drown in garbage up to our eyeballs." He said that his fight to save the Hudson had been the most fulfilling part of his life. He urged his audience not to try solving all the problems of the planet but to pick out a small piece of the world and defend it.

Among Garrett's new followers was Fred Danback, a union shop steward whose working-class credentials and strong attachment to the river typified the Fishermen's Association's membership. "The Yonkers waterfront was my playground," recalls Danback of his youth. "That's where I learned to fish and to swim." After the war Danback landed a job as a janitor at the Anaconda Wire and Cable Company in Hastings-on-Hudson, New York. Almost from the first day he had a broom in his hand, Fred realized his employer was dumping large amounts of oil, metals, and solvents into the river. "One day while I swept the floor I followed the washings from the machines through the floor drains and right to the river."

Danback is not your stereotypical environmentalist. He was driven to action by a broader sense of justice. "I was motivated because of what it was doing to the river and to the shad fishermen's business. In those days there was always complaints that the shad tasted of oil. I took it pretty hard when I seen what it was doing to them. I thought, This is my river, your river, our river. My God, we cannot let this happen."

He made it his mission to locate and map every pipe through which Anaconda dumped its poisons. When Fred took his complaint to management, company officials ordered him back to work. After he rose to be union president he badgered company officials about their discharges until they threatened him.

"Finally I called the Coast Guard to report the spill. They would show up, thank me for reporting it, and I wouldn't hear from them again. But I kept calling." One afternoon after the Coast Guard had left the facility following another of his calls, Fred noticed company officials through the large glass window of the local Italian restaurant. "They were sitting at a table laughing and joking with the Coast Guard. Right then I knew I had to find a better way." Ten years passed before he found one.

Anaconda held Fred back from promotions. With a wife and family to support, Fred brought his grievance to the international representative of his union. But the union dismissed his complaints as a "kook" issue. "I quit in 1969. The stuff was just pouring out of the place. I decided, 'Damn it, this has got to stop.' You weren't allowed to bring the company to court if you worked for them, that was part of the union agreement. So I quit. That's when I hooked up with the Fishermen." Fred laughs when asked where he found the courage to put his job on the line for the river. Wiry and tough at seventy-four, he rubs his callused hands together and recalls the heavy combat at the Battle of the Bulge during World War II. "Afterward, I figured that I was on borrowed time. If Patton didn't get me killed nobody could."

With Fred's information the Fishermen conducted their own investigation and brought the case and the evidence to the U.S. Attorney for the Southern District of New York. For the next two years they badgered the U.S. Attorney to prosecute.

Finally, in 1971, the U.S. Attorney charged Anaconda with one hundred counts of violating the Refuse Act of 1899. Two years later Anaconda Wire and Copper paid a record fine—$200,000—the largest ever imposed on any American company for polluting.

Anticipating the polluters they could pursue with their half of the fine, the Fishermen were ecstatic. But they soon realized that the government intended to welsh. They were shocked when high-level Justice Department officials, intent on depriving the Fishermen of their just desserts, arranged for the U.S. Coast Guard, which was practically a co-conspirator in Anaconda's mischief, to petition the U.S. Attorney for a portion of the reward. The U.S. Army Corps of Engineers and the Interstate Sanitation Commission followed suit and claimed a piece of the bounty. In the end, the Fishermen's share of the settlement was only $20,000.

In March 1994, the two of us found ourselves back at the Anaconda site—now a desolate industrial wasteland—twenty-six acres of untaxable riverfront surrounded by a chain-link fence, heaped with garbage, closed off to the public, poisoning the river, and mocking Anaconda's promise of pollution-based prosperity.

The Hastings/Anaconda debacle was familiar territory. Like many pollution cases it represented the worst of what corporate America was capable of: industrial abandonment, toxic contamination, tax dodging, loan abuse, destruction of property values. Once an international mining and manufacturing giant, Anaconda boasted the motto "From mine to consumer." The company was as good as its word. On the mining end, it had created the worst Superfund site in the nation, an open pit in Butte, Montana, that has killed fish and birds and poisoned children with arsenic, lead, and twenty-five billion gallons of contaminated water. On the consumer end was the Hastings plant, where eleven hundred workers once turned Anaconda copper into thousands of miles of wire and cable products. There the company had earned the reputation as early as 1965 for being one of the worst and most recalcitrant polluters on the Hudson River.

The eleven hundred jobs were now long gone. In 1977, the debt-ridden company was bought out by the oil giant Atlantic Richfield (ARCO), which inherited all of Anaconda's assets as well as its liabilities. ARCO drained the last of the profits from operations such as the Berkeley Pit while it unloaded liabilities like the Hastings plant without first cleaning up the toxic wastes Anaconda left behind.

Forty million dollars, ten years, and one national savings-and-loan scandal later, there was still no cleanup. The only thing the new owners had built was the protective cocoon of their limited partnership, which showed no assets. They carried a property tax debt of $1.9 million, and were the proud owners of a massive indoor garbage dump that they created to keep a stream of rent payments flowing to the partnership from a shady garbage carter. The tens of millions of dollars the new owners had raised to develop the site were gone without having so much as one decrepit factory building cleared or one new foundation laid. Physically, environmentally, and legally, Hastings was a mess. Building 15 carried at least a $5 million cleanup tag, and the cost of cleaning up the hazardous waste that contaminated the ground and water was estimated to be a minimum of $10 million.

The situation seemed hopeless, but we knew that where government fails to act, energetic citizens can fill the vacuum. Boyle had conceived the Riverkeeper idea in 1969. The Fishermen's Association created the Riverkeeper organization in 1983, and in 1986, the two organizations merged. Our mission was to complete the work of the

Hudson River Fishermen—to track down and prosecute every polluter on the river; to protect its biological integrity and return the Hudson to the public. The Hastings site was intimidating, but with role models like Fred Danbeck and Bob Boyle, nothing seems impossible. Using the confrontational style pioneered by the Fishermen, and using the legal beachheads that they had helped establish at Storm King and in the Refuse Act cases, we had, within a year from the day we inspected Building 15, orchestrated a court order requiring the cleanup of the Hastings site to be completed within eighteen months. As of publication of this book, the intractable 180,000 cubic yards of garbage have been almost entirely hauled from the site and a white-knight investor, Ted Kheel, has arranged to transform the site into a housing development, returning the shoreline to the public and the land to the tax rolls.

Sometimes, we look at a spot like Building 15 and consider the thirty years of effort that people like Fred Danback and the early Fishermen put into cleaning up the river, and all their work seems for naught. Boyle himself has admitted that at times he's felt "so overwhelmed that I am tempted to throw up my hands and surrender." But, he added instantly, "This would be a betrayal of trust and nothing positive will ever be accomplished if people despair or bow to the supposedly inevitable."

Once he advised a woman who said she despaired of ever seeing the river clean before she died, "We all have to fight so that when you die and I die, we can use as our epitaph those words from St. Paul to Timothy, 'I have fought the good fight, I have finished my course, I have kept the faith.'" Boyle's faith that the environment can be saved by people who steel themselves to fight one battle at a time for every inch of waterfront, wetland, and riverbottom has borne fruit in the resurrection of the Hudson. The single piece of wisdom most responsible for that miracle is Boyle's notion that the battle to save the planet begins within each of us, and progresses when we each resolve to take responsibility for preserving little bits of it—our backyards, our neighborhoods, our communities, our river valley. After all, our planet is being destroyed piece by piece. It will only be saved in the same fashion.

# CHAPTER 2

# John Cronin

The oil tanker I was tracking had anchored just off the river's main shipping channel directly across from the Franklin Delano Roosevelt home in Hyde Park. I took her measure from my own position one-quarter mile away. At 750 feet long and ten stories high, she dwarfed the twenty-five-foot Riverkeeper boat in which I rode. Her anchor chain was as wide around as a telephone pole, and the river's swells broke on her stern with all the effect of an open-handed slap on a sheer rock face.

I was responding to a state trooper's tip-off that foreign tankers were sailing seventy-five miles up the Hudson, filling up with fresh river water, and then departing for foreign ports. The story was Hudson River legend since the 1940s. Local historian William Geckle self-published a booklet in the late 1960s claiming there were "secret springs" at the river's bottom that produced water "as pure as diamonds" that was brought back by tankers to eagerly waiting Caribbean islanders.

I had always considered the tanker legend a river myth on a par with Washington Irving's Storm Ship, which haunted the rivermen of the Tappan Zee, or Captain Kidd's treasure, buried in the scuttled *Quedah Merchant* off Jones Point at the southern gate to the Highlands. But my trooper friend supplied details that lent the old yarn new credence. According to him, the tankers rinsed out their oily cargo holds into the river before loading up with clean water that was transported to the Caribbean to run oil refineries. And the brains behind the operation was the Exxon Oil Company.

Through my binoculars I could see voluminous discharges exiting three different ports in the sides of the rusty steel hull. A column of numbers climbing vertically from the waterline indicated that the tanker had risen three feet since I last checked. I collected my sampling gear, hung the fenders for sidling up next to the ship, started the engine, and pulled anchor.

I thought about the odd picture my diminutive patrol boat made pulling up to a huge oil tanker in the middle of the Hudson River. But to anyone familiar with my childhood, the image of me behind the wheel of a boat would be the stranger sight by far.

I grew up in the city of Yonkers. My father used to take my brother, sister, and me to a place he called the Ridge, a promontory that overlooked downtown, the river, and the western shore. I was thrilled by the view, by the bustle of the city and its sights—Getty Square, the Carpet Shop, Otis Elevator, the Sugar House. We watched the river flow in the distance.

Yonkers kids of my generation knew only three things about the Hudson—it was the boundary between New York and New Jersey; the dark, vertical Palisades on the opposite shore got their name from an amusement park that sat atop them; and the waters of the river were too polluted for swimming.

My parents had enjoyed a very different relationship with the river when they were young. My father learned to swim in the Hudson, one of a boatload of terror-stricken St. Peter's parish boys who were instructed by Monsignor Brown. The monsignor would tie the stout bowline around the waist of the nearest boy and throw him into the drink with the command, "Swim!"

On summer weekends my father's family would congregate twenty-five miles upriver on the Buchanan shore for swimming, eating, family business, and general carousing.

My mother's father was an avid fisherman and kept a boat at the Yonkers waterfront. Usually he brought home eel, which he kept alive in the bathtub. He trained my mother and her five brothers to gut, clean, and skin the eel. My grandfather's fish, the rabbits he raised, and the garden he harvested helped keep a family of seven well provisioned through the lean Depression years.

When my parents were courting in the late 1940s, boats were readily available and rowing was a popular pastime. My mother, not a swimmer back then, happily entrusted her safety to my father at the oars. A riverfront bonfire and crab-bake reunited friends and sweethearts who had been separated by the war.

When my brother and I were very young, my mother would bring us down to the river to cool ourselves on a hot summer day. This was the early 1950s, just before we learned that the water was too polluted for swimming, in the days when the river was still a part of our lives rather than a boundary.

The Hudson was about one mile from our apartment on Morris Street. We would pick up soda and sandwiches from Pomerantz Delicatessen, stroll through the elm-lined streets, past the large Victorian homes that my parents so admired, and cross the railroad to a small beach not far from Ludlow Station. We waded in the shallows and watched far-off tugs move along the river. At that time, the Hudson was not a destination but another point in the circle of our lives. It was a part of our neighborhood and family.

Rowing with your date, children wading on a hot summer's day, even eels in the bathtub—how sad that I would later think such things quaint and old-fashioned. But these were not sentimental pursuits for which we had become too sophisticated. They were our rightful inheritance, which was taken from us when eel became so laced with toxins that it was illegal to fish them, when most of the piers and docks that dotted the river for the first half of the century finally collapsed, when pieces of open shore became the site of factories, landfills, and railroad yards, and when the waters off Yonkers and many other communities were declared unfit for swimming.

What happened to my family's river?

That was a question I wouldn't think to ask for years. Born in 1950, I was part of the first generation that grew up apart from the Hudson, the generation of kids who were taught in school to add plumes of black smoke to the chimneys of the buildings we drew; the generation raised on the taste of chlorinated drinking water; the generation whose feet were X-rayed by shoe salesmen, whose biggest concern about smoking was that it stunted growth, and whose family cars were filled by only a few dollars' worth of gasoline.

Baseball was my childhood passion. My father, a former city all-star pitcher, was my hero and my own personal coach. The summer that Mickey Mantle and Roger Maris chased Babe Ruth's home-run record was the most exciting of my childhood. Hitting the long ball in Yankee Stadium was a feat for which I could imagine no equivalent sense of accomplishment in the human experience.

After high school, I spent one unsuccessful year at college. My whole young life I believed that I would graduate and perhaps study law. Instead, I joined the restless hordes traveling across the country. I was a stablehand at a mid-Hudson resort in upstate New York, a door-to-door book salesman in South Bend, Indiana, a dishwasher in Phoenix, Arizona, and a grocery sacker in Boulder, Colorado. Eventually, I returned to New York, lured back by the beauty of the mid-Hudson Valley. I set up shop as a roofer and house painter.

One October day in 1973, while pounding asphalt shingles and listening to the radio, I heard that the 106-foot *Clearwater*, a full-size replica of a historic Hudson River sailing sloop, would be docking at the city of Beacon waterfront carrying a cargo of pumpkins. The annual *Clearwater* "Pumpkin Sail" was a popular autumn event. I knew of the *Clearwater* though I had never seen her. Since high school I had been a fan of folksinger Pete Seeger, who was one of the vessel's founders. The boat served as a floating environmental classroom for children, and the Clearwater organization named for it advocated the restoration of the Hudson River.

The *Clearwater* pulled up to the ferry dock and the crew passed the pumpkins bucket-brigade style to the rhythm of Pete's five-string banjo. It was a magical evening. The magnificence of the huge gaff-rigged mainsail, the warm and friendly crowd, Pete's music, and the autumn sunset stirred me deeply. The smells and sounds of the river evoked memories of walking hand-in-hand with my mother along the Yonkers shore. I experienced a sense of belonging, a sense of place that was at once new and familiar.

When Pete called for volunteers to help rebuild the crumbling dock, I was the first to sign up. For the next three weekends, Pete, four others, and I dismembered an old barn and hauled the lumber down to the waterfront. For the next two weekends Pete, two others, and myself started replacing dock timbers. For the last two weekends Pete and I worked alone.

While he hammered Pete would burst forth with occasional sea chanties and work songs, interspersed with passionate asides about the extraordinary things people can accomplish if only they "work together." He urged me to volunteer for Clearwater and join the fight to clean up the Hudson.

I was resistant. If I had learned anything as a city kid it was the old adage that you can't fight city hall; the little guy didn't stand a chance. Besides, I had little inclination toward environmental issues. The environment seemed a problem of such extraordinary dimensions that I could only consider it in broad and abstract terms. Pete's solution was to start locally, at home, one thing at a time. To solve the big stuff you had to tackle the small.

The message struck a chord. While I was living in Boulder I attended a lecture given by the late Réné Dubos at the University of Colorado. A Pulitzer Prize–winning microbiologist, Dubos was a brilliant humanist, philosopher, and environmental thinker. He authored the expression "Think globally but act locally."

During a lecture tour of college campuses across Canada and the United States, Dubos was distressed to find students and faculty indulging themselves in a preoccupation with social problems at the global level while their immediate environment and their personal social affairs were deteriorating. Dubos said that in order to "contribute to the welfare of humankind and of our planet, the best place to start is in your own community and its fields, rivers, marshes, coastlines, roads, and streets, as well as with its social problems."

Dubos' message was borne out by my travels. In each place I lived— the Great Plains, the American desert, and the Rockies—the worst crimes against nature had been caused not by global cataclysms but by local decisions.

Where to start? Right where you're standing, according to both Dubos and Seeger.

It is difficult to imagine the abuses that were inflicted on the nation's waterways leading up to the 1970s. As early as the 1870s, *Harper's Weekly* had featured regular editorial commentary on the state of the river in the form of a white-bearded cartoon character called Father Hudson who would complain about the filth plaguing the lower river. By 1970, the industrial and chemical boom that followed World War II had introduced new forms of pollution that would have stripped the flesh from Father Hudson's bones. The river was littered with the pollution and castoffs of industry. Stories of the General Motors assembly plant in Tarrytown were legend: fishermen could tell what color the cars were being painted by simply looking at the river. The grounds of the local branch of the Diamond Candle Company were covered in wax.

The twin lures of my newfound relationship with the river and Pete's positive message proved irresistible. I took his challenge and volunteered for a Clearwater project called the People's Pipewatch. The Pipewatch was the idea of Tom Whyatt, a brilliant and creative activist who was the first Hudson Riverkeeper. Its objective was straightforward. The new federal 1972 Clean Water Act required polluters to abide by permits that specified what they were allowed to discharge and in what amounts. I worked with a Vassar College student named Karin Limburg evaluating whether polluters were abiding by the 1972 Clean Water Act and complying with their permits. Our first case was against the Tuck Tape company.

At the Tuck factory we found barrels of thick, white waste adhesive that had been poured out the back doors. The company had a permit for only two discharges. We discovered twenty-three that poured hot solvents, adhesives, sewage, latex, and titanium dioxide. Broken sacks of chemicals littered the banks of the creek, and leaking steel drums sat unsecured and rotting in a holding area immediately uphill from the water. Inside the plant unprotected workers carried chemicals by the armfuls to the large mixing vats.

We spent two months collecting evidence and sampling each discharge. Under the leadership of teacher Richard Knabel, a group of Yorktown high school students operated a laboratory called the Student Educational Workshop in Environmental Research—SEWER— where we brought the samples for analysis. We shot slides and monitored truck deliveries into the plant. We drew a map of the plant pinpointing all twenty-three discharge points.

Following the path beaten by Bob Boyle and the Hudson River Fishermen's Association, we brought our evidence to the office of the U.S. Attorney in Manhattan. On the train ride down I joked with Karin Limburg that it was we, not the company, who were headed for trouble. I told her that when we had finished presenting our evidence to the U.S. Attorney, he would quietly usher us into another room where federal marshals would take us away, never to be seen again by family or friends.

I was only half joking. Despite Pete's indefatigable optimism, I was convinced that the deck was stacked against little guys like us. It was unthinkable to me that a couple of volunteers could bring a polluting company to justice.

We met with assistant U.S. Attorneys Chris Roosevelt and Anne Sidammon-Eristoff of the environmental division and presented our slide show and our discharge analyses. When we uncapped one of our samples, an ugly odor filled the room. I tried to surmise the impression we were making: Two nuts off the street? Malcontents looking for attention? Trespassers who belong in prison?

The attorneys said that they would like to confer privately and asked us to step into an adjoining room, where I waited for the federal marshals to materialize. Roosevelt called us back in and asked if we had ever testified before a federal grand jury. One jury had just finished hearing evidence about a pornography ring and he thought it would be perfect for the Tuck case. He was confident the grand jury would return charges—if we would testify. I went home in a state of shock.

Within a matter of weeks, we were subpoenaed and had testified, and the U.S. Attorney had charged the company with twenty-four counts of violating the Clean Water Act and the Federal Refuse Act. A Tuck spokesman sneered to the *New York Times* that we were "boy scouts with binoculars," but the company soon pled guilty to half of the counts and was fined $205,000. It was the first successful prosecution in New York State under the 1972 Clean Water Act.

I was elated. I felt like I had just sent a four-hundred-footer into the Yankee Stadium bleachers.

Because of the Tuck case, Clearwater offered me a regular staff position to run the Pipewatch project. I had no idea I was embarking on a lifelong career. During the next ten years I would switch jobs four more times. In different ways, each job would prepare me for becoming the Hudson Riverkeeper.

I cut my teeth as a full-time environmental advocate while working for Clearwater. My job regularly exposed me to the dirtier side of human nature, but I relished the intrigue of our investigations and the satisfaction of halting environmental lawbreakers.

The early 1970s was an exciting period of experimentation and discovery in the environmental movement. The new laws were untested. Despite the warnings of Rachel Carson and others, we were unprepared for the magnitude of the toxic nightmare that industry had created.

By the summer of 1975, it appeared that a decade of Hudson River activism had paid off handsomely. There was a general sense of optimism, even elation, about the condition of the river. The fishery was in better condition that it had been in years. Federal and state grants and loans for constructing public treatment works had eliminated discharges of raw sewage from most communities. New York State voters had over-whelmingly approved $2.15 billion in bonds to stop water pollution. Industry was learning to comply with the new federal laws. There was talk that public swimming beaches would soon open again. Cities and towns were developing plans to restore their waterfronts. Hudson Valley media were trumpeting the proud news that the river was undergoing a renaissance.

But on August 6 hope and pride were dashed when the *New York Times* reported that the state had found dangerous levels of a toxic chemical compound called polychlorinated biphenyl (PCB) in Hudson River fish. The General Electric Company had discharged as much as two million pounds of PCBs into the Hudson River since 1946 from its Fort Edward and Hudson Falls factories. A chlorinated hydrocarbon similar to DDT, PCB is a suspected human carcinogen associated with liver, kidney, and nervous system disorders. Most recently it has been linked with developmental and reproductive abnormalities and with disruption of the endocrine systems in mammals, thanks to its disturbing ability to mimic the body's natural hormones.

Because of its extraordinary stability and its flame-retardant qualities, PCB was heralded as one of the miracle chemicals of the twentieth century. The oily compound was used as an insulating fluid in capacitors and transformers, such as those manufactured by GE at its Hudson River plants, and to produce scores of household products including appliances, carbonless carbon paper, and baby bottles. By 1975, more than two billion pounds of PCBs were loose in the global environment, but nowhere had an ecosystem been subjected to higher doses than the Hudson.

Environmental Conservation Commissioner Ogden Reid warned the public to refrain from consuming the river's striped bass. By February 1976, after a program of state testing, that warning was expanded to include an outright ban on the commercial harvest of bass, eel, carp, catfish, and perch. At the time, the allowable level of PCBs in fish, according to the federal Food and Drug Administration, was five parts per million. It has since been lowered to two parts per million. One Hudson River eel was found to have 559 parts per million of PCBs in its flesh. Because they spend most of their lives at sea, American shad and sturgeon were exempt from the fishing ban.

The public's hopes, raised so high by the Hudson's improvement, were replaced by fear that the river had become a toxic threat. Bob Boyle remembers that "it was like the rug had been pulled out from under us. We'd been on this fantastic winning streak. We were beating all the polluters. The river was improving and then PCBs hit. After that, the Fishermen's membership dropped off and some of those people just walked away from the river and never came back."

Commercial fishermen were especially devastated. For centuries they had lived a quiet and simple existence far from the spotlight of controversy. They had endured the vagaries of weather, catch, market price, even pollution, but PCB was a chemical predator that they could not elude.

General Electric's response was to issue threats. The ink was barely dry on the *New York Times* story when the company told Governor Hugh Carey that it would remove all of its operations from New York State if it was held responsible for the contamination of the Hudson. It issued notices to its workers at Fort Edward and Hudson Falls that PCBs were a phony controversy cooked up by environmentalists to destroy their jobs. It refused to comply with an order by Ogden Reid to phase out the use of PCBs at its plants.

GE's most cogent defense was that it had government permission to dump PCBs into the Hudson. Indeed, GE had procured a Clean Water Act permit from the EPA and the DEC to discharge up to thirty pounds per day. GE had also obtained permission from the DEC's predecessor, the Conservation Department, as well as from the state's Department of Health. Federal and state officials were aware of the extent of the PCB problem years before the 1975 announcement but failed to take action.

In 1970, Bob Boyle captured five striped bass in a net off Verplanck, packed the filets in dry ice from the Good Humor plant in Mount Vernon, and sent them to the Warf Institute Laboratory in Madison, Wisconsin, for analysis. The lab found abnormally high levels of PCBs in the fish—11.4 parts per million in striped bass eggs and 4.01 parts per million in striped bass flesh. On October 26, 1970, Boyle published his findings in a lengthy *Sports Illustrated* article entitled "Poison Roams Our Coastal Seas." Boyle did not know where the PCBs were coming from since, at the time, GE had disguised its discharges by renaming the chemical "pyranol." Boyle sent his article and a formal report of his findings to State Conservation Department Fisheries Director Carl Parker. "These are grim figures," Boyle wrote, "and we certainly think that the state should warn fishermen not to eat striped bass eggs." Although the DEC knew what GE was discharging, Parker replied with a derisive letter ridiculing Boyle's "so-called" test results as impossible. Parker secretly ordered the state lab to replicate the tests, and when Boyle's findings were confirmed, Parker suppressed the results. The Conservation Department allowed GE to continue its discharges.

On the day of the *New York Times* story, I went directly to the regional office of the EPA in New York City where I filed a freedom-of-information request for all the agency's documents regarding PCBs and the Hudson. I later filed the same request with the mid-Hudson Valley regional office of the DEC. Among the documents I received from the agencies was an internal 1974 EPA memorandum by Alan W. Eckert of the EPA Office of General Counsel warning that based on the size of the GE discharges, Hudson River fish would be expected to have concentrations of PCBs of 37.5 parts per million. Another 1974 EPA report by Dr. Royal Nadeau confirmed Eckert's prediction that river fish were indeed contaminated. One bass showed levels of 350 parts per million, according to Nadeau, "a new record for PCB contamination of freshwater fish." Neither Eckert nor Nadeau ever informed the state or the public of their findings. But the state had already secretly gathered its own PCB data. We forced the DEC to release a survey Carl Parker had conducted in response to Boyle's earlier findings. It showed that PCB contamination of Hudson River fish was in excess of FDA limits in fifty-two of ninety-nine samples collected between 1970 and 1975. We also later learned that Ward Stone, the DEC's own Wildlife Pathologist, had issued more than 100 memos to his superiors warning of the dangers of PCBs and specifically of the contamination of the Hudson.

Despite the apparent government complicity, Reid announced an administrative enforcement proceeding against GE. State law forbids the discharge of pollutants in amounts that are injurious to human health or the resources of the state, irrespective of what a permit may allow. In addition, the Monsanto Company, which was the sole manufacturer of PCBs, had warned GE that PCBs were environmentally harmful. GE chose to disregard Monsanto's warnings.

The Hudson River Fishermen's Association, Clearwater, and the Natural Resources Defense Council participated as intervening parties on the side of the state. Reid, concerned about possible GE accusations of bias against a DEC hearing officer, called in an outside judge, Abraham Sofaer. The DEC presented exhaustive testimony regarding the extent of the contamination, the toxicity of PCBs, and the economic effect on the Hudson River fishery. GE's star expert, Dr. Gerald Lauer, testified that his PCB analyses of fish caught near the plants showed no contamination above the allowable FDA limits. The next day NRDC attorney Sarah Chasis forced Lauer to concede that decimal points had been misplaced in his report and in fact all of the fish were highly contaminated.

After four months of hearings Sofaer issued an "interim opinion and order" that laid the blame for PCBs on "corporate abuse and regulatory failure; corporate abuse in that GE caused PCBs to be discharged without exercising sufficient precaution and concern; regulatory failure in that GE informed the responsible federal and state agencies of its activities and they, too, exercised insufficient caution and concern." He found GE guilty of two of the three charges brought against it, but Judge Sofaer's attention to government's failures had set the stage for settlement of the case.

In the wake of the decision faulting both parties, General Electric and the state agreed to create a $7 million PCB research and clean-up fund—$3 million in cash each from the state and GE and $1 million in in-kind research from GE alone. Additionally, GE would construct pollution abatement facilities at Fort Edward and Hudson Falls and phase out its use of PCBs statewide by July 1977.

The proposed settlement generated some controversy among environmentalists. Even though $7 million was considered an enormous amount of money for a pollution case in 1976, the actual costs to clean up GE's PCBs promised to total in the tens of millions if not hundreds of millions of dollars. But Sofaer warned us at a confidential meeting that if the case went to appeal, GE's liability was unlikely to be sustained in New York's highly politicized state court system. He also noted that throughout the appeals process, which could take years, GE's discharges of PCBs might continue. After all, the company had already proven itself very adept at environmental blackmail. I held out against the settlement. I believed then, as I do now, that the gamble was worth the risk. The state should have fought GE for the entire cleanup and itself put up the $7 million fund as a hedge against the GE appeal of the state's case. I also believed that GE would eliminate the discharges on its own. Public excoriation over the continued dumping of PCBs into the river was more than even GE's corporate flaks wanted to handle.

Ultimately, the boards of directors of each of the parties approved the settlement. Bob Boyle, who also opposed the settlement, was asked by *Sports Illustrated* to recuse himself from board participation since he was covering the story for the magazine. The state announced the agreement in September 1996 to much praise by the media and the environmental community.

Nothing in the PCB settlement could improve the lot of the Hudson's rivermen. Experts agreed that the bulk of the fisheries would stay closed for several generations. The timing of the PCB issue had been particularly cruel. By 1975, the Hudson River renaissance had extended to the marketplace as well, and rivermen had every reason to look forward to prosperous times. The river's eel, bass, and shad no longer carried the taint that the label "Hudson River" once brought with it. Demand for the river's harvest was at an all-time high. The catch was up and prices were good. During the early days of the PCB controversy, my Clearwater colleague Chris Letts and I made the rounds of fishing camps and saw the evidence of the rivermen's investments in the Hudson's future. At Stony Point the DeGroats had built a new covered pier and spent thousands of dollars on eel traps. At Nyack the Gabrielsons had laid in thousands of square feet of bass net. In Dutchess County Ivar Andersen had built the most lucrative eel fishery on the river. He didn't even have to truck his catch. Tank trucks from Boston and Baltimore would come to his dock to pick up his eels live.

When the state was ready to issue the February 1976 report that would close most of the fisheries, I was asked to be the messenger who would inform the commercial fishermen. Commissioner Ogden Reid called me at home to convey the news. He wanted me to be able to say that I had gotten the information directly from him. He went over the PCB concentrations with me species by species. When he had finished the mostly bad news I told him that he had not mentioned eel. He asked me to hold for a moment and after a muffled conversation with his aide returned to say that the DEC had not yet decided whether eel were fish or snakes. Though Reid had personally pledged his agency's assistance to the rivermen, I knew then that the DEC was institution-ally incapable of caring about the livelihoods it had helped destroy.

The DEC's announcement heralded the end of an industry that had enriched New York's palate, economy, and culture for centuries. The Hudson's fishing industry would last only as long as rivermen were willing to fish the shad and sturgeon fisheries that remained open. In all likelihood it would cease before the end of the century as their chil-dren lost interest and the current generation quit or died. Before 1976 there were approximately two hundred rivermen making at least part of their living on the Hudson. By the spring of 1997, there were fewer than twenty-five.

To my knowledge, after two decades neither the DEC, nor the EPA, nor GE have ever apologized to the rivermen for the roles they played in destroying the Hudson's commercial fishing industry.

I left Clearwater after three years. My next three jobs came in quick succession. For two years I was an advocate and lobbyist for the Center for the Hudson River Valley. For nine months I worked as an aide to the late Congressman Hamilton Fish, Jr., a Republican conservative, and for a year and a half as a legislative aide to state Assemblyman Mau-rice Hinchey, a Democratic liberal, now a congressman. This was my four-year crash course in government.

As a lobbyist I learned the labyrinthine ways of the legislative process while continuing my interest in the commercial fishery. I drafted and lobbied into law the Hudson River Fishery Management Act that required the state to develop a plan to restore the fishery. As Fish's dis-trict coordinator I represented the congressman on a wide variety of federal matters including labor, housing, environment, and energy and was involved in federal issues surrounding the nuclear disaster at Three Mile Island in Pennsylvania. While I worked for Hinchey, he tackled a breadth of issues from coastal management to organized crime involve-ment in toxic waste disposal. I worked on several investigations includ-ing the U.S. Army's role in Love Canal, where I helped expose Manhattan Project contractors who had pumped radioactive wastes into drinking water aquifers.

In government, we measured success by the treatment technology we could require or by the blame we could assign. Rarely were we able to help the victims. I was reminded often of the Hudson's rivermen. Their story haunted me.

I had stayed in touch with the rivermen, occasionally appearing on DeGroat's or Gabrielson's dock to look over their catch and to satisfy my curiosity about their well-being. One day Gabrielson finally told me, "The next time you show up, you better be ready to put on foul-weather gear and go out on the boats." Back at my Albany desk, I pictured myself arriving at Bob's dock unannounced, ready to work, and being given a job on the spot.

When I told Maurice I was leaving to be a commercial fisherman he was bewildered but wished me the best. I left my job, my apartment, my medical and dental plans, and moved into the back of a pickup truck. I drove 125 miles south to Bob Gabrielson's in Nyack, New York, and reported for work. It never occurred to me that Bob might turn me down, and he didn't.

I was thirty when I walked onto the Burd Street dock. I had never even operated a boat and had little idea about the demands of life on the water. I soon learned that the lives and methods of the Hudson's rivermen had changed little in three hundred years. They worked out of small open boats using the techniques that the Dutch settlers learned from the Algonquin Indians. They had made concessions to technology—outboard motors, synthetic line, fiberglass hull boats — but for the most part they used the time-honored methods and frequented the same fishing locations of the generations of family and friends who preceded them. Their centers of operation were wood shanties on pieces of shoreline littered with evidence of their trade—nets, scales, oilskins, grapnels, hawsers, rope, buoys, traps, seines, oars, anchors.

When they could fish freely, before the PCB crisis, they harvested and marketed a wide range of river delicacies—American shad and roe so prized for size and quality that fish markets ceased buying from other waterways when they became available; the caviar and smoked meat of sturgeon that ranged up to ten feet in length; striped bass from the most abundant population in the mid-Atlantic; blue crab that, claw to claw, could not be beat for heft or flavor; and American eel as big around as a human arm.

The Hudson is best known for its shad. Riverfront shad bakes are a centuries-old tradition and the deep-bodied, iridescent fish, the largest member of the herring family, is one of the most readily identified of the Hudson's two hundred species. Typically a shad fisherman works twice a day, on both flood or both ebb tides depending on his method of fishing. His routine is unmechanized and labor intensive. He hauls his nets hand over hand, across the boat's bow, removing the fish from the mesh one by one, hoping to fill the deck of his twenty-foot skiff with a ton or so of fish. After bringing his catch to shore, he boxes it in sixty-pound lots, ices it down, and loads it on a market-bound truck. The fishing and shipping effort, combined with maintenance of gear and marketing of the catch, allows a riverman perhaps three hours of sleep for every twelve he works at the height of the season.

Life in the back of my pickup was spare, lonely at times. Bob Gabrielson took me home for meals often. We lived by a tidal clock, fishing at six in the morning and six in the evening one day and midday and midnight by the following week. Two weeks into the season, time of day had little to do with what meal we ate. Chowder and beer tasted as good at sunrise as it had at sunset ten days before.

We fished the Tappan Zee where we set three thousand feet of net in two-hundred-foot "shots" between long ash poles driven deep into the river's bottom. I worked with Bob's son Robert. Some tides we would load as much as three thousand pounds of shad, allowing no more than twelve inches of freeboard between our gunwales and the water during the trip back to the dock.

By law, we had to remove our nets for thirty-six hours during the weekend to allow the fish to swim freely up the river. The remainder of the week the nets were in the water around the clock, and we "picked" them twice a day at each high tide. We fished no matter the weather; otherwise the force of the river against nets full of fish would tear the gear apart.

One night the north wind was howling against the incoming tide, lifting up the river in swells twice the height of the boat's bow. I leaned over the gunwale for a third try at the pick-up buoy we used to haul the net when the bow bucked so high and dropped so fast that I was still in the air when the bottom of the boat hit the water. I landed hard on the gunwale and toppled forward, my center of gravity shifting to the dark empty space between bow and water. Just as I was going in, I felt Robert's strong hand at my neck. He managed to cover the twenty feet between us, haul me aboard, and return to the tiller in time to prevent our skiff from being broadsided by the next swell. That night it took five hours to pick three hours' worth of net.

When we got back to shore Bob Gabrielson asked me if I still loved the river. There was a point to his jibe, which I understood right away. While Robert and I were out there struggling, we hated the river, we cursed the river. It was as threatening an enemy as either of us had met. The Hudson was no longer an environmental issue to me. My life was in its hands. Love for the river was replaced by respect.

Fishing with the Gabrielsons was difficult, sometimes backbreaking work. But the weather was pleasant more often than not and the job carried with it an exquisite sense of freedom and purpose. There were evenings of heartbreaking beauty, riding the bow of the skiff toward sunset, all cool spray and balmy air, when I never wanted the trip back to shore to end.

I worked the blue crab season with Bob that summer. We fished 120 Chesapeake-style crab pots, big box-style traps about two feet on a side with funnel-like openings that crabs entered easily but from which they could not escape. We rigged twelve separate lines of ten pots each and placed them all over the Tappan Zee. We let the pots sit on the river bottom overnight, baited with the menhaden that we netted every morning. Bob refused to mark his lines with buoys, fearful that curious boaters might help themselves to his catch. He memorized the location of the pots by using north-south and east-west coordinates taken from onshore structures, buoys, or stanchions of the Tappan Zee Bridge. To retrieve the pots we rode to an approximate location, threw out a grapnel, and dragged blind until we caught the line. Bob almost always located the line within thirty seconds.

Life is thick, slow, and sultry during crabbing season. Cool river breezes are rare; the Hudson's water temperature rises above eighty by August. Breezes blowing from the south bring New York smog into the valley. But spending the summer in cutoffs and T-shirt, aboard a boat, amid the warm embrace of river water and air, was my own piece of heaven.

The following shad season Chris Letts and I decided to work together as independent fishermen. Bob Gabrielson didn't have room for another boat and so the DeGroat family offered us a place at their Stony Point shanty. We asked Henry Gourdine, an African American fisherman from Ossining, to help us build our shad boat. Henry's obsession with the Hudson started as soon as he could walk; to keep him from the river, Henry's mother clothed him in a red dress, hoping he'd be embarrassed to leave the yard. At ninety-three, Henry is the most accomplished fisherman on the Hudson, still sought out by rivermen and novices eager to learn tricks of the trade. A master net maker and boatbuilder, he once ran the largest fishing operation on the river. During the '30s and '40s, Henry employed over twenty men whom he billetted on a barge. One lunch break while we huddled around the woodstove in my garage, which Henry had converted into a boatbuilding shop, Chris and I bantered about the riches that awaited us when we finally worked for ourselves. Henry smiled patiently and sobered us with stories of seasons past. "One season was so bad I had to sell my Cadillac to pay the grub bill. Went down to the river riding and went home walking, without a dime in my pocket." Another time, a riverfront fire burned all his boats. He recalled the disastrous season that shad dropped to ten cents per pound, and of course, the dark year of 1975 when DEC closed the bass, eel, and perch fisheries. Reading our grim reactions, Henry laughed. "If I was lookin' to get rich, I wouldn't be a fisherman and neither would you."

The boat Henry helped us build was a handsome twenty-foot, flat-bottomed, lapstraked, copper-riveted Hudson River shad boat. Henry said it would easily hold two tons of fish. We had our chance to find out at Stony Point.

Turk DeGroat was the patriarch of the Stony Point shanty where he, his sons, grandsons, and friends held camp all year 'round, using the shanty for weekly poker games during the off seasons. When the shad were running, the lights and stove burned through the night and we kept ourselves warm with the "Lucy Jug," which contained a concoction of blackberry brandy and anisette and, according to tradition, was never washed between refillings.

The DeGroats have been fishing out of Stony Point for so many generations they have lost count. Tim believes they date back to the original Dutch settlers. Turk's grandfather was a river captain in the days when they still used schooners. "He never worked a day onshore," said Turk. As a youth, Turk would hitch a rope to a northbound tug and chase the shad schools fifty miles upriver to Kingston, and when the fishing died there, catch another fifty-mile tow to the Albany pool. "All my brothers fished," Turk said. "There was never a DeGroat who didn't."

Chris and I enjoyed the unpredictable adventures of novice fishermen. One afternoon our outboard cut out in the middle of Haverstraw Bay in four-foot rollers with almost two tons of shad onboard. And on one humiliating Saturday, we trimmed a shot of net lengthwise instead of crossways.

At the shanty, there was always a sturgeon to be skinned and a crisis to be resolved—a broken outboard, nets torn by an errant tug or clogged with oakum, a boat with a busted seam. We learned our trade by watching the DeGroats solve each problem with the wisdom of the collective experience of a dozen generations of Hudson rivermen. At the end of the season, Chris and I retired our nets in arrears to Henry, Turk, and the boys at Stony Point for their patience and generosity and for the cold nights when they warmed us with camaraderie and the Lucy Jug.

The summer of 1982 marked my last fishing venture, as a drift netter for sturgeon with Dave White, the last of a long line of Garrison-based shad fishermen. Dave and I fished out of the small Putnam County hamlet in the shadow of West Point Military Academy. I was Dave's oarsman. We used an engine only rarely, only when we felt like having an adventure in another stretch of the river.

Both Turk and Dave have since passed on. As the rivermen die out, it is increasingly likely that their culture and skills will die out as well. Of the many rivermen we have lost, the death of Jake DeGroat was perhaps the most tragic of all. Jake was the youngest and quietest of the DeGroat boys. He served in Vietnam and returned withdrawn and troubled. The two certain things in his life were his family and their fishing business. During the brief river renaissance of 1975, Jake invested heavily in gear and made plans to fish full-time. The PCB crisis was a severe blow. Over the years he grew more angry and taciturn. When filmmaker Robert Nixon and I collaborated on *The Last Rivermen,* a documentary about the demise of the commercial fishery, Jake was the only fisherman who refused to be interviewed. Eventually, he became so despondent that he committed suicide. It can't be said with certainty that Jake would still be alive were it not for General Electric's PCBs. It can be said that his chances would have been better if his family business had stayed intact.

When I was fishing with Gabrielson, other rivermen began to ask for my assistance with political matters. The state had broken every promise it had made to help keep the endangered industry alive. The state had failed to implement the Hudson River Fishery Management Act, and the officials who were in charge of fishery policy believed that commercial fishing was a threat to proper resource management. In

1981, the New York State Commercial Fishermen's Association asked me to become the business agent for the rivermen.

My mind increasingly turned to the issues that made the rivermen's lives ever more difficult. Through my work as their business agent I was able to assist with regulatory problems, assure that PCB testing of fish was being performed, and monitor river fishery management. But I was again drawn to the investigative work, the lobbying, the politics and the controversy of the larger issues that formed the Hudson's future. I didn't want to give up life on the water, however. I had come to enjoy the feeling of a boat deck underfoot. I still wanted to negotiate the river's narrows, round its bends, traverse its bays, explore its shallows, land on its islands.

That's when Bob Boyle offered me my dream job. Bob had $25,000 in the Fishermen's treasury from the Indian Point settlement. He called me in 1982 and told me that the Fishermen wanted to hire me to help collect striped bass for a research project. And, he added, he would like me to start thinking about how the Fishermen could have a "presence" on the river. I wasn't quite sure what he had in mind until he called again several weeks later. "How would you like to be the Hudson Riverkeeper?"

In his book about the Hudson he had called for a Riverkeeper: "out on the river the length of the year, nailing polluters on the spot . . . giving a sense of time, place and purpose to people who live in or visit the valley . . . with the idiosyncrasies, migrations, and workings of the Hudson engrained in his mind. We need someone like this on the Hudson and on every major river in the country." The Fishermen had started a Riverkeeper program in 1972 and appointed Tom Whyatt to the job. Tom was responsible for an impressive string of successes, but after three years the program languished for lack of funding. Bob decided it was time to try again.

No group on the river had a better reputation than the Fishermen for going after polluters. They were fearless in the face of big government and big business. They understood the importance of the legislative process and worked with a cadre of the area's best lawyers and scientists. The Fishermen's ranks included commercial fishermen, sport fishermen, biologists, writers, and everyday people. They understood the universal message of effective local action. They had money in the bank.

"You'll need a boat," Bob told me.

"Of course," I said. I sat down to gain my composure.

"You'll track down polluters, stay on top of government agencies, be a presence on the river. Do what needs to be done. Think it over." It didn't take me long.

We couldn't find the right boat so we decided to have one custom-built. The *New York Times* got wind of our plans and, before we could even get the keel laid, ran a story headlined "New Riverkeeper to Patrol Hudson."

Within a week I got a phone call from Mark Kusnetz, then a producer for Tom Brokaw at *NBC Nightly News,* who had seen the *Times* article. He said he wanted to film the building of the boat, the launching of the boat, and my first day on the job. About a week later I received another call, this time from a producer for Charles Kuralt, who then hosted *CBS Sunday Morning.* He also had seen the *Times* article. He said he wanted to shoot the building of the boat, the launching of the boat, and my first day on the job. For the next five months my main responsibilities included making sure that the boat construction stayed on schedule, organizing the launch party, and keeping the two competing networks from learning about each other. I was afraid that if either knew of the other's interest, one or both would cancel.

The construction of the boat proceeded apace but devoured our entire budget, including my $50-per-week salary. We were left with no money to buy an engine or refreshments for the two hundred people who would be attending the launch. I still didn't have a plan for handling the two networks. But providence continued to shine. NBC anchor Tom Brokaw personally attended the launch party, inspiring his rivals at CBS to redouble their efforts to get the story. Local businesses donated the food and drinks, and a local riverman appeared with smoked shad.

The skies were clear, a warm breeze wafted us with the fecund smells of springtime on the river. We launched the boat to much fanfare, a rousing barnstormer from Bob Boyle, and a great flood of champagne. The champagne, the spectacle, and the engineless craft prompted famed television hunter Joe DeFalco to find a donated engine and to make us a gift of the money it would have cost to buy a new one.

There was, however, another trial ahead from which no grand gesture of generosity could deliver me: my first day on the job. NBC planned to accompany me and wanted something dramatic to report. I was beginning to regret the metaphors that Bob Boyle and I had drummed up to explain our program: David and Goliath, St. George and the Dragon, Robin Hood and the Sheriff of Nottingham.

My dread began to diminish when the trooper called me about the tankers. After spotting one at anchor during a sailing trip, he had gotten a tip that tankers were rinsing themselves in the river. His boss told him it was outside his beat. "You're the Riverkeeper, John. It's your job now."

I called NBC producer Kusnetz and told him I was ready to take him out on the job.

"What will we be doing?" he asked.

"Looking for oil tankers."

"Are there some missing?"

I explained the story and two days later, we headed up the river. I acted confident about our mission though I had no way of knowing if there would be a tanker on the river that day. But as the river curved west there it was: a 750-foot oil tanker, at anchor, liquid gushing from its ports.

"There's the tanker I've been looking for," I told Mark, hiding my relief but recognizing the irony of a Riverkeeper grateful to find someone polluting his river.

I picked up my marine radio microphone to hail the tanker's captain. The cameraman got in position to shoot my discussion. The soundman boomed a microphone to hover between my mouth and the speaker of the boat's radio. Mark cued me.

The tanker's name was *Palm Beach*. I used the usual etiquette of repeating the vessel's name twice and then identifying myself.

"*Palm Beach, Palm Beach,* this is . . ."

As I looked up at the enormous vessel that loomed ever closer, it occurred to me that I had never before identified myself as the Hudson Riverkeeper. It suddenly sounded like an enormous title, presumptuous, grandiose. I wasn't St. George versus the dragon. I was the mouse that wanted to roar. I summoned up my nerve and mumbled, ". . . the Riverkeeper."

But the tanker captain had heard me just fine.

"Yes, Riverkeeper, what do you want?" he asked officiously.

"I would like to know what you are discharging."

"Under what authority are you asking me this question?"

"I'm the Hudson Riverkeeper," I said firmly now. "I would like to know what you are discharging."

"Fourteen thousand tons of seawater, Riverkeeper."

As we got closer, we could smell the petrochemicals in the air.

"Under what authority are you discharging?" I asked him.

"Under the authority of Exxon International," he replied with impunity. "If you have any further questions, contact Exxon International. They have many answers for many questions."

I would have broken out in a war dance were it not for the camera. Mark was pleased too. After all, what are the chances that a network news crew would take a ride with some guy claiming to be a River-keeper and catch the largest corporation in the world polluting the Hudson in broad daylight?

It took months of grueling investigative work and some good luck to uncover the full story. Exxon tankers would leave the Lago refinery in Aruba loaded with petroleum products such as jet fuel. They would off-load at Bayway, New Jersey, or elsewhere on the East Coast and journey ninety miles up the Hudson to anchor off Hyde Park. There they would rinse their oil tanks and load up with fresh river water for use in Exxon's Aruba refinery.

In order to prove that Exxon was polluting, we had to obtain and analyze samples of their discharges. Working alongside the tanker was a dangerous business. Powerful discharges burst from twelve-inch-diameter ports in the hull ten feet overhead. On our first try, I handled the boat while Andra Sramek, a new co-worker, grabbed the sample. I had rigged a boat pole to the handle of a screen-bottomed pail and placed a bottle inside. The excess discharge would flow through the bottom rather than knock the pail out of Andra's hands with its tremendous force.

Maneuvering next to the tanker was an adventure. A stiff breeze pinned our boat against the tanker's side. When we tried to back away the stern swung under the discharge and the boat started to swamp. I put the engine in slow forward and we pushed hand-over-hand along the rusted steel hull toward the tanker's stern where her half-exposed propeller—eight feet across—threatened to grind us into fish food at one command from the captain.

Our second try was successful. We brought our samples to Carpenter Environmental Associates, a laboratory that had volunteered to perform the analysis. They contained toluene, xylene, ethylbenzene, and benzene, a known carcinogen associated with leukemia. When I unscrewed the lid of an extra sample jar to give Bob Boyle a sniff, hydrocarbon fumes filled his living room. "What's that smell like to you?" I asked. Bob's deadpan reply was, "Oh, about $2 million."

Next we learned that some of the water that the company was sending back to Aruba was going to the island's public water supply. One of our board members, Arthur Glowka, was an Eastern Airlines pilot. While in Aruba he asked his hotel manager if he had ever heard of the Hudson River. The manager brought Art around to the back of the hotel and, pointing to the swimming pool, said, "That's the Hudson River."

Next I called the head of the Aruba water works. He explained that in addition to Exxon's petroleum-laden tankers, independent tankers under contract to Exxon were traveling to the United States empty for the sole purpose of picking up Hudson River water for Aruba. He sounded proud of the arrangement.

I called Exxon headquarters, posing as an academic researching the secret springs that Bill Geckle had written about. A shipping department clerk told me that he knew nothing of secret springs. He said that the government of Venezuela had decided to charge for the water that Exxon had been getting from the Rio Orinoco. Exxon switched to the Hudson, he said, because "there the water is free."

In addition to the Hyde Park anchorage, Exxon tankers were dumping their poisons almost directly into Port Ewen's drinking water. Twice I saw tankers anchored within fifteen hundred feet of the village's water intake.

After I discovered the Port Ewen situation we moved quickly. Boyle and I decided on a three-pronged attack: to seek the intervention of the federal government, to begin legal proceedings against Exxon, and to go public with our story. Under the Clean Water Act, the U.S. Environmental Protection Agency usually has federal jurisdiction over pollutant discharges into the nation's waters. One exception is that the Coast Guard has jurisdiction over the "normal operations" of vessels. And though we considered the Exxon tanker operations in the Hudson to be anything but normal, the Coast Guard and the EPA agreed that the Exxon tanker case would come under Coast Guard purview.

73

This was distressing to us because the Coast Guard maintained that Exxon was doing nothing wrong.

That's when assistant U.S. Attorney Susan Campbell came in to our rescue. A bright, aggressive, and energetic prosecutor, Susan joined us in pursuing Exxon with the blessing of her boss, then U.S. Attorney Rudolph Giuliani. Susan gave us a cloak of respectability even though she was operating mainly by bluff—she had no real authority since technically she was not representing a federal agency.

As required by the Clean Water Act, we notified Exxon of our intent to sue. We immediately released the simple facts about our suit—our tests of the discharges and the transport of water to Aruba. We would release the remaining revelations over time in hopes that interest in the story would build.

In a sharply worded news release, we accused Exxon of polluting the Hudson with toxic petrochemicals and stealing Hudson River water. Nothing had prepared us for the wave of publicity that followed. NBC aired its piece. The *New York Times* ran an article. National radio covered the story and a variety of magazines and newspapers ran features. Of course the Exxon case made front-page news throughout the Hudson River valley. It was also picked up by all the major wire services and papers from Montreal to Sydney. Exxon received the "Screw of the Week" award from a popular HBO show called *Not Necessarily the News.*

After initially denying everything, Exxon finally acknowledged "occasional" tanker trips into the Hudson. When pressed for a number, the company admitted to about twenty-five trips. But it claimed it had done no polluting and broken no law.

A reporter with the *Albany Times Union,* Ron Kermani, took our information as a starting point and distinguished himself with aggressive reporting, developing firsthand sources that even we didn't find. The Exxon story was a regular installment on the paper's front page.

Due in no small part to the continued heat generated by the *Times Union* series, Exxon's version of events started to crumble. At first, the company vociferously denied selling water. Later, a company spokesman clarified that statement with a bizarre distinction: the company had not sold water, it had received money for water. Exxon maintained that the tanker trips were rare and that its withdrawals had been lawful. These positions also crumbled when Susan Campbell's investigation revealed one hundred Exxon tanker trips up the Hudson in two years, and when Nicholas Robinson, then general counsel to the New York State Department of Environmental Conservation, released his legal analysis that the exportation of water outside New York State boundaries without explicit permission violated state law.

The story had become a public relations nightmare for Exxon. Finally they decided to meet with us. Tense from start to finish, the meetings were a microcosm of what was happening in public: denials, countercharges, and brinkmanship. We demanded that the tanker traffic cease and the company pay retribution. Exxon agreed to stop the tankers temporarily but flatly refused to make payment. We wanted the company to create a fund for the river; Exxon wanted us to go away.

Whenever the company rolled out the threat of combating our organization with its publicity and legal machinery, Susan Campbell, tough as nails, reminded Exxon that the Justice Department was listening. She also reminded Exxon that "These people live on the river and you don't. You weren't even doing business up there." She was right. Foreign crews guided Exxon tankers upriver under foreign flags and conducted no business on the Hudson, other than to pollute and pirate the river's water.

After four or five meetings we were deadlocked. The most reprehensible aspect of Exxon's conduct—and the charge that Exxon continued to adamantly deny—was its discharges at the Port Ewen anchorage. For all parties, the possibility that the company had unloaded benzene near a drinking water intake was a defining issue. Susan Campbell's list of Exxon tankers did not indicate where those vessels had anchored. I had seen tankers at Port Ewen only twice and Exxon knew it. Exxon's attorney admitted that Port Ewen may have been mistakenly used once or twice but denied any regular practice and refused to discuss the issue.

The day before our next-to-last negotiating session, I received a politely worded note from a riverman named Frank Parslow. He explained that he spent a lot of time in his Port Ewen home looking out at the river. He was suspicious when he saw oil tankers discharging, so he got out his binoculars. The previous autumn he had recorded the names of a dozen discharging vessels, and the date and time each had anchored. He had read about the Exxon case and was enclosing the list in hopes it might be helpful. A cross-check with Susan's list showed that each had belonged to or been contracted by Exxon.

We resumed the Port Ewen discussion at the next meeting. I took out Frank Parslow's card and went through the list. When I finished, Exxon's attorney and its vice president for shipping looked crestfallen. The attorney asked for a break to talk with his client. Upon returning they announced that they were prepared to take our proposal up to the next level of the company and suggested that we meet again in a few days.

The next meeting, at Exxon headquarters, would determine whether the case would be decided by litigation or by settlement. On my way to Exxon's headquarters I opened the *New York Times* to find an editorial lambasting Exxon's water caper by Sydney Schanberg, an internationally respected journalist. The Schanberg column had signaled to the oil giant that the story would continue to generate bad publicity. Its effect was apparent as soon as we entered the room.

The posturing was over; the horse trading had begun. In a deal worked out with the U.S. Attorney, New York State, and the Fishermen, Exxon agreed to cease its tanker traffic and pay $1.5 million to the state and $500,000 to the Hudson River Fishermen's Association. Governor Mario Cuomo had told us he would support using the state's share to establish a private independent fund that would benefit the Hudson. Half of the money that went to us funded the Riverkeeper program and the rest went immediately to a series of environmental projects on the river. The first project to receive money was the Village of Port Ewen Drinking Water Plant for the replacement of antiquated equipment. The Hudson River Improvement Fund was established by state appropriation of the Exxon money and continues to this day to fund physical improvements to the Hudson.

The Exxon case put the Riverkeeper program on the map. We had funding, international notoriety, and inquiries about starting similar programs. Judged by the interest it generated, the case lasted for years. Magazine and television stories, and even a children's book, delighted in telling the tale long after it had concluded. Yet I felt that the true Riverkeeper mission was not yet in sharp focus.

A short time later, I received a note from Pete Seeger, with whom I had not spoken in months. Enclosed was a small reproduction of Winslow Homer's 1892 watercolor *Boy Fishing* that he had cut from a magazine. The note read, in part, "When I saw this picture, I thought of you and wanted to let you know how much I appreciated what you are doing. I feel very proud I may have been one of the influences in getting you to settle along the Hudson, and I'll never forget the days we spent hammering nails into the Old Beacon Ferry dock."

I was flattered and moved by Pete's kind words. Homer had painted the image of the straw-hatted boy during his time in the Adirondacks, perhaps in the upper Hudson watershed. I realized that Riverkeeper was really about the right of any child to cast a line in the river and catch a fish for the family table. Of all the complex issues we would endeavor to solve—power plants killing fish, landfills destroying wetlands, sewage treatment plants polluting drinking water—none would prove a greater challenge than that small, simple dream.

Riverkeeper was not just about stalking Goliaths. We had to prove our mettle in the local communities that bore the brunt of environmental abuse. Our first opportunity would come with the addition of Robert F. Kennedy, Jr., as our chief prosecuting attorney and his investigation of Quassaic Creek in Newburgh, New York. A natural-born advocate with a brilliant mind for complex scientific and technical matters, Bobby would, in the space of five years, go on to become one of the nation's preeminent environmental attorneys and the voice of a generation of lawyers who believe that the pioneering days of environmental law are not yet over.

# CHAPTER 3

# Robert F. Kennedy, Jr.

I can't name the exact time that nature got a hold on my thoughts. My first memories are of the dogs at our house in Georgetown, but my mother told me recently that when I was in my crib in the garden I spent hours staring at ants and beetles. When I was three months old, we moved to Hickory Hill, an antebellum estate that had been General McClellan's Civil War headquarters in McLean, Virginia, across the Potomac from the capital. My mother, Ethel Skakel, bought it from her brother-in-law, Jack Kennedy, in the spring of 1957 as he began his run for the presidency. I was raised in that house, the third of eleven brothers and sisters, drawn from the beginning to nature and wilderness, and lucky enough to be able to see some of the prettiest places on earth.

The Skakels, a clan of unruly Republican outdoorsmen, might provide a genetic antecedent to my predispositions. My grandfather George Skakel, a quiet railroad traffic controller from South Dakota, made a fortune by discovering a process for turning coal waste from steel smelting into commercial graphite. Before my grandparents died in a plane crash in 1955, they produced three sons and four daughters. My mother was the sixth child. The boys—tall, large-boned, and brawny—spent their time hunting and fishing at Grandfather's ranches in Utah, Cuba, and Canada. My uncles, Jimmy, George, and Rush, sometimes disappeared for months on camping and pack trips to wild places. All were accomplished fishermen with spinning or fly rods, in freshwater on the flats, in surf, or offshore. Crack shots and graceful athletes, they loved back-country skiing at Mont Tremblant and the Bugaboos, shooting dove at Cabo San Lucas on the Mexican Baja, canoeing at their salmon camp in Newfoundland, and trout fishing at Lake Certo in Ontario. My grandfather would disappear for a third of the year on hunting expeditions to places unknown. My uncle Rush was mauled, some say deservedly, during a grizzly hunt. Uncle George, who dropped from a helicopter to ride eight-hundred-pound musk ox on one of his famous trips "above the dew line," died in a plane crash during an Idaho hunt in 1969. He kept live mountain lions at his home. He had darted or lassoed them in Canada and brought them across the border in the trunk of his El Camino. Uncle Jimmy's house in Bel Air was filled with giant aquariums housing sharks, abalone, octopus, and other creatures he had captured diving in the kelp beds of the Humboldt current. He would don his tank and enter the aquarium to feed the fish. In 1961 he harpooned a sperm whale from the bow of a dory rowed by Portuguese fishermen off the Azores and went on an eight-mile "Nantucket sleigh ride" before dragging the cetacean to the beach to be butchered. After an expedition in western Canada, he had mysteriously promised us "Christmas seals." When the crate came off the truck on Christmas Day out came a young California sea lion, who took up residence in our swimming pool and joined the growing menagerie that I had collected from the countryside around Hickory Hill.

When I was nine my *tiergarten* included raccoons, possums, squirrels, mice, and rats, and various reptiles and amphibians. I spent my monthly allowance on the two thousand crickets needed to feed my lizards, which were housed in the aquariums that lined the bookshelves in my bedroom. A giant leopard tortoise wandered the rooms of Hickory Hill. I had captured it in Kenya's northern frontier in 1963 during a safari with my cousin Bobby Shriver and his father, Peace Corps director Sargent Shriver, and brought it home in a suitcase under diplomatic protection. My mother complained that the suitcase was afterward unuseable. At the barn we had chickens, ducks, and geese. Each of the children had a horse—mine a Pinto, Geronimo. I had a 4H calf and pheasant runs near the barn.

In the evenings, our Costa Rican nanny, Ena Bernard, would read heavily accented versions of Uncle Remus and Brer Rabbit, *Aesop's Fables,* Kipling's *Just So Stories, Peter Rabbit,* and *The Wind in the Willows.* But my favorites were her tales of jungle life in Costa Rica—she had once straddled an alligator's back and another time fled a threatening tortoise— which gave me a lifelong hankering for Latin America and the rain forests. When I grew a little older I read Edgar Rice Burrough's twenty-four

Tarzan novels, C. S. Lewis' *Chronicles of Narnia,* and Hugh Lofting's *Dr. Doolittle.* The common thread in these books was talking animals.

Our groom and gardener, Bill Shamwell, taught me how to make baling twine snares and box traps to capture starlings and English sparrows, and how to trap field mice by putting cracked corn in a Coke bottle from which, fattened, they could not escape. Sometimes I would hide in the oats in a dark feed bin, lid closed, until I heard the mice emerging from a hole, moving around me. Using a tin-can top I would quietly plug the hole to block their escape and leap up to catch them with my hands, pulling them from the grain, my trouser legs, or my boots.

Our neighbor Mr. Zemo also encouraged me. A wily man with a dull razor, a Panama hat, and the slouch of *Green Acres'* Mr. Haney, he lived in a tiny farmhouse adjacent to ours where he kept homing pigeons, gamecocks, hunting dogs, and a few sickly horses. He liked fighting roosters and racing pigeons, and started me at age nine breeding Hungarian homers for competitions.

While I still keep pigeons, my obsession with birds found its focus when, at age eleven, I read T. H. White's Camelot tale *The Once and Future King* and knew instantly that I was to be a falconer. Falconry is the sport of training wild hawks for hunting. I bought every book available on falconry and wrote the authors. When I nearly severed my foot in a 1965 accident that kept me on crutches for months, my father bought me a red-tailed hawk from a pet store as a consolation. I named it Morgan Le Fay, after Mallory's witch, King Arthur's stepmother. Miraculously I found a local falconer, Alva Nye, to teach me the sport. Nye, who died in 1991, lived in Falls Church, five miles from Hickory Hill. An aviation engineer employed by the Pentagon, he was one of the pioneers of falconry in America and was often asked by the State Department to entertain visiting Arab dignitaries who wished to fly hawks.

I had few friends outside my household and family. On weekends and after school my brothers David, Michael, and I would dig for Civil War relics or wander nearby woods and streams with my sister Kerry, searching for frogs and crayfish, mud puppies and snakes. When I was nine, Uncle Jack invited me to the White House for a private audience in the Oval Office. As a gift, I brought him a seven-inch spotted salamander I'd captured the previous afternoon. We spent a good deal of our meeting discussing the salamander's health. I still have a picture of myself seated across from the president in my shorty shorts looking into the large crystal vase I had between my legs. The president is reaching across his desk and probing the salamander with the dull end of a pen. Afterward, we went outside and released it in the White House fountain.

We spent each summer on Cape Cod at the family compound on the Hyannisport shore where the twenty-eight cousins were raised communally and subjected to a daily regimen of athletic training supervised by a rotund former Olympic diver, Sandy Eiler. Three times a week we would have riding lessons at my grandfather's farm in Osterville or go on long rides through the scrub pine forests and sandy marshlands with him and his horse, Killarney. Every day my mother and father took us on the *Victura,* a twenty-six-foot wooden day sailer, for a picnic lunch on one of the nearby islands where we would fish for sand sharks, scup, flounder, puffers, and sea robins; gather hermit crabs, periwinkles, and scallops; or dig for the steamers that showed their presence on the tidal flats by squirting.

My cousin Bobby Shriver and I rode our bikes to the tidal inlets at Kalmus Beach to crab or to the salt marshes at Squaw Island to catch fiddler crabs, killifish, and mummichogs in a wire trap. We went dip-netting for painted turtles and baby catfish from a dinghy on Anderson's Pond, or beach seining for eels, shiners, skipjacks, and Atlantic needlefish that hid in the sargasso weed on the shores that bracketed the harbor. We snorkeled for scallops and held them hostage in an underwater cage anchored in the harbor until we had enough to feed the whole family—a formidable task, despite the scallops' abundance.

In the winters we went to the mountains or stayed at Grandpa's house at Palm Beach, where I would catch anoles, blue-tail skinks, and northern curly-tailed lizards and, with his encouragement, keep them on the screens in my grandmother's cabana. The high point of our Palm Beach vacations was our annual visit to Trapper Nelson in the nearby Loxahatchee. We helped him peel the softshell turtles and alligators and bullheads he caught on trotlines that we checked in his prop boat. On Grandpa's boat, the *Marlin,* Captain Frank would bring us out for a picnic lunch in the Intercoastal where we looked for manatees and porpoises or to the Atlantic, where I caught my first glimpse of flying fish and the cormorants, which, along with egrets and ospreys, had been nearly eradicated by DDT north of the Mason-Dixon line. During one visit we watched green turtles hatch on Grandpa's beach. Each day we stood on the flying balustrade that extended over the surf from the seawall and fished for pompano and spots while watching the nurse sharks in the waves.

In the spring while I was attending fifth and sixth grades at Sidwell Friends School, my father arranged for me to work in the Washington Zoo for a few dollars per week, making and distributing food, washing cages and polishing brass handrails, cleaning glass with a squeegee and bucket at the reptile house, or feeding rats to the raptors.

On autumn weekends we would often visit Camp David. While Daddy conferred with Uncle Jack, we wandered the mountain woodland, sometimes with Secret Service guards, turning over logs and rocks, capturing red and dusky salamanders, and trying to get a glimpse of a pine martin or the wolverines whose legendary ferocity we discussed and exaggerated at length.

On other fall weekends I would go with my brothers and sisters to trap vultures, sometimes crouching for hours beneath a piece of plywood that was suspended on two sawhorses and covered with carrion. At night we climbed with flashlights and burlap sacks up into the rickety rafters of local barns capturing pigeons to breed or to use for trapping hawks. When anybody asked me about my future plans, I replied without hesitation that I wanted to be a veterinarian.

My mother had a gentler version of her brothers' love of the outdoors. She was a superb horsewoman and had unofficially broken the world-record high jump on her quarter horse. Each morning before breakfast she and my father took us riding on breathtaking gallops through the Virginia woods and over fences near Pimmit Run as it cascaded north toward the Potomac, or in the woodland and hills surrounding the nearby CIA headquarters. Like my father, she couldn't stand any form of cruelty to animals. Once on a morning ride she heard the whinny of a starving horse and broke into a neighbor's barn in a futile effort to save the animal. The horse died, the neighbor pressed charges, and she was tried and acquitted for horse thievery by a Virginia jury. When she was very pregnant or accompanied by children too young to straddle a horse, she drove the younger children in a buggy behind my father, escorted by her older children on horseback and half a dozen giant dogs.

Her devotion to her Roman Catholic faith was the central tenet of her life. She always carried a rosary and led our kneeling family through the decades each evening. We made a morning offering and attended daily mass with her throughout the summer and holidays, sometimes twice. We fasted on Sundays, fainted from hunger at High Mass, ate fish on Fridays, and bracketed each meal with prayers. We read about the lives of the saints and prayed with particular fervor to St. Anthony and St. Francis of Assisi, the patron of animals who was a family patron as well. My mother was a strict disciplinarian and expected us to arrive at each meal on time, hair combed, fingernails clean.

My father, whose devotion rivaled my mother's, read us the Bible at night. His devotion to country came a close second. We knew every patriotic hymn and the fight songs for the army, navy, air force, and marines as well as Harvard and Notre Dame, and belted them out in the car rides to and from church in convertibles and station wagons overflowing with dogs and children. Whining was forbidden, toughness admired. "He's got guts" was my father's greatest compliment. We were admonished with "Kennedys don't quit" or "Kennedys never give up." Our parents supplemented our parochial school instruction in the Catholic creed by emphasizing the lives of the saints and particularly the joys of martyrdom, secular or religious. A picture of Daddy's brother Joe in his air force uniform hung over the dining room mantel, the flak-filled London sky silhouetting his B-25. He had flown fifty missions before volunteering to pilot an experimental flying bomb that vaporized over the English Channel. His sister, Kick, killed in a plane crash just after the war, had flown to England to join the nurse auxiliary at its outbreak. Her husband, Billy Cavendish, the Duke of Devonshire, died heroically on the Maginot line.

My father's strongest love was for democracy, because it elevated the human soul above all things. He saw it as the only system on the planet that could harness the energies of all our diverse peoples to solve the problems that faced our growing population. He admired the Greeks because they invented the democratic system and celebrated humanity in their politics, art, and literature. He often quoted from them or had us read poems of Aeschylus and Euripides. On Sundays each child would memorize a poem or biography, then recite it during dinner. Sometimes, he or my mother would read us poetry. He was a good military historian and would tell us, as he ate his dessert, the stories of the Battle of Bunker Hill or other skirmishes that changed history.

Both parents always reminded us that this country has been good to our family and that we therefore owed it a reciprocal debt. They frequently quoted St. Paul's admonition, "to whom much is given, much is expected." We children wanted to please them and give them our best. My father was always gentle with us, and there was always laughter when he was around. Only rarely did he have to discipline us. I remember one such occasion—when the Dolly Madison Highway was built, skirting our property and blocking our paths to Pimmit Run, and filling a local pond where we'd once caught tadpoles. David and I, at twelve years old, sensed that our paradise of horse farms and woodlands and feed and saddle shops was drowning beneath the rising suburban tide. In protest we dislodged some stacked highway culvert pipes and smashed them down an embankment, a crime for which we were soon caught. My father punished us severely. David and I swept boardwalks all summer to work off the debt. At other times, however, he supported my environmental instincts; at age ten, I announced I would write a book on the environment and began the work with his encouragement. A well-connected uncle arranged for me to interview Cabinet Secretary Stewart Udall, the nation's leading environmentalist, in his cavernous offices at the Department of the Interior. I brought my tape recorder and asked him questions about air and water pollution. I was grateful for the attention when the story of my impending work made *Time* magazine, though the actual writing has eluded me until now.

In good weather we weren't permitted indoors during the daytime. We played football, tennis, capture the flag, kick the can, guerrilla tag, chase-one chase-all, or went horseback riding and regularly made long walks through the woods. My father abhorred cruelty and would not permit us to keep guns or live feeders. I recall discovering him seated one afternoon on the grass beside the tennis court striving with tweezers to straighten the naturally curved bill of a red crossbill, believing it to be the result of an injury.

On vacations he took us on white-water rafting trips on the Colorado River, the Snake, the Salmon in Idaho, the Yampa and Green Rivers in Utah, or the upper Hudson in the Adirondacks. Daddy would ask us each morning to survey the horizon for a high peak, which we would then climb before breaking camp. When I was eleven my father and his friend Supreme Court Justice William O. Douglas, the nation's greatest environmental jurist, led David and me on a twenty-mile walk and bird-watching expedition on the C & O Canal between Washington and Baltimore. In 1962 Justice Douglas took us kids, many of my cousins, aunts, and uncles, and my father and mother on a ten-day pack trip to Whiskey Bend in the San Juan range on Washington's Olympic peninsula. We lived on trout that we caught with salmon eggs and drank from the streams. Afterward we fished for salmon in Puget Sound and caught more fish than I'd ever seen.

Several of us would accompany my father on most of his campaign trips. Whenever he landed in a new city he would ask to tour nearby Indian reservations. Many of us were given Indian names by tribal leaders on visits to various reservations. Indian or Eskimo leaders often visited the house, bringing gifts from great chiefs, peace pipes and headdresses, objects my father treasured. One winter a contingent of Alaskan Inuit arrived for lunch during an unusual Virginia snowstorm and spent the afternoon with my father in the backyard building a great igloo.

Viscerally he admired the Indians for their courage and toughness. But the conditions in which most Indians lived offended his sense of justice and his notion of America's mission in history. He believed in America's unique destiny. We were not united by common history, language, or culture. We were a collection of peoples from around the globe, united by an ideal: to build a community that would be an example to other nations of the best that humanity was capable of accomplishing. To help us accomplish this task, God had blessed us with the greatest natural resources of any nation, and the founders had given us the gift of democracy to harness the talents of all our diverse people. But this system relied on a foundation of justice. We would never fulfill our destiny, he believed, if we didn't first go back and address the fundamental injustice upon which the nation was founded. The Indians' condition put the lie to all his heartfelt beliefs about this country.

He spoke directly to us about these things at dinner when he returned from his trips. Once he told us that on the Pine Ridge Reservation he had seen an entire Sioux family living in the burned-out hulk of an abandoned car. Another night when he arrived from a junket to Appalachia for his Senate Hunger Committee, he recounted how he had visited a home where two large families lived in a single room with no heat or running water. Their children had one meal each day. "When you're older," he told us, "I hope you will help people like this."

When he was away for prolonged periods, he would call daily and would send each of us regular letters, with excerpts from poems or updates on his political battles. For example, in a 1962 letter to Michael, he wrote: "Today we sent the National Guard to bring James Meredith to school in Mississippi. I hope this doesn't happen when you grow up." Shortly after he died, we found in his desk a prophetic excerpt from Keats in his hand: "While we are laughing, the seeds of some trouble is put into the wide arable land of events, while we are laughing, it sprouts, it grows, and suddenly bears a poison fruit which we must pluck."

I was fourteen years old when my father was killed. On the morning of June 5, 1968, Georgetown Preparatory School's disciplinarian, Father Dugan, woke me up at 6:00 A.M. and told me there was a car waiting outside to take me to Hickory Hill. I was boarding at Georgetown and had not joined my father on the campaign trail as had David, Michael, and Courtney. At home someone told me Daddy had been shot. There were seven of us children home at the time—Kathleen, Joe, Kerry, Christopher, Max, and me. Douglas was an infant. My mother was pregnant with my sister Rory. The older children, myself included, flew to Los Angeles on Vice President Humphrey's plane, Air Force II. At the hospital the floor had been cleared except for close friends, family, and a security force of U.S. marshals. My father's head was bandaged and his eyes were black. His face was bruised, especially around his eyes. My mother was beside him, holding his hand, where she stayed all night. Each of us spent time with him that night, holding his hand, praying, saying good-bye, listening to the pumps that kept him breathing. In the morning, my brother Joe came into the ward where all the children were sleeping and told us, "He's gone." We all cried.

We flew his body back to New York on one of the presidential planes.

On June 7, Saturday, we held a wake for him at St. Patrick's. I stood vigil near the casket as a red-eyed crowd numbering in the hundred thousands, some having waited all night, filed quietly past saying their good-byes.

In Washington our funeral procession passed by the Mall on the way up the hill to Arlington Cemetery where thousands of homeless men organized by the late Martin Luther King, Jr.'s poor people's campaign were encamped in shanties and raggedy canvas tents with their new leader, the Reverend Ralph Abernathy. As we passed they came to the sidewalk and stood there quietly, heads bowed and holding their hats against their chests. We buried my father near his brother, beneath a simple black slab engraved with his name and the years he lived.

My aspirations to be a vet changed at that time as I began to take a greater interest in the issues of my father's crusade: civil rights, the cities, the Cold War, and the war in Vietnam. I felt some obligation to pick up the flag where he'd dropped it.

Still, I retained my interest in wildlife. The summer after his death, I spent a safari in East Africa traveling with Uncle Jack's best friend, LeMoyne Billings, who became a surrogate father to me. I transferred that autumn to Millbrook School, an all-boy boarding school in upstate New York where the chief attractions were the school's zoo and its natural history and ornithology programs. I joined the school's informal falconry program led by a fellow student, Peter Jenny. Jenny, whose parents were well-known veterinarians at the University of Pennsylvania, had been hawking since the age of seven in the company of the old-guard Pennsylvania falconers who had pioneered the sport between the wars.

In the autumn we captured and trained kestrels, red-tails, and immature "passage" hawks on their first migration. We used bow nets, *bal chartris,* or harness pigeons, contraptions that bristled with monofilament snares and nooses we found diagrammed in Beebe & Webster's *North American Falconry and Hunting Hawks,* or we used large mist nets of Japanese silk baited with live mice or pigeons. With these I've caught upwards of fifty hawks in a day squatting atop a ridge line on Schunemunk Mountain in the Hudson Valley in autumn.

By the time the leaves fell in the third week of October, we had trained the birds to come when we called and to follow like dogs, flying high in the canopy from tree to tree over our heads. We beat bush below them for cottontail and pheasant or worked the corn stubble for giant Belgian hare. We flew wild red-tails, falcons, and goshawks and pioneered many of the game-hawking techniques still used by American falconers.

We talked about hawks every spare moment, at meals, between classes, and after chapel. At night we fashioned hardware, hoods, jesses, gauntlets, and bewits out of tough, pliant kangaroo hide and marked in our memories the raptor nests we found during our daily hunting excursions in the winter months. In the spring we banded baby red-tails, crows, and owls in their nests, which we had found when no leaves obstructed our view of the upper canopy. The bands would help federal fish and wildlife scientists to trace migration patterns. We learned to use ropes and climbing spurs to scale the giant trees where the large raptors nested. At Millbrook I learned taxidermy and basic veterinary skills, how to determine disease, check for worms, give injections, and diagnose a range of illnesses and parasites that afflict raptors and other mammals.

Since Millbrook I have flown hawks nearly every autumn, and I continue to trap, band, and release hawks every year on Schunemunk Ridge overlooking the black-dirt farms of Orange County and the Hudson River. I breed hawks and owls at my home as well as quail, pheasant, and occasionally turkeys, and operate a wildlife rehabilitation center with a state and federal license that allows me to take in orphaned and injured wildlife and prepare them for release.

In the summers during high school I traveled to the Rio Meta region of the Colombian Llanos in South America to work on a ranch managed by Lem's nephew, Sandy Fisher, a former Peace Corps volunteer. For two dollars per week I worked from dawn clearing fields with machetes and fire, branding the skeletal Brahmin steers in a rough plank corral, and riding fence lines to check for breaks in the wire or for squatters. We ate yams and potatoes and fried plantains and only occasionally beef or capybara—a giant rodent. We drank sugar water. At night we slept beneath netting in bunkhouse hammocks. During high school and college I made frequent trips to Latin America as a journalist and as a guide for my brother Michael's white-water rafting company on first descents of rivers in Colombia, Peru, and Venezuela.

I had never seen such an abundance of life. Odd-looking fish, caiman and anacondas, wild peccary and capybara filled the ranch lagoon, and vast flocks of parrots and ibis flew from the lake to their evening roosts at twilight. On trips to Colombia I would sometimes hire canoes or string a hammock in a stall of a cattle boat and ride up the Meta River for four days to Cravo Norte, a roadless jungle cow town on the Venezuelan frontier, and then find my way back to Puerto Lopez over land.

At the same time, I followed my father's path through Harvard and the University of Virginia Law School. After law school I went to the Manhattan District Attorney's Office where I spent a year prosecuting misdemeanor cases, assaults, prostitutes, and fare beaters.

Everyone, a friend has observed, is given something to overcome. My biggest battle was with addiction to drugs. Soon after my father's death I made a series of choices involving drugs that started me down a road from which I had to struggle to return. Addiction is a progressive malady. It gets worse with time. Like many other addicts, I was functional while using and able to put down drugs for long periods of time, months and even years, but I always went back.

An addict's other characteristic is denial. My ability to put drugs aside for long periods and my strong willpower in every other area of my life fueled my denial. My life experience with public scrutiny and an aggressive and nosy press made me wary of attending public twelve-step programs, where I might otherwise have found recovery.

The process of recovery is also a process of restoring self-esteem. Self-esteem comes from doing estimable things. On my own part I had accepted as a child a very religious moral code which forbade dishonesty, and illegal activities in general. My addiction caused me to devote less energy to pursuing the principles that I was taught as a child. The addiction increasingly challenged my capacity to live up to my values and the dictates of my conscience.

In September 1983 I was arrested by South Dakota police as I was leaving a plane in Rapid City on my way to treatment. They found a small amount of heroin in my bag. My arrest generated tremendous publicity and, ironically, neutralized my fear of scandal, allowing me to get help.

Part of the process of recovery from addiction is focusing on your own conduct and taking responsibility for that conduct: paying bills, driving the speed limit, putting water back in the ice tray, making the bed—getting up when the alarm goes off and trying to live your life as an ethical and moral example. Following my arrest and during my early recovery, I began to rethink my life. In January 1984, I obtained a volunteer job in upstate New York working on a project for the Natural Resources Defense Council's (NRDC) executive director, John Adams. My decision to work on environmental issues was consistent with my other efforts to retrace my steps to that point where I had started off on the wrong path. I decided now to explore job opportunities in areas that felt truer to my earlier aspirations. The NRDC was the national environmental group of lawyers and scientists that was best known for having written and successfully lobbied and litigated the nation's most important environmental laws after Earth Day 1970. It had served as legal counsel for the Hudson River Fishermen since 1970. It wasn't long before that job brought me into contact with the Hudson River Fishermen and its Riverkeeper, John Cronin.

Using prison labor provided by the state and funds from the settlement of the Storm King case, I was transforming a compound of farmhouses on the Osborn family estate into a scientific field station for the study and protection of the Hudson River. The Castle Rock Field Station would include a fully equipped laboratory, overnight quarters for field scientists, and offices for environmental advocacy groups. The first tenant, the Hudson River Fishermen's Association, was due in mid-February.

I had heard about the Fishermen from Ross Sandler and Al Butzel, two environmental lawyers who had represented the group in several cases. They had enormous respect for the blue-collar coalition of recreational and commercial fishermen and scientists led by Bob Boyle. The Fishermen operated like a lightweight cavalry unit in enemy territory, relying on mobility and offensive tactics against larger, better-equipped forces. After eighteen years of existence, their only headquarters was the home of the recently appointed Riverkeeper, John Cronin. Castle Rock would be their first real office.

I met John Cronin in mid-February. I liked him instantly. Six-foot-two, with piercing blue eyes, he was eloquent, thoughtful, and utterly committed. He had a great sense of humor and an extraordinary talent for politics. He thought about tactics and strategy in a way I found familiar. But John only grudgingly settled in at Castle Rock. I remember his unease at changing his mailing address, certain that when the state officials administering the estate realized its new tenant's subversive mission they would find a way to terminate the lease.

Indeed, John was a militant environmentalist. But he always put humans first. He saw human beings as part of the landscape he sought to protect, and he saw the Hudson as a community—where sports fishermen, commercial fishermen, river pilots, oil tankers, barges, and pleasure boats enjoy the beauty and support their livelihoods.

When I began working with the Fishermen, our approach was

kamikaze. John had almost no cash flow and yet he was delivering legal broadsides to the biggest corporations and most powerful institutions in America—Con Edison, the U.S. Army, Westway, Exxon Oil, and New York State. Early on he explained his philosophy. He told me that if he had only a few thousand dollars and came upon a polluter, he would attack even if it looked like the effort might jeopardize the organization. This apparently self-destructive strategy made sense at second glance, when one considered that their opponents could always outspend them. The Fishermen relied on stronger spirit, conviction, idealism, and tenacity to prevail. The organization's purpose, John often reminded me, was to protect the river, not to build an institution.

From my Millbrook days I already knew and loved the Hudson Valley and fell easily into life in Mount Kisco, New York—forty miles north of New York City, but still rural enough to support expanding ranges of coyote, turkey, and white-tailed deer, and plenty of game for my daily hawking.

Two things made me fall in love with the river itself. First, I read Bob Boyle's book, *The Hudson River: A Natural and Unnatural History,* which advocated an in-the-muck, waders-on environmentalism. Second, I took Boyle's advice and acquainted myself with the river firsthand.

During my first spring in the Hudson Valley, I fished with Bob Boyle and some of his friends for stripers, black bass, and white perch from boats and from the shore. We went fly-fishing on the tributaries for brown and brook trout. We beach-seined for exotics and shrimp with everything from window screens to a one-hundred-foot net off Croton Point or Senasqua Beach. We went scuba diving from canoes in Iona Marsh, and hiked in the woods to watch the yellow perch spawn on a tiny creek at Constitution Island. Inspired by these expeditions I hiked, swam, fished, netted, and even snorkeled or scuba dove many of the river's tributaries on my own.

Exploring my new surroundings was more than an interesting diversion. It was a way of getting my bearings—of adapting to a new home by systematically developing the same sort of familiarity with my surroundings and its indigenous plants and animals as I'd had with the Virginia and Cape Cod homes of my youth. Plumbing its depths, exploring its richness, finding and surveying its special places, inventorying its species and recording the rhythms of their appearances and disappearances were my way of staking my claim. I learned to think of the Hudson Valley as my home, my place.

The Croton River quickly became a favorite spot. Several times during my first years as a Hudson Valley resident I snorkeled or scuba dived from the rail yard at the river's mouth upstream to Quaker Rock below the first dam. The pool there is about twelve feet deep during high water in the spring. Lying on the bottom and hugging a big rock to stabilize myself in the current, I could sit and watch the pool fill up with fish. Near the mouth of the Croton, the bottom is carpeted with barnacles and other marine invertebrates and crustaceans interspersed with thick groves of eel grass. Blue crabs and green crabs scuttle along the bottom and glass shrimp fill the water column almost anytime during the spring or summer. Atlantic eels four-and-a-half feet long hide between the rocks and crevices, having migrated from their spawning grounds in the North Atlantic. They feed in the Hudson River for a number of years and then run back to the Sargasso Sea to spawn. In the early spring the water turns to quicksilver as thousands and thousands of alewives or "sawbellies" come up the Croton on their spawning run from the Atlantic. You can see great striped bass that swim up to feed on the herring schools or to spawn. Ravenous schools of snapper bluefish, which I used to catch on Cape Cod as a boy, snatch mayflies in their vicious little teeth, competing for food with the Croton's abundant trout populations—rainbow, brown, and brook. The freshwater species—largemouth bass, smallmouth bass, white perch, yellow perch, bluegills, beautiful pumpkinseed sunfish that are as colorful as any of the tropical fish that adorn pet-store fish tanks—congregate in large numbers in the aerated waters beneath the spillway. Giant carp, weighing thirty to fifty pounds and resembling mustachioed goldfish, darken the bottom as they swim overhead in pairs or trios. Proper goldfish also live and swim in the Hudson, though they are less abundant than in former times. They grow extraordinarily large—up to four pounds—and at least one commercial fisherman, Everett Nack of Claverack, New York, supplements his income by capturing them for collectors.

I was surprised to find large numbers of tropical fish in the estuary. They are funneled into the Hudson in large cells of warm water that break off the Gulf Stream as it flows north past Long Island. In the Croton, you see odd creatures like sea horses and a fish called a moongazer, which emits an electric shock when you touch it. Jack crevalle and Atlantic needlefish, whose home waters are in Florida and the Caribbean, are abundant in the Hudson. Hudson fisherman Tom Lake wrote me recently to say that he had caught a permit, a Caribbean pompano, the Hudson's two hundredth confirmed species. A few years ago, Bob Boyle netted a mangrove snapper, also at home in the Congo River, on Senasqua Beach just north of the Croton's mouth.

The Hudson is both diverse *and* abundant. One March a few years ago I was out with a commercial fisherman under the Tappan Zee Bridge pulling up ten thousand pounds of fish on every lift. With each tide the nets were filled—every six hours—day and night, week after week, month after month, all springtime. That spring the State Department of Environmental Conservation asked the commercial fishermen to drive their boats slowly in the shallows because at high speeds they were hitting too many fish.

Because of its relative diversity, health, and abundance, the Hudson is the Noah's Ark of the East Coast and perhaps of the entire North Atlantic. As the great estuaries of the North Atlantic—the Chesapeake, the St. Lawrence, the Sea of Azov, the Rhine, Long Island Sound, Narragansett Bay, and the Carolina estuaries—decline, the Hudson grows in importance. It is the gene pool, the last safe harbor for species that face extinction elsewhere.

Yet despite their abundance, striped bass and other fishes cannot legally be sold because they are contaminated by PCBs. Pollution and poorly planned development continue to threaten the river along its length. Although many environmental victories have been won, the pressure from increasing population and development assures that the greatest battles lie ahead. Ironically, it seems the cleaner we make the Hudson, the greater the interest that developers take in paving, developing, and polluting her watershed. The Hudson River Fishermen's Association (HRFA) and its successor, Riverkeeper, stand at the center of the battle to clean up and protect the river.

My professional affiliation with the Fishermen's Association began almost accidentally because of the intervention of a man neither John Cronin nor I had actually met. Joe Augustine of Newburgh, New York, was the most persistent and frequent among the army of tipsters—including fishermen and boaters, government employees, factory workers, marina operators, property owners, and railroad commuters—who kept ringing Cronin's phone off the hook with updates on river pollution and requests for help. Joe was a jeweler and pawnshop operator, with a giant Afro and energy as abundant as his notable girth, both of which he maintained with a nearly insatiable taste for Mallomars, Oreos, and Coca-Cola.

On weekends Joe would bid for the contents of unpaid self-storage bins. He hawked the goods at outdoor Hudson Valley flea markets or sold them in his junk store on Main Street in Newburgh where he worked feverishly with his wife and three generations of the Augustine family. The rest of the week, he was a full-time environmentalist with a grassroots group, DECEPA—an acronym suggesting a conspiracy of deception between New York State's Department of Environmental Conservation (DEC) and the federal Environmental Protection Agency (EPA).

Augustine showered the agencies with a fervent deluge of daily complaints. He demanded, for example, to know what the DEC was doing to remove forty-four drums he'd found on Newburgh's Quassaic Creek. The Plattekill Rod and Gun Club, he noted, was discharging lead shot into a lake. Contaminants from the air force base at Stewart Field were leaching into Newburgh's drinking water at Washington Lake. He reported a shoreline pipe draining blood and formaldehyde into the Hudson River from a cluster of funeral homes.

In addition to the barrage of letters and complaints, he circulated petitions and harassed DEC employees with continuous phone calls and the agency's commissioner with unrequited demands for a meeting. He organized petition drives and paid from his own pocket for advertisements in local newspapers blasting the DEC engineers as "liars." He appeared at virtually every town board meeting as well as meetings of the planning board and zoning board of appeals. He cultivated friendships with idealistic clerks and agency bureaucrats who shared gossip and sensitive information. Local newspapers frequently carried glowing letters with heroic descriptions of Augustine from his fans and people he had assisted.

His boundless energy and indignation made him a thorn in the side of government agencies, but his information was too good to be dismissed. He knew the DEC's procedures and the office and field hours of its inspectors. He could recite various environmental laws and regulations. He knew the administrative permit process and proper protocols for sampling and analysis. By continually asking simple, common-sense questions, he developed a sophisticated knowledge of basic sanitary engineering. He knew soil types, aquifer depths and locations, and how a sewer plant worked.

Joe's most consistent complaint was that his community was being destroyed by polluters and that government was doing little to prevent it. His expectations were not unreasonable; environmental enforcement agencies should enforce environmental law and protect public health. In the spring of 1984, Joe sent one of his letters to John Cronin accompanied by a hefty scrapbook containing carefully annotated dossiers on thirty-five Newburgh-area polluters, each with photographs and disparaging captions blasting his perpetual villains—the DEC, the EPA, Wehran Engineering, and corrupt politicians.

Along with his scrapbook, he sent the Fishermen a letter in which he pleaded that: "We have been begging for help for so long that we feel no one out there cares about the environment except you and us. The biggest problem we have is the DEC. They just don't give a damn." I offered to go to Newburgh to meet with Augustine and determine if his complaints were justified.

The town of Newburgh and the adjacent city of Newburgh, each with approximately twenty-two thousand residents, are located on the banks of the Hudson in northeastern Orange County. The historic city of Newburgh regularly leads the nation in virtually every criterion used to measure urban decay and is famed for producing local politicians with elastic ethics and a knack for plundering the public trust. The main thoroughfare, Broadway, is as squalid and dangerous as the worst streets in the South Bronx. In the words of its current police chief, Newburgh is a "mean, sick, nasty, fetid little city."

As squalid as the city streets are, Newburgh's waterfront gives new meaning to the word "depressed." Since the days of Rockefeller's Hudson River Commission in the early 1960s, Hudson River advocates have used photographs of Newburgh's shoreline to illustrate the depths of the river's affliction. The only active shoreline industries are the city's sewage treatment plant and the Consolidated Metal Junkyard where twisted hulks of metal and crushed and rusted automobile wrecks lie in heaps, at times half in and half out of the river. Junkyards and incinerators dominate the once proud Hudson River vistas. The remaining shoreline is a defoliated and depopulated wasteland where truckers come for illicit sex and drug dealers sell their wares. The river itself is littered with burned-out barges; it bristles with the skeletons of broken piers and rotting pilings. The Washington Street boat ramp is the one cheerful outpost on this dreary shore.

John and I were particularly concerned by Augustine's story that the city of Newburgh had arranged to sell its Washington Street boat ramp and three adjoining acres of public parkland to certain acquaintances of the mayor for the bargain price of $30,000. The new owner, Mr. James Cracolicci, a local baker and developer, intended to start a floating restaurant at the site. John saw this transfer as a threat to the River-keeper's mission to maintain public access to the river for the fishermen and boaters who were the strongest constituency for clean water. The boat ramp was the only public access to the Hudson in Orange County. It was heavily utilized by small boat owners who often had to wait in long lines to launch or retrieve their boats. On any Saturday and Sunday during boating season, the parking area was filled to its capacity of twenty-five trailers. The ramp was also used by many of Newburgh's low-income and minority population for fishing and wading.

The property's appraised value at that time was $75,000. The private developers stood to benefit substantially from the $140,000 spent by the state on shoreline stabilization, paving, dredging, and bulkheading. When we asked Mr. Cracolicci and his partner whether they intended that the public would still be able to use the boat ramp, his partner replied with striking candor: "We are not going to have spades drinking and screwing and swimming around our *new* boat ramp, if that's what you mean by the public!" At that moment I knew I wanted to be an environmental lawyer. Any ambivalence I'd felt about having abandoned the battle for social justice when I took up arms for a clean environment was gone. Mr. Cracolicci's partner's remark confirmed my instinct that the battles were the same. In fact, the battle for the environment was the ultimate civil rights and human rights contest, a struggle to maintain public control over publicly owned resources against special interests that would monopolize, segregate, and liquidate them for cash.

That case also inaugurated my career in environmental law. Prior to that time, I knew little about civil litigation and next to nothing about environmental law. The civil law I'd studied in law school I'd long since forgotten. I never so much as took a course in environmental law.

My training and experience weighed heavily in criminal prosecution. So I started out by doing the things that seemed obvious.

John and I obtained copies of the deed and lease to the boat launch property as well as Newburgh's City Charter. Both contained limitations affecting alienability. Reading through the minutes of various city council meetings, we discovered that the city had ignored a provision requiring a four-to-five council vote on all sales of city property. The council vote had been three to five. We also found another provision requiring competitive bidding on all sales of city property.

I called the city's corporation counsel, William Kavanaugh, and pointed out the city's noncompliance with the provision that required a four-to-five council vote. Kavanaugh agreed that the vote should be retaken. I then notified him that Riverkeeper intended to submit a competitive bid. This was John's idea, and he was undeterred by the fact that we didn't have the money. We would simply have to scramble around the Hudson Valley to raise it, even if it meant our selling the boat and John's contributing his own paycheck and turning volunteer. Our offer put the city government in a temporary quandary. We were able to stall the vote in city council, giving ourselves time to devise a strategy to save the boat ramp.

In the meantime, John and I decided to take a closer look at Newburgh. Augustine's parade of Newburgh polluters dovetailed with our growing realization that the Hudson's apocalypse was less likely to come from a catastrophic mega project like Storm King or Westway, but rather, in Bob Boyle's words, from "the death by a thousand cuts." The problem we saw in Newburgh was endemic to the Hudson Valley.

Even in the Hudson Valley, where enforcement was generally more aggressive than anywhere else in the state, most polluters had little or nothing to fear. When they enforce against polluters at all, the DEC and EPA and other environmental agencies tended to focus their resources on a few high-profile polluters. Less visible dischargers rarely received enforcement attention. For example, both federal and state agencies, as a matter of official policy, would not even inspect polluters whose discharges were less than one million gallons a day and would not enforce against developers who filled wetlands less than twelve acres. An accumulation of such garden variety dischargers, dumpers, and bank disturbers could destroy an entire tributary without attracting any enforcement attention.

We decided to help Joe focus his scattered approach with a concentrated enforcement effort targeted at a single Hudson River tributary. Joe had complained all summer about sewage discharges at the foot of Quassaic Creek. His scrapbook presentation included several other violators along the length of the creek. Our project would be to identify specific illegal sources of pollution, and the Fishermen would then act as a catalyst to get government agencies to set a precedent of assuming regulatory responsibility over less prominent violators.

The Quassaic Creek is a troubled urban tributary, flowing through the town and the city of Newburgh and forming the border between the city and the neighboring town of New Windsor. Damming and industrialization typifies much of the creek's seven-mile length from its source, Chadwick Lake, to its mouth at the Hudson. New York DEC had awarded Quassaic Creek a "D" classification—the agency's lowest rating.

In August, and over the next several months, Joe and I and two local HRFA volunteer investigators, Patrick Gilligan and Karl Shwartz, documented twenty-four polluters, including three municipalities. Wearing waders I walked, at various times, every foot of its seven-mile length. Our investigation took us into pipes and culverts and underneath ancient factories. We mounted twenty-four-hour surveillance of intermittent pipes. We sat for days on lawn chairs to sample factory and sewer plant outfalls, and set traps to catch liquids being dumped at odd hours. We interviewed neighbors and factory workers and other eyewitnesses. We took photographs, invaded historical archives and dusty agency file cabinets, and traced underground pipelines on ancient sewer maps. We scuba dived in the Hudson to collect evidence of illegal dumping and donned wet suits to swim across a pond on a cold winter night to collect samples from an unpermitted pipe. We carried backpacks filled with sampling vials, flashlights, maps, notepads, a camera, and, occasionally, fishing rods to avoid suspicion. We collected sediment samples and fishes to use in our cases. As some of our cases headed for trial, I accompanied scientists retained to prepare formal stream surveys to assess environmental damage.

Despite the years of abuse, we found the Quassaic to be beautiful in some of its reaches, and abundant and rich in diversity. Below the Chadwick Lake Dam, the creek flows over a stony bottom through a series of small rapids and deep pools shaded by deciduous forests.

Walking the upper stream was almost always a pleasant task for me. Certain stretches reminded me of Pimmit Run where I spent some of the best days of my boyhood. A mile below the dam the terrain changes abruptly into an open, grassy floodplain, unusual in the Hudson Valley, and then, after half a mile, back into forest from which it emerges at the city's outskirts and meanders through a series of braided tributaries into Brookside Pond. Brookside is surrounded by a nineteen-acre cattail and red-elm-wooded marshland fed by streamlets. Mute swans and other waterfowl breed in deep stands of reed canary grass and tussock grass, speckled alder, red osier dogwood, and American elm. Designated as "protected" on the DEC's state wetlands map, these streamlets consolidate above the Arma Dye House, where Quassaic Creek runs beneath a parking lot and a series of textile mills and factories that historically utilized the creek as their private waste conveyance. The creek emerges from this darkened culvert to make the final stretch through channelized urban blight, passing over three dams and their impoundments, then beneath River Road and the Amtrak railroad bridge to enter the Hudson estuary at Quassaic's vegetated delta bracketed by oil storage tank farms.

Along the banks and in the creek we found wood turtles, painted turtles, and snappers; water snakes, garter snakes, milk, brown, and deekay snakes; green-tailed, wood, and leopard frogs; red salamanders and stream salamanders.

Every sweep of a small stream seine would net us chain and redfin, pickerel, yellow and brown bullheads, pumpkinseed sunfish, and bluegills. We saw the female red-breasted sunfish guarding their nests, and common and golden shiners, white suckers, tessellated darters, black-nosed dace, and giant goldfish. In the evenings we could see the carp congregate in our lights below the bridges and the spawning herring and alewives gathering at the base of the Quassaic's lowest dam. In late August I swept the vegetated delta at Quassaic's mouth with a sixty-foot bag seine. When I reached the shore the bag was alive with sunfish, crappie, Johnny darters, and a two-pound largemouth bass.

The bobbers and monofilament webbing that festooned the trees in some places like Christmas lights told us that fishermen still used the creek intensively. In our travels we met them going down the intertwining paths in the forested buffers or trying every trick to catch giant carp below the dams. We watched Hispanic fishermen catching catfish from twisted metal perches at Consolidated Metal Junkyard and cutting off the poison dorsal spine in preparation for the table. We saw kids with crab traps or fishing poles and treble hooks for snagging the alewives. In the heart of the city people desperate for open space could be seen camping and swimming in the lower reaches along the well-used network of foot trails.

Despite the stream's biological resilience, our investigation had its Dantean aspect. Quassaic had become a conveyance for industrial and municipal waste. Just south of Quassaic's mouth, Consolidated Metal Junkyard's cranes towered over giant heaps of scrap iron and wrecked and compacted car bodies. Crushed cars, drums, tires, bicycles and baby carriages, pallets and paint cans, rusted machinery, and demolition debris moved glacially into the river beckoned by a listing barge lashed to the shore. The site occupies the view from Washington's Revolutionary War headquarters, which perches on a hanging delta a hundred feet above the junkyard. When I seined the Quassaic in August I noticed so many pipes and drains emptying into the mouth that I wondered that there was anything alive in this part of the creek. Among the fish I found long strings of toilet paper and what we euphemistically called "brown trout" or "river pickles": human fecal material. After a short time cuts on my hand began to fester.

Walking upstream I found the source of the sewage—a concrete flume hidden between the railroad bridge abutments, belching milky liquid and solid fecal matter. Near the pipe the searing stench of volatile chemicals obscured the sewage odors. I followed the buried pipe upstream along the bank for three-quarters of a mile to a hole through which the pipe's concrete roofing had fractured and fallen. Overpowering mothball scents wafted from the deep culvert below. I returned with John Cronin and safety equipment and rope. John lowered me into the pipe where I sampled the phenolic dregs. Analysis showed high quantities of naphthalene, a chemical used in the dye and textile industries that is known to cause mutations, blood disorders, and other ailments in animals.

Neither city sewer maps nor DEC engineers nor the town and city officials had any explanation for the source of the effluent. After additional research we traced the naphthalene to Arma Textile, which had illegally hooked its discharge to a manhole. Arma was discharging unadulterated textile waste, first into the city sewer and then directly into Quassaic through a defective sewer regulator. We decided to take a closer look at the company.

In early September, John Cronin, Joe Augustine, and I visited Arma's dilapidated complex of twenty interconnected structures. Blue-brown peroxide fumes veiled the factory. Inside, workers breathed the abominable vapors that did not escape through the structure's many illegal stacks to pollute the neighborhood. Nearby Locust Street residents complained of the rotten egg smell of sulfur and the persistent odor of bleach and formaldehyde that hung over their schoolyard, causing sore throats. John and I climbed Arma's roof to check the emissions sources. We were undeterred by trespass laws, since "necessity to stop a crime in progress" is a defense to trespass in New York State. We found plenty of crimes in progress on Arma's roof. Altogether, there were twenty-four illegal pipes and stacks discharging liquid and chemical fumes. Some of them were jerry-rigged through broken windows or breaches in the wall and ramshackle roof. One pipe from the shipping building discharged liquid into a holding pond at fifty gallons per minute. We took samples by swimming the pond in wet suits at night.

Arma was only one of many environmental offenders in Quassaic's dreary urban corridor. On the same day that I found sewage in my seine net, I discovered an illegal pipe protruding from a railway headwall through which Mobil Oil was pumping fifteen thousand gallons per day of contaminated groundwater into Quassaic's mouth from its shoreline oil storage terminal. Joe and I determined the flow by measuring the time it took to fill a five-gallon bucket. Analysis of the water showed a brew so volatile that a spark would have caused a catastrophic explosion.

Just up the bank from Mobil, we counted half a dozen unpermitted pipes, bilge holes, and scuppers leading from American Felt and Filter's factory walls or protruding from the stream banks in the adjacent woodlands. One pipe vomited shredded filter paper and trailed a possum-colored plume highlighted by an iridescent sheen.

A half mile upstream, Federal Block was perched a hundred feet above on Quassaic's left bank. Concrete rubble and thousands of discarded blocks covered the debris-strewn slope, spilling into the creek and obstructing its flow. We found a plastic painter's dropcloth that nearly obscured a twelve-inch pipe near the summit, discharging petroleum waste from machinery cleaning operations.

I stumbled onto the grounds of Hudson Valley Tree, a plastic Christmas tree company, as a bulldozer was pushing fill into Brookside Pond, Quassaic's largest wetland. A hundred-foot wall of fresh earth was poised at its edge to inter the wetland. The construction supervisor told me that the owner had not obtained necessary permits under the state Wetlands Law or the federal Clean Water Act.

Some of the violations were rather droll and resulted more from carelessness than from deliberation, like a washing-machine discharge from an unpermitted drain at Economy Cleaners. A floor drain at Resnick Warehouse spat frothy brown cleaning fluid into the creek. Zayre's Shopping Center had allowed heaps of discarded wire-mesh shopping carts to accumulate in large piles in the creek. Tires and pallets from Harvey Brothers Tires littered the Quassaic ravine just downstream.

Other violators were aware of their wrongdoing. In the last week of August, Joe and I were exploring Quassaic's Brookside tributaries and were drawn by a startling stench of putrescence and chlorine to the sewer pipe of the Justgold Shopping Plaza. Emerging from a thickly vegetated bank in a wooded thicket, the broken pipe blasted a steady stream of soapy black film. Above the pipe Brookside Stream was gin clear; below it was smelly and cream colored. Fecal matter bobbed in pools and carpeted the back eddies. Below the pipe the streambed was scarlet red. Mindful of our experience with the funeral homes, I said, "Jeez, Joe, it's blood." I looked more closely and realized I was staring at masses of scarlet tubifex worms densely packed and undulating with the current like red liquid. I had collected tubifex in ponds as a boy as food for salamanders, but I'd never seen them in such densities. Today they are harvested from highly fertilized Mexican sewers and freeze-dried in cubes for sale in pet stores for fish and amphibian food. Thanks to Justgold, Brookside had its own potential cash crop.

Each time Joe and I returned for samples, the conditions were as bad or worse. Sometimes the creek was tar black, topped by a spaghetti-like scum. The neighbors told us that the choking stench kept them inside all summer, windows locked.

Justgold's own self-reporting records, which we obtained from the DEC, showed hundreds of violations in 1984 and 1985 in virtually every category of pollutant. The company's own tests indicated that they were exceeding their pollution permit limitation for solid matter by ten to twenty times. But Justgold's records did not tell the full story. Joe and I brought our samples to Ronald Bayer, the owner of a local lab called Envirotest, for analysis. Joe insisted that we code the vial labels since he didn't trust Newburgh-area labs. Bayer's independent testing showed the plant exceedance was much worse than it was reporting—as high as one hundred to one thousand times the permitted levels. In one instance, Envirotest's analysis showed settleable solid levels at an astounding six thousand times the plant's permit level! The high values could only be explained if the plant was discharging primary sludge. If this were true, whoever was responsible could be criminally liable.

One day when the effluent was particularly offensive, Joe and I made our way up to the sewer plant through a quiet grove at the edge of the mall's parking lot. In our indignation we put caution and judgment aside and climbed an eight-foot chain-link fence topped with barbed wire. We confirmed that the sand filter was broken and the plant was bypassing the entire filtration process. Furthermore, there were large sludge accumulations in the primary tanks, and it appeared that this sludge, instead of being dried and hauled away, was simply being dumped into the creek. As we examined the primary tank, a pickup truck hurtled into the compound and Joe and I headed for the fence, which I vaulted, and then awaited Joe's more conservative ascent, slowed by his 280 pounds and Mallomar-laden pockets. He was still climbing when the driver approached the gate, saw Joe, and fled. I recognized the man as Ronald Bayer, the owner of Envirotest, and realized that the same man who was performing our tests was also operating the plant. He must have recognized us and been horrified to realize that the samples he was testing were from his own plant. The following day he reported to the DEC that Justgold's plant had had an "accidental" spill and immediately thereafter resigned his contracts to operate the plant.

In the urban corridor between Brookside and Arma, the Quassaic runs beneath a string of factories, parking lots, and warehouses. In its most abused stretch just below Arma, the working courtyard of the Al Cam mechanic's garage backs onto old wooden warehouses that straddle Quassaic Creek. I visited Al Cam a half dozen times, hiking the creek through this long dark crawl space, and always found a car parked above an oil drain cut between the joists and girders above me.

Motor oil stained the bank, bleeding into the creek. Puddles of aquamarine antifreeze rested gloomily in grim pools. Thick sludge deposits covered the creek bottom. Clearly, Al Cam's mechanic was dumping used automobile fluids into the creek. Two Salvadoran employees of the adjoining dye house told us that, three mornings each week, the Al Cam mechanic dropped a barrel of oil from the Stroock Bridge into the creek or into the gravel parking lot. We dug where they indicated and struck deposits of motor oil.

We often found that the creek emerged from the underground stretch stinking of mothballs and colored purple, blue, or green. In mid-October a Riverkeeper volunteer, Patrick Gilligan, and I followed the vapor and a colorful plume into a culvert beneath the Valmar Dye House, where the creek bed turned spongy. We made our way through the dank culvert with flashlights and breathing apparatuses. Bubbly brown algae clung to slimy rocks. We followed the stench up a stone catacomb into the factory's underbelly where steaming dye vats drained through spitting valves and a pipe hole into the creek. I took a sample from the stream and tested the oily loam sediments in the culvert. These samples yielded high levels of naphthalene, chlorobenzene, and other hazardous chemicals.

The most egregious violators were the municipalities. Red dye and raw sewage from the town of New Windsor's pump station regularly blew the covers off the River Road manholes and cascaded into the creek, dyeing Quassaic's mouth red. The city of Newburgh discharged raw sewage and untreated industrial waste into the creek from a collection of defective stormwater regulators. The city's sewer plant near Quassaic's mouth had hundreds of self-reporting violations. But the adjacent town of Newburgh was worse.

In late August Joe and I visited Gidneytown Creek, a Quassaic tributary, to confirm neighborhood complaints that the town of Newburgh's Gidneytown sewage treatment plant had turned the creek charcoal black. The neighborhood smelled like a urinal. We spotted a pipe emerging from a stepped bulkhead discharging a hundred gallons of milky water per minute. Above the pipe, the creek was crystal green; below it was a turbid soup, cream colored or black. Thick foam bloomed at its base where long brown streamers of filamental growth festooned the rocks. We posted volunteers on lawn chairs in the woods, near the pipe and out of sight of plant workers, to collect composite samples, and Joe and I visited the plant over a dozen times during the next weeks.

We obtained and examined the plant's daily self-reporting records (called DMRs). These confessed to violating standards, but rather less dramatically than we suspected from the creek's milky discharge. Our own sampling results consistently showed much higher values—generally double or triple the reported numbers. We decided to bring our evidence to the DEC, hoping for a criminal investigation. The DEC's Regional Water Engineer, Cesare Manfredi, appeared at our meeting with Regional Counsel Judith Ferry and scoffed at our sampling results. The numbers were impossibly high, he said. We must have mishandled the samples. His deputy engineers had checked the plant numerous times, and the violations were nowhere near as bad as our numbers suggested. John and I dug out photographs of the creamed-coffee discharge. Manfredi examined the photos with a puzzled look. Pointing at the masonry bulkhead, he said, "This isn't the Gidneytown outfall." We stared at each other blankly for a moment before realizing the town had installed a sneak pipe.

Before the end of the day we confirmed that the plant had two outfalls, an official pipe from which the operators sampled and which they showed visiting DEC inspectors. A second sneak pipe ran through the woods, bypassed treatment altogether, and discharged raw sewage downstream.

The town's two other sewer plants followed suit. Meadow Hill South discharged 200,000 gallons of untreated sewage from its own sneak pipe, producing an odor around the local mall that would, in Joe's words, "gag a maggot." Self-monitoring reports showed that even its legal pipe had 342 violations over the preceding three years. Its sister plant, Meadow Hill North, exceeded its permit parameters 80 percent of the time during the same period.

In December Joe, Patrick Gilligan, and I found the creek bed buried beneath two to three feet of caramel-colored sludge with an oatmeal consistency. The creek was barren of life except for two fish struggling through the narrow channels in the gelatinous mass. A mile upstream we found the culprit pipe protruding from the town of Newburgh water treatment plant.

I realized that the sludge must be alum, a common by-product of the process by which drinking water treatment plants make dirty lake or river water potable. Under the law, the plant must carefully collect the sludge—which is dangerous to fish and aquatic ecosystems—and haul it to a landfill for disposal.

Approaching the plant compound with my fishing rod in hand, I stopped at the chain-link fence and hailed a plant operator. He conceded that there were no fish left in the creek but said he would lose his job if he revealed where the "silt" was coming from. When I asked him if it was alum sludge in the creek he went into the plant, closing the door behind him. A few minutes later Mr. Lawrence "Butch" Goodrich, the plant manager, emerged.

Goodrich confessed to us that there was no place to dump his alum. He had complained, he said, to Town Supervisor Robert Kirkpatrick to no avail. Rather than shut down the plant, he dumped into the creek "at least forty thousand gallons of alum." He conceded that the amount could be considerably greater. Our research supported that contention.

Using the state's freedom-of-information law, we quickly obtained the sludge hauling and alum purchasing records for the town of Newburgh's Chadwick Lake filtration plant. Those records showed that while the plant had produced over a million gallons of alum sludge during 1984, none had been hauled away. It could only have been dumped into the creek. Records for the previous five years also showed giant discrepancies between alum sludge produced and the amount hauled away. We immediately informed the DEC about the illegal dumping, hoping for a criminal prosecution against the town.

It was disappointing to me that the DEC responded instead by writing the town a temporary permit to discharge alum backwash into the creek. I had read just enough environmental law by then to recognize that the purported permit was utterly illegal under the Clean Water Act. The permit had not been subject to public notice or comment, as the act requires, and it allowed discharges of pollutants that the act flatly forbade. There were no penalties and no requirement that the town clean up the creek. The town happily signed this order on April 11, 1985, and thumbing its nose at the Fishermen and the law, sent the "permit" back to the DEC for final signature by the regional director. I was still naive enough to be shocked that a government agency, charged with protecting the public from pollution, would so blatantly intervene to protect a polluter from the public and the law.

Angered at such collusion, John and I drafted a letter to the U.S. Attorney demanding a criminal investigation of alum dumping by the town of Newburgh. Although the EPA has delegated its permit-issuing authority to the state DEC, the federal agency still retains independent enforcement authority over Clean Water Act violators. At the request of a friendly deputy U.S. Attorney, Susan Campbell, Federal EPA grudgingly agreed to inspect the plant.

On Thursday, May 16, I arrived at the Town of Newburgh Water Treatment Plant at 11:00 A.M. to meet EPA inspector John Mac. Two hostile DEC engineers were waiting with Mac at the plant. During a private meeting before my arrival, Goodrich and the other plant operators had claimed that a small alum spill from a broken board near the sludge lagoons accounted for any alum in the creek. I walked with John Mac to show him the gelatinous mass in the creek. He was skeptical when I told him that Goodrich had confessed to dumping forty thousand gallons; a story Goodrich now denies. Mac said that he would need more evidence than my word. As I took this in, a young plant operator approached and motioned us to follow him to a corner of the compound, out of sight of the other workers. His name, he said, was Paul Miller, and he was a seven-year plant veteran. He said he was happy "somebody was finally doing something about this mess." He told us that deliberate dumping had been standard plant procedure for years. "Sometimes," he said, "the whole creek bed is filled with the stuff." He said Goodrich had often ordered him to dump alum from the upper lagoons in the creek. A memo from Goodrich instructed the operators to dump only at night. When Miller refused to dump a particularly large load, Goodrich threatened to fire him. Miller said the town dumped the alum to save money on hauling fees and that Goodrich was trying to keep it quiet. When he left, Miller gave us his home number and urged us to contact him later.

Miller later recanted his statements, citing his personal friendship with Supervisor Kirkpatrick and his fear for his job. However, John Mac was, by then, convinced that the alum discharges were the result of deliberate wrongdoing. One week after the inspection, the EPA ordered the DEC's wastewater director to initiate appropriate enforcement action against Chadwick Lake Filtration Plant.

Simultaneously John and I sent a letter to the DEC's Hudson Valley Regional Administrator Paul Keller requesting that he not issue any permit or order until the creek had been cleaned up. Keller agreed to postpone signing the proposed permit with the town of Newburgh until after John and I had the opportunity to speak to him face to face. We told Keller that in addition to Chadwick Lake, we had a series of cases in Newburgh about which we wanted to confer. We set up a meeting for October 30.

In the interim, John and I assembled sufficient evidence in twenty neat accordion files to successfully prosecute twenty polluters on Quassaic Creek. Many of the cases were potential criminal actions. We loaded our work into cardboard boxes and took it first to Susan Campbell in the U.S. Attorney's office. She selected four cases she considered most promising and assigned attorneys to prosecute them: Al Cam enterprises, American Felt and Filter, Valmar Textile, and Consolidated Metal Junkyard.

On October 30 we lugged our remaining cases up to New Paltz for our meeting with Paul Keller at the New York State Department of Environmental Conservation regional headquarters. Keller's brand-new regional attorney, Judi Ferry, attended the meeting along with the regional engineers in charge of water, air, and solid and hazardous waste. John and I reviewed each of our remaining cases for the group and then proposed a joint enforcement sweep by the Fishermen and the DEC. DEC would bring enforcement actions and administrative prosecutions, while conservation officers would issue tickets to polluters. The Fishermen would bring simultaneous citizen suits in federal court and intervene in DEC's proceedings. Half of the fines collected by DEC would go to the State General Fund and the other half to a specially created "Quassaic Creek Fund." All settlement moneys and fines won by the Fishermen would go to this fund. Our objective was to see that those responsible for the creek's defilement would shoulder the responsibility for its rehabilitation.

It's hard to describe the discomfort that this proposal caused the DEC staff. The engineers stared at us as if we'd just uncovered a chum bucket of stinking fish guts and invited them to eat. They were openly hostile and disparaging. They clearly viewed our proposal as a turf challenge. To them the Fishermen were not a natural ally but a dangerous opponent.

But Paul Keller and his Regional Attorney Judi Ferry restored some of my faith in government officials. Wearing the carefree smile of a bureaucrat about to retire, Keller dismissed their reservations and announced that DEC would be delighted to participate. He was ready, after thirty-five years of carefully repressed idealism, to reclaim the values that had brought him to the agency as a young man.

Judi Ferry, fresh from the snake pits of medical malpractice litigation, had an iron gut and an instinct for the jugular. This was precisely the kind of opportunity she was looking for when she left a successful private practice to go into public service. Captain Washburn, the agency's chief conservation officer, rolled his eyes, swallowed his bile, and reluctantly agreed to provide a conservation officer to issue tickets. Keller also agreed to refrain from signing any permit in the Chadwick Lake case until the town cleaned up the creek and paid fines for its deliberate dumping.

Three weeks later, John stood shoulder-to-shoulder with Paul and Judi at the Coliseum Restaurant in Newburgh, at a podium lined with one-liter sample jars filled with red dye and sewage and alum sludge. Before a large gathering of Hudson Valley press they announced an unprecedented joint enforcement sweep of twelve Quassaic Creek polluters, including Mobil Oil, the town of Newburgh, and some of the most powerful financial and political interests in the Hudson Valley, for violations ranging from filling of wetlands to the discharge of toxic waste. Keller explained that the DEC had joined forces with the Fishermen and that each would contribute their technical and legal resources in a fight to rehabilitate a Hudson River tributary "where lawlessness has become the norm." I opted not to attend that press conference, fearing that press interest in my involvement might distract from the central issue. This was the policy I adopted during my first five years at Riverkeeper.

The local papers all covered the story with end-of-the-world-sized headlines listing the polluters and their crimes on the front pages. As the weeks went by, Riverkeeper announced federal lawsuits against four more polluters. Because our evidence was strong, all sixteen of these cases (and the four cases by the U.S. Attorney) settled before trial. The DEC assessed a total of $350,000 in penalties against the polluters and collected $75,000. The U.S. Attorney collected $50,000 in penalties. The Riverkeeper collected payments in lieu of penalties for the Quassaic Creek Fund totaling $150,000 and fees totaling $50,000. Altogether the polluters contributed a total of $200,000 to the Quassaic Creek Fund.

In addition to paying penalties, each violator agreed to stop polluting and to remediate the creek where possible. American Felt and Filter, Mobil, and Federal Block plugged their discharge pipes. New Windsor constructed a new power source to stop its manhole overflows and cleaned up the one-mile stretch of the creek that passed through the town. Consolidated Metal Junkyard removed its barge and shoreline debris. The city of Newburgh, Justgold, and Meadow Hill rebuilt their sewage plants. Al Cam eliminated their oil discharges. Hudson Valley Tree moved its proposed building out of the wetland. Zayre's removed all their shopping carts, Harvey Brothers removed its tires from the creek, and Arma eliminated all twenty-four of its unpermitted pipes. The town of Newburgh cleaned the alum from Quassaic Creek, hired a responsible outside consultant to manage its water treatment plant, demoted those responsible for sludge dumping, and found a hauler to remove alum sludge.

The results of the Quassaic Creek cases were particularly gratifying because they were my first successes as an environmental lawyer. I'd discovered powerful tools for making polluters clean up after themselves. Suddenly I felt competent in a new profession, but I confess also to a kind of primal satisfaction. The destruction I'd seen on Quassaic Creek revived childhood memories of the highway men destroying my boyhood refuge on Pimmit Run. They had taken a little paradise, where my brother and I knew every meadow, hill, and glen. We knew where to catch tadpoles and crayfish, and where the snapping turtles laid their eggs each September, and which rock *always* hid a greensnake—and they had leveled the hills, filled the streams, and cut the forest, burying it all beneath a tract development and strip mall that was indistinguishable from every other strip mall in America. I recalled how David and I had waged our misguided battle to stop them by rolling their pipes down the bank. As we signed the orders and watched the cleanup begin, I thought of my brother David, who died in 1983, and I imagined a faint voice saying, "Aha! Now here's a good way to stop 'em and make them clean up their mess!"

Among the most gratifying was the settlement with the city of Newburgh. As we embarked on this project, John and I had vowed to each other and the DEC that we would not settle without monetary penalties from each polluter. Our rationale was that settlements requiring cessation of the polluting activity without monetary penalties created an incentive to others in that industry to continue polluting until they were caught and prosecuted, thereby delaying costly expenditures on equipment and personnel until the eleventh hour. We were vocal critics of the DEC's unwillingness to levy penalties against polluters.

However, the city of Newburgh was so utterly impoverished, and the poverty of its citizenry so stark, as to make us reconsider. Instead of demanding monetary penalties from the city, we asked that it permanently abandon its plan to sell the Washington Street boat ramp. The city accepted the compromise. Furthermore, Newburgh granted the Fishermen and its successive organizations a "conservation easement" perpetually protecting it from sale to any private party. The city agreed to maintain the property as a public boat ramp and park.

The polluters' reactions to our suits ranged from enthusiastic cooperation to outright war. Steve Miron of Federal Block planted wildflowers at his own expense on the stream bank following removal of the discharge pipe, cinder blocks, and debris. Others like Plaza Materials and Mobil brought in outside counsel to fight our lawsuits, and settled after a brief exchange of motions and legal papers. Frederick Massini, president of Arma Textiles, failed to show up to answer charges in the Newburgh City Court, which promptly ordered his arrest. On February 21, 1986, the local police blotter reported that Massini was "arrested on a bench warrant for using an outlet to discharge waste without a permit" and published his name beside those of other criminals on the front-page police blotter. John was especially thrilled by this case's conclusion, because he has long believed that people won't think of environmental crime as true crime until the government treats environmental violators as criminals.

The most troublesome defendants were the municipalities and particularly the town of Newburgh, whose boisterous, combative supervisor, Robert Kirkpatrick, regarded the Fishermen as interlopers and made the suits a personal vendetta. Our escalating confrontations with Kirkpatrick were proof of the magnitude of resistance to environmental law among those who believe they have a right to pollute. Unconstrained by the financial considerations of private businesses, Kirkpatrick and his attorney, Donald Becker, fought us bitterly in the courts, the press, the agencies, and before the state legislature. Kirkpatrick publicly condemned the Fishermen as "blackmailers," "burglars," and "extortionists." He railed against third-party involvement in the environmental concerns of the state, and refused our generous settlement proposal. Instead, Kirkpatrick and Becker spent hundreds of thousands of dollars of public money on attorneys' fees and were finally forced to accede to all our demands. Their ill-conceived crusade changed the town's political landscape and caused them political wounds from which they could not recover. A grand jury found that Kirkpatrick had engaged in criminal activity at the water treatment plant. A disparaging report by the state inspector general suggested that he had deliberately lied in public accusations leveled against John and me. A series of brutal editorials by town newpapers lambasted him for mishandling the suits. In the end, his friends in the state legislature whom he had enlisted to participate in his battle against us abandoned him. He inadvisedly fought and lost half a dozen lawsuits filed by us, the DEC, and the U.S. Attorney. His antics precipitated a full-scale revolt by town ratepayers whom he had initially riled against us. In the end, they turned on him, descending by the hundreds on the town hall one evening to denounce him as a "liar" and demand that Kirkpatrick settle the suits on the generous terms offered by the Fishermen. Frightened by the near riot, his formerly compliant town council mutinied against him and agreed to negotiate directly with the Fishermen. The episode ultimately cost Kirkpatrick his political career.

Following the mutiny, it took only a few days for us to reach a final settlement with the town board. The town agreed to retire the Meadow Hill North and Meadow Hill South sewage treatment plants and hook up to a nearby municipal plant with excess capacity. The town would rebuild the Gidneytown plant and contract with independent outside consultants to run their Chadwick Lake water filtration plant. They agreed to a plan to clear their alum from the creek and paid $23,000 to the Quassaic Creek Fund to benefit the creek—a tiny fraction of the nearly $150,000 they paid their own attorneys to fight us.

The Quassaic Creek cases had a lasting impact on the Newburgh area. We forced twenty polluters to clean up their messes and come into compliance, and we extracted for the creek an additional $200,000 for further rehabilitation. We brought attention to a badly neglected public resource and helped make the environment a political issue in Newburgh. In the 1987 campaign immediately following our settlement, Russ Chatham, a politically unknown environmental engineer running as a green candidate, lost to Kirkpatrick by a mere twelve votes, forcing Kirkpatrick, now bedeviled by more environmental law-suits, to resign in 1988, prior to the next election. Town Councilman Robert Kunkel, formerly the low man on the totem pole, who had led the mutiny against Kirkpatrick during the lawsuits, won the election to succeed him.

There were also indirect victories. We raised environmental con-sciousness a notch in Newburgh and in the Hudson Valley. Stories about our cases dominated the front pages of Orange County's papers and reg-ularly inspired supportive editorials. The popular Newburgh weekly *Sen-tinel* ran at least one and often two or three front-page stories on our cases in virtually every issue between November 1985 and May 1986.

According to DEC's Regional Director, Paul Keller, the Quassaic Creek sweep and resulting publicity changed attitudes toward the DEC in the Hudson Valley, making both business and municipalities more responsive. "It used to be I'd have a hell of a time getting them on the phone," Keller told us of Hudson Valley polluters. "Now they call right back and say, 'Tell us what you need, just don't tell the Fishermen.'"

For me there were personal revelations as well. In part our investi-gation confirmed Joe Augustine's conviction that government officials were not vigorously enforcing environmental law despite the idealism and energy of many individuals within the agencies. We saw how insti-tutional cultures within the environmental agencies encouraged routine acquiescence to pollution and to a gradual decline in environmental quality.

Perhaps the most encouraging lesson I learned was that where gov-ernment agencies failed to act, citizens could seize the opportunity and take the law into their own hands to protect a public resource. Under the laws of our country—unique in the world—individuals have the right to stand in the shoes of the U.S. Attorney, to bring lawsuits against polluters, and levy penalties to the U.S. Treasury. At the outset my switch from criminal to civil law was daunting. Environmental law and civil litigation were new frontiers for me. I was unfamiliar with rules of discovery, many unwritten procedures in civil law, and the complex regulatory and statutory schemes of environmental law. Yet I found myself litigating against some of the most sophisticated envi-ronmental practitioners in the country.

At that time there was not much case law governing lawsuits against polluters. For example, there was no reported case against unpermitted discharges prior to 1984. No one had ever applied the Clean Water Act to cinder blocks or automobile tires before. However, the statutory wording was in clear English, and I assumed it meant what it said. We brought half a dozen cases against unpermitted dischargers on Quassaic Creek under the Clean Water Act. Our lawsuit against Mobil was one of the first cases under the Resource Conservation and Recovery Act (RCRA) that governs the disposal of hazardous wastes.

Because of my lack of experience in environmental law, I was stuck with taking a direct, common-sense approach. By this I mean applying my own simple internal sense of right and wrong. In walking Quassaic Creek I contrasted the scene in my mind with the pristine stretches of Pimmit Run I'd walked as a child, or the rivers and streams I'd rafted with my father. I saw cinder blocks and pipes and automobile tires and knew it was wrong, as would most seven-year-olds. After all, we are taught as children to clean up after ourselves and to pay our way. My primary reference, then, was my own conscience. I found these things that conflicted with my sense of right and wrong, and I assumed that there must be a legal approach to redress the situation.

I went to the law books and found a way to sue the polluters. I learned that common sense and honesty, a willingness to read the law, and a strong sense of entitlement to a clean environment are the only necessary qualities for a good environmental advocate or lawyer. This is the approach that had worked for John in the Exxon case. When he caught Exxon stealing Hudson River water he assumed that the theft must be illegal even though no law specifically prohibited it. He reasoned that New Yorkers had not spent millions of dollars to clean up the Hudson to benefit Exxon. John had only his moral indignation, his strategic skills, and his sense of bravado when he went up against the biggest corporation on earth. He brought the action under a range of statutes, utilized publicity and federal agency interests, got the legislature involved, and finally forced Exxon to back down.

Lastly, the Quassaic Creek project gave me some personal direction. I was certain by the end that I wanted to be an environmental lawyer. Since my father's death when I was fourteen, I'd been torn by the tension between the part of me that wanted to spend my life pursuing and protecting nature as a conservationist or veterinarian, and the obligation I felt to my father's vision of justice for all people, particularly those who are less advantaged. This tension was aggravated by my vague thought that the environment was "out there" in those places I had been privileged to visit on vacations as a child—and the battle for justice was "back here" in the cities where the struggle for justice and the democratic ideal, the disparities in wealth and opportunity, problems of race and civil rights, community and quality of life, were all displayed in their starkest relief.

The Newburgh cases helped me reconcile the two divergent strains in my own history and character. I recognized that environment is not something distant and inaccessible to most Americans. It is not an issue that can be separated out and dealt with on its own. The environment is our neighborhood, our community. It is our quality of life.

Newburgh's quality of life was certainly affected by the way it cared for its environment. Rather than celebrating its proximity to the Hudson River and Quassaic Creek, Newburgh allowed its resources to become dumps and sewers, spoiling their value for the rest of us. Its lack of care for its environment was reflected in the disheveled and hopeless character of the city itself. Newburgh's morale followed its shoreline. Just as the restoration of Baltimore's waterfront led the way to that city's revitalization and moral rejuvenation, the destruction of Newburgh's waterfront clearly paralleled its moral and physical bankruptcy.

In Newburgh, I began to see the environment not as a privilege that was part of my affluent background, but as a right for every American, one that was being subverted by greedy, powerful, and corrupt interests within our society. When we first proposed the Quassaic Creek projects to the agencies, John and I told them that our goal was to return to every Newburgh child his or her right to go down to the creek with a fishing pole and pull out a fish for dinner. We might have added, or to turn over a rock and catch a pet frog or salamander or swim in the swimming holes without danger of being poisoned. These are entitlements that no one has a right to subvert.

# CHAPTER 4

# *Keepers*

On Christmas Eve 1985, John received a call from a fisherman who had learned that workers for Westchester County would be pumping toxic liquid from Westchester County's Croton Point Landfill into the Hudson River on Christmas Day. "They chose Christmas," he said, "because they figure you guys won't be around."

Croton Landfill was an environmental nightmare—hundreds of thousands of tons of domestic garbage and one billion pounds of industrial wastes, including a radioactive building, buried in two hundred acres of Hudson River tidal marsh.

After forty years of operation the landfill had reached 135 feet in height and sunk 45 feet into the wetland muds. It had destroyed sixty acres of tidal wetland that had once provided a habitat for bald eagles, osprey, heron, and egrets; dozens of waterfowl species; muskrat and river otter; and recreation for hunters, trappers, and canoeists. The Hudson River Fishermen's Association had turned the site over to the U.S. Attorney for prosecution under the Refuse Act of 1899. The resulting 1972 federal court order required the county to phase out the landfill, restore the remains of Croton Marsh, and collect and treat toxic leachate, a deadly mixture of solvents, viruses, and bacteria created when precipitation flows though a landfill and picks up contaminants from the decaying contents inside. The Croton Landfill produced leachate by the tens of millions of gallons per year. Contamination of the waters around the landfill had caused bizarre effects such as double-headed cattails and killifish with spines so bent the fish could only swim in circles. So daunting was the prospect of collecting and treating the pestilential brew that Westchester County endlessly recirculated it instead. Leachate that ran into the collection moat at the landfill's base was pumped back up to a pond at its summit to run through again, like a toxic percolator distilling an ever more lethal concoction.

As official memories of the federal case faded, Westchester allowed the landfill to grow past the court-ordered boundaries and the pumps that fed the upper pond to fall into disrepair. We asked Laurie Marchan Silberfeld, a student intern from Pace University School of Law, to investigate the county's compliance with the 1972 court order at the Croton Point Landfill. She documented many violations and petitioned the U.S. Attorney to reopen the case. When Laurie learned that the leachate pumps were broken, we suspected that workers were using portable pumps to pump leachate from the backed-up collection moat directly into the river. But we had no hard evidence.

The Christmas Eve tip-off was an exciting development, though it was difficult even for environmentalists to explain to their families why they must spend Christmas Day at a garbage dump. It was bitterly cold at Croton Point, with a bone-chilling wind blowing across the river. In fact, it was too cold to run a pump, so the workers never showed. But we found their equipment. A trailer carrying a large portable pump was set up with fire hoses leading directly from the leachate moat to the river. John and volunteer Mark Sramek documented the setup with photographs that we then turned over to the U.S. Attorney as further evidence of the county's violations of its federal court order. We also discovered a storm sewer discharging leachate into the river just one hundred feet from a public swimming beach. Chemical analysis of samples that we took from the storm pipe showed that it contained bacteria, toxic volatile compounds, and other chemical and biological pollutants. When John returned for more samples, county workers called the police and John was taken into custody for trespassing. After they discovered he was the Riverkeeper, county police headquarters ordered him released. The arresting officers apologized earnestly and wished him luck, but the county kept his leachate samples.

By spring the Croton case was growing in complexity. We had collected enough evidence of unpermitted discharges from the storm sewer into the river to start our own citizens' suit. The U.S. Attorney had filed a contempt action against the county for other violations of the 1972 order. Both cases required our full attention because the U.S. Attorney intended to build the case around our investigation. John was to be their lead witness. In addition, we were still immersed in a series of ferocious legal battles arising from Bobby's Quassaic Creek investigation and in an ultimately successful lawsuit to stop New York State from closing the Hudson to all fishing. We had printed posters with the phrase "Report the Unusual" emblazoned above the Riverkeeper logo and the Riverkeeper hotline, 1-800-21-RIVER. We hung them at marinas, bait shops, and public access points along the Hudson. Citizen tip-offs and complaints were deluging the new Riverkeeper headquarters. We needed nothing less than a team of prosecutors to meet the public demand for our work.

By 1987, Pace University had built one of the most highly rated environmental law programs in the country at its law school in White Plains, New York. Bobby had been attending night school at Pace for the two years since joining Riverkeeper, and that spring was awarded the university's first master's degree in environmental law. Our successful Exxon case, the Newburgh prosecutions, and the investigation of the Croton Landfill by Pace student Laurie Marchan Silberfeld had caught the faculty's attention. When Professor Nicholas Robinson and other members of the environmental law faculty proposed that Pace and the Riverkeeper form a partnership to create a student litigation clinic, the timing could not have been better. Unencumbered by the political liabilities of public funding, staffed by a faculty that included some of the most important names in environmental law, Pace was attracting environmentally committed students from across the country.

We met with a group of Pace law professors and agreed that Bobby would supervise a clinic of students who, under a special court order, would be allowed to practice law as if they were full attorneys. The Hudson River Fishermen's Association and the Hudson Riverkeeper would provide a steady stream of cases, guarantee that litigation costs would be paid, and provide technical experts to assist in the litigation. Pace would contribute office space and support staff, its considerable faculty and library resources, and its on-line services. Students would benefit from the invaluable experience of real-life litigation, including arguing cases in court. Riverkeeper would get the free services of energetic young attorneys. The Pace Clinic opened for business in September 1987, and we began work on the Croton case.

Bobby and the students filed a Clean Water Act citizens' suit against the county while the U.S. Attorney began the contempt-of-court proceedings. The county's outside counsel, Rosenman and Colin, filed papers with the court claiming the discharge at the Croton swimming beach had been stopped and therefore the Riverkeeper lawsuit was moot. But we knew that there was just too much liquid at the site for the county simply to turn off the pipe. The leachate was going somewhere and the river was the only place for it to go.

What we found at the landfill when we went to investigate the county's claim was almost comical. The county had attempted to plug the eighteen-inch-diameter storm pipe with a gigantic rubber stopper. But the pressure of the discharge had forced the stopper out and leachate was flowing as freely as ever. We took photographs of John standing next to the discharge holding a copy of that morning's *USA Today* to verify the date. Two hours after the judge received the county's papers claiming the discharge had ceased, our students had on his desk eight-by-ten photographs of the belching pipe with our reply brief attached. The county lost both its motion to dismiss and its credibility with the judge. Undeterred, Rosenman and Colin filed another motion to dismiss, protesting that the foul-smelling liquid was only storm water, which is often exempt from the permit provisions of the Clean Water Act. This was a clever ploy since all leachate can technically be classified as storm water. The clinic students answered with an untested legal theory: storm water, when channeled through a pipe and when proven to contain pollutants, is not entitled to the exemption. The judge agreed. Calling the landfill a "time bomb" he reaffirmed the right of the Fishermen to stop its pollution, whether the liquid was "storm water" or leachate.

On the first day of the U.S. Attorney's case against Westchester, we traveled with our students and the clinic's support staff to the New York City courtroom of Federal District Court Judge Constance Baker Motley. John was to be the first witness for the United States.

The clerk announced Judge Motley with "All rise." Before John could be called to the witness stand, the attorney for Westchester County abruptly rose and informed the court that his client was prepared to settle the matter according to the terms demanded by the U.S. Attorney. It was a stunning turn of events and shortly thereafter, Westchester agreed to a settlement with Riverkeeper as well. The discharges were halted, tank trucks began to regularly pick up the leachate for disposal at a treatment facility, the landfill was shut down and a plan for its remediation agreed upon, and a program for the restoration of the remains of Croton Marsh was established.

The county also agreed to pay all our legal fees. The Clean Water Act requires such payments to "substantially prevailing parties." As a matter of practice the law clinic's students and professors keep track of their billable hours on each case, and, when we win or settle, the defendant pays the total. The Pace Clinic and Riverkeeper retain the fee awards for operating expenses. In the Westchester case our fees totaled $75,000. At a joint press conference announcing the settlement, Westchester County Executive Andrew O'Rourke compared the clinic's fees favorably to the $150,000 bill the county had paid to its own attorneys for losing the case. Tipping his hat to the Pace students, O'Rourke promised that, in the future, when the county needed environmental counsel, it would search out clinic alumnae so as to get twice the legal talent for half the money. It was a proud day for the students and an auspicious inaugural victory for the clinic program.

Over the coming months and years, Pace Clinic students would argue cases for Riverkeeper that would stop New York City from discharging chlorine and aquatic pesticides into a drinking water reservoir; force the Federal Bureau of Prisons to rebuild its sewer system at the Otisville Federal Correctional Facility; and get the New York State Women's Prison to switch to cardboard tampon containers when our analysis showed that the unusual number of plastic dispensers had destroyed treatment organisms in its sewer plant.

We sued a chemical company for illegal discharges of ammonia into a tributary and forced the federal EPA to stop unregulated sewage discharges from vessels into the Hudson. We forced Orange County to spend $60 million moving its new landfill out of a protected wetland. We sued dozens of Hudson Valley cities and towns for violations at water and sewage treatment plants. New York City was our most frequent defendant. At one time, in 1989, we were involved in nine separate proceedings and lawsuits against New York City, including a successful suit to reopen the permits for all fourteen of New York City's sewage treatment plants that discharged into the Hudson River, East River, Long Island Sound, and New York Harbor.

As Riverkeeper's reputation spread, grassroots and citizens' groups increasingly asked us for legal assistance. Pace Clinic quickly evolved into a legal aid agency for many small community environmental organizations. We took on cases representing a local chapter of the NAACP, two mothers from Newburgh concerned about the quality of their drinking water, a local archaeological organization trying to protect historic Indian gravesites from developers, two different neighborhood associations, and several stream watch groups.

By 1990, students were enrolling at the law school for the chance of being accepted. In 1992, Steve Solow of the New York State Organized Crime Task Force became the first codirector of the clinic with Bobby. Steve was a natural-born prosecutor under whose influence the clinic docket took on all the dimensions of a major crime-busting campaign. When Steve moved on to the environmental crimes division of the United States Department of Justice two years later, he was replaced by Karl Coplan, a partner in Berle Kass and Case, Al Butzel's environmental boutique that represented the plaintiffs in the Storm King and Westway cases, among others. Karl, a former clerk to United States Supreme Court Chief Justice Warren Burger and a brilliant litigator, had worked with us as pro bono counsel in several cases against Long Island Sound sewage plants. At Berle, Karl had argued a series of landmark cases protecting private property against polluters and protecting the public trust. One of his victories made national news when he forced a developer to lop the top twelve stories off a forty-two-story Manhattan apartment building constructed in violation of zoning codes.

Pace has devoted an entire building to clinic operations, with file rooms, conference rooms, and offices. Each semester ten students are selected for the clinic from three times that number of applicants. Clinic students are drawn from the second- and third-year classes and are invariably highly motivated. Many are environmental careerists. The clinic becomes a second home to most interns, who frequent the offices in groups from early morning until late evening. Each class develops a strong *esprit de corps*. Interns have access to Riverkeeper's stable of battle-tested scientific and technical experts, and Riverkeeper maintains a revolving fund at a local laboratory for sampling and analysis. We all meet officially twice a week—attorneys, clients, and student attorneys—to review the hot cases and plot strategy and practice for court.

The Pace Clinic gives Riverkeeper the resources to go up against the best corporate litigators in the world. The students' talent and enthusiasm and access to the Pace faculty puts us at par with the best law firms. In fact, clinic students have argued and won cases against some of the best law firms in the country—Coudert Brothers, LeBoeuf Lamb Greene & Macrae, and even Sive, Paget and Riesel. In 1993 a third-year law student, Tom Humbach, assigned to a power plant case, went head-to-head with Peter Bergen, the world-famous utility lawyer who argued both Storm King and Westway cases, and won handily. With this kind of track record the clinic became the centerpiece of the Hudson Riverkeeper program.

Soon after our merger with Pace, news of our successful battles against pollution spread outside the Hudson Valley. In April 1988, a small crew of burly lobstermen from Norwalk, Connecticut, came up the Hudson River to buy buck shad for lobster bait from the commercial fishermen in the Tappan Zee. As they loaded their truck, they told Hudson riverman Bobby Gabrielson that chlorine discharges from Norwalk's sewage plant had killed the oyster beds in Norwalk Harbor. Furthermore, Connecticut state law shuts down most Long Island Sound shellfish beds after rain of more than one-quarter inch, due to sewage overflows from the cities. Fishermen once enjoyed the rain, especially in the summer; now it is their enemy. They lamented that you couldn't sue a city for pollution. Gabrielson, a Riverkeeper board member, told them he knew some guys who were doing just that.

A few weeks later, we were standing with fishermen Chris Stablefeldt and Terry Backer on the rickety pilings in Norwalk Harbor watching a foaming plume of sewage effluent billow from a submerged pipe. By the time we traced the brown foam to the roaring discharge pipe of the City of Norwalk Sewage Treatment Plant, we were ready to do whatever we could to help. "This is just one tributary to the Sound," said Terry. "I can show you as much of this as you want in Bridgeport, New Haven, Milford. Name the place."

Long Island Sound had seen dramatic changes in twenty years. Commercial fishermen like Terry and Chris watched their oyster catch drop from three million bushels per year to less than fifteen thousand. The flounder catch was down from forty million pounds in 1983 to one million pounds in 1987. In the summer as much as half the water was dead. Dissolved oxygen levels along the eastern half of Long Island sank to zero. The fin fish left the area or perished by the millions. Barnacles disappeared and animals that could not leave simply asphyxiated. Lobstermen found their lobsters dead in their traps. Smelt that once could be scooped out with a bucket had vanished. Blue crabs were gone as were razor clams, and steamers that were once common on every mudflat.

Industrial pollution and farm runoff caused some of the Sound's pollution problems, but the principal culprit was municipal sewage plants, which accounted for nearly 50 percent of the nitrogen that was robbing the Sound of its oxygen. Chlorine and sewer discharges from New York City and dozens of smaller municipal plants in New York and Connecticut had killed local oyster beds and regularly closed shell fishing even in healthier sections of the Sound. Like other families on the Sound, fishermen endured closed beaches, health warnings, and the effects of pollution on property values. Now they also faced the loss of their livelihoods. Many were leaving their ancient profession, finding jobs as carpenters, road pavers, truckers—any occupation that did not depend on clean water.

We sat down with Terry and Chris in the back office of the Talmadge Brothers Oyster House in Norwalk Harbor and hatched a strategy.

First, the commercial fishermen would form an alliance with Long Island Sound sportsmen. Creating such a coalition would broaden the issue's public appeal. Robert Nixon, a Darien, Connecticut, sports fisherman and hunter, had just started an informal association called the Connecticut Coastal Sportsmen's Association to fight pollution threatening ducks and fish. When we introduced Bob to Terry and Chris, they decided to combine their efforts and renamed the group "Connecticut Coastal Fishermen's Association." This alliance was new territory for the commercial fishermen, who traditionally endured an uneasy—and sometimes combative—relationship with anglers.

We would investigate the plants. If, after viewing our results, the fishermen wanted to sue, we would help. One month later, at the same table at the Oyster House, we related the findings of our initial investigation. Pace students had uncovered more than three thousand violations of the Clean Water Act by the cities of Norwalk, Bridgeport, and Milford, with indications of similar records in a half dozen other cities. Chris shook his head in resigned disgust. The news was more or less what he expected. But Terry's outrage was palpable to all at the table.

The fishermen wanted to know how we had uncovered this incriminating evidence. We didn't make clandestine visits to the plants to sample discharges or rely on employee tip-offs. Every violation had been documented in writing in monthly discharge monitoring submitted to the state of Connecticut by officials of the cities themselves. Federal law requires the state to make the reports available for public examination.

Terry was appalled. The fact that the cities had sent evidence of their wrongdoings to the state and then continued to violate with impunity was almost more than he could bear. As a fisherman he made it his business to maintain friendly relations with state officials. He was always cooperative, honest, and forthright with the state's biologists, wardens, and researchers. Now, he felt betrayed and used. Terry spoke the mind of each fisherman at the table when he said that they had no choice but to sue the cities, if only to retain their own self-respect.

Given the number of new cases, we invited the environmental law firm Berle Kass and Case in New York City to act as pro bono cocounsel with Bobby so that he could focus his attention on the Hudson. They assigned Karl Coplan, a young associate who would later become codirector of the Pace Clinic. The well-respected Connecticut Fund for the Environment announced that it was throwing its formidable influence behind the fishermen's suits, rounding out our coalition. The local shellfish house, Talmadge Brothers, offered to help finance our efforts.

As soon as the lawsuits were ready for filing, we organized press conferences. We met the press on the fishermen's home turf, the SoNo seafood restaurant on the Norwalk Wharf. A standing-room-only crowd of reporters and supporters downed complimentary chowder as Terry and Chris, with scraggly beards hugging their faces like sargasso weed, displayed liter bottles of sewage effluent and talked about the Sound and the livelihoods they saw coming to an end. They said that pollution of Long Island Sound was a violation of their rights. They announced their suits against Norwalk, Bridgeport, and Branford and vowed that every city and industry on the Sound that was violating the Clean Water Act would be found and prosecuted.

Terry—with his maritime squint, anchor earring, and worn skipper's hat that smelled so much of fish and the sea that one wondered that the gulls didn't flock behind it—became an instant folk hero. Bumper stickers appeared spontaneously in Norwalk nominating "Backer for Mayor." To keep the pressure on, we persuaded Talmadge

Brothers to take a full-page ad in the popular *Stamford Advocate* with bold letters declaring "If Pollution Put Mayors out of Work, Long Island Sound Would Be Clean." It went on to explain that in fact pollution puts fishermen out of work and degrades communities. All readers were encouraged to join the Connecticut Coastal Fishermen's Association. Terry had copies of the ad made into placards that he placed, along with membership applications, in stores all over the Sound. Citizens began to sign up and the mayors began to wear down. Terry began talking to reporters from the major local newspapers, educating them on the issues, and keeping them abreast of breaking developments with regular calls and press releases.

The campaign had its desired effect. Our first settlement was against Norwalk. The city agreed to rebuild its plant to achieve permit compliance. After much resistance and some litigation, the city made a payment of $270,000 in lieu of penalties. The money would go to fund a Long Island Soundkeeper. Terry took the job as Soundkeeper and moved into a donated office that was right out of the pages of *Cannery Row*—a small, two-story, cedar shake shack on a pier overlooking Norwalk Harbor. Soon he was patrolling in the new *Soundkeeper,* a twenty-seven-foot Mako sportfishing boat donated to the organization by a friend of Bob Nixon's.

A third-generation lobsterman and a high school dropout, Terry is arguably the most effective advocate yet to emerge on behalf of Long Island Sound. By 1990 he had successfully run for the state legislature. He was later appointed to the Environment Committee and the powerful Appropriations Committee, where he now wields his substantial weight on state environmental policy.

One by one, we settled cases against each of Connecticut's coastal cities from New Haven east. Our litigation docket read like a Metro North commuter schedule—New Haven, West Haven, Branford, Stamford, Stratford, Greenwich, Bridgeport, and Norwalk. Our Pace Clinic also represented the Soundkeeper in a groundbreaking lawsuit against DuPont Corporation, which operated the Remington Gun Club on Lordship Point, a small peninsula at the confluence of the Housatonic River with Long Island Sound.

Shooters at Remington's twenty-six ranges fired at targets that were mechanically hurled over the water. According to Remington's own figures, the range deposited as much as 70 tons of lead and 270 tons of toxic target material *per year* into the mouth of the Housatonic River. The Lordship Point shooting range was seventy years old.

Sediments in the Housatonic's mouth contained lead levels as high as 64 percent, probably the highest concentrations of lead in the nation. Shellfish and aquatic vegetation were grossly contaminated. According to Remington's tests, over half the black ducks in the area had lethal levels of lead in their blood. Although many Soundkeeper supporters enjoyed the sport of target shooting, they were unhappy that Remington had not followed the example of the hunting community and halted the use of lead shot. We obtained documents from Remington showing that Remington had refused to market safer steel shot for trap and skeet shooting because of pressure from the National Rifle Association.

The Housatonic's intertidal area was littered with "clay" targets that made the shallows glow from their neon orange paint. "Clay" is a misnomer; the targets are actually composed of highly toxic coal tar and polyaromatic hydrocarbons that are also carcinogenic. Each box of traps was labeled with the warning "Toxic to hogs." In fact, the chemical constituents were toxic to a wide range of animal and fish life.

The state of Connecticut refused to order Remington to cease polluting because of its fear of the gun lobby. The EPA, also fearful of tangling with the NRA, tried its best to ignore the issue, adopting a policy of nonenforcement against shooting ranges.

Finally, we filed a complaint in April 1987 on behalf of the Connecticut Coastal Fishermen's Association in federal court alleging that the twenty-six shooting stations at the Remington range were discharge "point sources" under the Clean Water Act. It was a novel theory. No court or agency had ever considered a gun to be a regulated point source. Our argument was simple: Is there a difference between a big pipe and a little pipe? Remington denied all liability but immediately closed the club, depriving the federal court of Clean Water Act jurisdiction over the site. The court, however, gave us a victory on a second citizens' suit that we filed simultaneously under the Resource Conservation and Recovery Act. That statute (RCRA) makes it illegal to dispose of hazardous wastes in quantities that might cause harm to the environment. The court ordered Remington to remove the massive contamination at their site.

The publicity surrounding the Remington case generated pleas for help from communities as far away as California and Illinois and along the Chesapeake, all struggling with water pollution caused by gun clubs. The following year, we brought Clean Water Act cases against a New York City–owned shooting range in Pelham Bay Park in the Bronx and another against Westchester County's Blue Mountain gun range, which was discharging into a Hudson River tributary. Geese and even frogs had died from lead contamination in the stream that flowed through a school yard just below the Blue Mountain gun range. A range instructor had suffered serious lead contamination and his children, who lived at a house near the site, were also poisoned. At Pelham Bay, a police officer who frequented the range suffered lead levels so high that his blood had to be removed and replaced. We filed letters of intent to sue both sites under the Clean Water Act, but in each case, the ranges adopted Remington's defensive tactic of closing the club, mooting our Clean Water Act cases.

We were delighted that they stopped polluting, but in these cases, unlike most others, we would have preferred to litigate. Federal and state agencies were hiding from this issue. We wanted a judgment that, once and for all, would declare such discharges illegal. That way, we would answer the many inquiries about gun clubs from across the country with a published federal court decision that the agencies could not ignore.

Finally, in a lawsuit against the New York Athletic Club gun range, we got our decision. Lawyers for the club were so confident they would prevail against Soundkeeper and a local group called New York Coastal Fishermen's Association, that they advised their clients to continue shooting at the site as our action proceeded. This gave us the foothold to maintain our action in federal court. Judge Robert P. Patterson held that the NYAC's discharges violated the Clean Water Act and ordered the club to stop shooting over water. The decision was particularly gratifying since Tim Cox, the student attorney who successfully argued the case in court, was going up against a team of attorneys from Coudert Brothers, probably the highest-paid lawyers in the United States. The NYAC is now in the process of cleaning its contamination from New Rochelle Harbor. As a result of our victory, an embarrassed EPA had no choice but to begin development of a national policy for gun ranges, which, at this writing, has yet to be completed.

With the Pace Clinic in full swing and a second Keeper established, we were receiving calls from people all over the country who wanted to apply for Riverkeeper jobs on their local waterways. Of course we had no jobs to offer. We were interested, however, in assisting people who were themselves willing to do the organizing work necessary to start programs in their own communities. In June 1988, at about the same time Terry Backer was formally named Soundkeeper, Cynthia Poten, a writer and environmental activist, became the Delaware Riverkeeper after working for about two years to start a program. The following year, Mike Herz, a former senior scientist at the Center for Environmental Studies at the University of San Francisco, started the San Francisco Baykeeper project.

Mike and Terry were a study in contrasts. While Terry's approach was instinctive, Michael's was deliberate.

Michael devoted a year to researching whether a San Francisco Baykeeper was necessary. He interviewed John and Terry. He distributed a questionnaire to other environmental groups in the Bay Area seeking their opinions. He investigated who the polluters were, which agencies were enforcing environmental laws and which weren't. In the end, he produced an extensive report that concluded a San Francisco Baykeeper was warranted and viable.

There was a method to Mike's meticulousness. Armed with his research report he made the rounds of charitable foundations and asked for their financial support. By the time we traveled out to California for the launching of the San Francisco Baykeeper, Mike had already procured a boat, a waterfront office, and a full year of funding.

An army of press attended the launch. Mike and John christened the new Baykeeper boat with both San Francisco and Hudson River waters and declared that the symbolic joining of waters marked the beginning of a new era of direct citizen custodianship of the nation's rivers, sounds, and bays. They predicted Keeper programs from coast to coast. By the following day the San Francisco Baykeeper toll-free hotline for citizens to report pollution sightings —1-800-KeepBay— was ringing off the hook.

Mike Lozeau replaced Mike Herz as Baykeeper in 1996. Lozeau is a former attorney for the Sierra Club Legal Defense Fund and the NRDC. He has developed a reliable battalion of twenty-two Bay Area attorneys who handle cases for Baykeeper. His program rivals our own for its aggressiveness and effectiveness. He has a small patrol force that includes kayakers, boaters, and pilots who regularly patrol the harbor for polluters. In 1996 Lozeau spun off Deltakeeper with its own office in Stockton and a patrol boat to cover the delta area. In six years Baykeeper has responded to over 750 incidents and resolved 78 substantial legal cases. Its current docket includes 40 cases. Among its many accomplishments Baykeeper wrote and lobbied through passage the first municipal citizen enforcement ordinance in the nation, allowing San Franciscans to prosecute violators of city pollution laws and collect rewards.

After reading an article about the Baykeeper in *Audubon Magazine,* Terry Taminen, a swimming pool maintenance company operator with his own boat and a passion for the water, inaugurated the Santa Monica Baykeeper in 1993. Keepers from the Hudson, Delaware, San Francisco Bay, and Long Island Sound, along with three new Keepers from Casco Bay in Maine, New York–New Jersey Harbor, and Puget Sound attended the christening and baptized Terry's boat with water from each of their waterways. Terry intended to start a modest part-time operation until he had a serendipitous meeting with the Walt Disney Company's CEO Frank Wells. Wells, who liked the aggressive philosophy behind the Keeper movement, agreed to fund the new Baykeeper and another Keeper on San Diego Bay. It was on a stormy plane ride home from our initial meeting with Wells that we decided to write this book. Wells was an inveterate outdoorsman, skier, kayaker, and mountaineer who had climbed the highest peak on every continent in a twelve-month period. He was six-foot-four, impressively handsome, and brilliant. Wells never saw the San Diego Baykeeper inaugurated. In April 1994 he died in a helicopter crash while backcountry skiing with his family in Nevada. Wells' wife, Luanne, continued her support of both Santa Monica and San Diego Baykeepers and the programs flourished. The Santa Monica Baykeeper and the NRDC won the historic *CalTrans* decision that forced the California Department of Transportation to prevent runoff from its highways and maintenance facilities, as required by the Clean Water Act amendments of 1990. The federal court ruling marked the first time a public agency had been held to the new Clean Water Act standards.

Beside Wells, the largest individual supporter of the Riverkeeper movement has been CNN founder Ted Turner, whose Turner Foundation provided funding for the upper Chattahoochee Riverkeeper. Wells and Turner were both tough, visionary businessmen who understood environmentalism as a high-stakes struggle for control of natural resources, pitting the public interest against greedy businessmen with the assistance of compliant government officials. They were well aware of the cutthroat tactics employed by our opponents. For this reason, they were among the few environmental funders willing to underwrite litigation.

Many of the existing Keeper programs were started as subsidiary projects by existing environmental groups. The American Littoral Society, which had hired activist Cynthia Poten as Delaware Baykeeper, appointed boatbuilder Andy Willner as New York–New Jersey Harborkeeper. Rhode Island's premier environmental group, Save the Bay, also launched a Narragansett Baykeeper. Today, there are Keepers on the Hudson River, Long Island Sound, Delaware River, Hackensack River, San Francisco Bay, New York–New Jersey Harbor, Puget Sound, Casco Bay, Santa Monica Bay, Neuse River, Narragansett Bay, Upper Chattahoochee River, Lower Chattahoochee River, San Diego Bay, Cook Inlet, Schuylkill River, Peconic Bay, and the Willamette. While each group has its own personality and agenda, all of the Keeper programs are making their mark on the local waterways they seek to protect.

In Seattle, the Puget Soundkeeper sued the U.S. Navy for illegally discharging untreated sewage into Sinclair Inlet and for allowing spilled wastes including PCBs, paint, detergents, gasoline, battery acid, and dissolved metals to wash into Puget Sound. The Pace Clinic served as cocounsel in that case. As a result of a settlement, the U.S. Navy is completing an $8.5 million sewage-treatment system, and has repaired broken pipes and devised a plan to reduce hazardous spills.

On the Delaware River, Riverkeeper Poten has succeeded in launching a Schuylkill Riverkeeper project to protect one of the Delaware's major tributaries. Poten says she hopes to create a model for river restoration with this tributary and eventually place Keepers on all of the rivers that feed the Delaware.

The San Francisco Baykeeper took an anonymous tip about suspicious activities at a shipyard known as Donco Industries and turned it into the first federal criminal prosecution for dredging in California's northern district. Donco Industries' president and chief financial officer both received jail terms and fines.

In 1997, the San Diego Baykeeper, Kenny Moser, settled his first case against Wassco, the bay's largest shipbuilder, which he caught dumping toxic wastes directly into the bay. In 1996, the Upper Chattahoochee's Riverkeeper forced the city of Atlanta to agree to invest $250 million in upgrading its sewer plant by 2001.

Wherever there are Riverkeepers, a legal arm like the Pace Clinic is never far behind. A litigation clinic at Widener University Law School in Chester, Pennsylvania, modeled on our clinic at Pace, represents the Delaware Riverkeeper and is cotaught by Pace alumni Professor Jim May and Maya van Rossum. Another Pace Clinic alumnus, David Moore, worked with Emory Law School to help start a litigation arm of the Upper Chattahoochee Riverkeeper. Billy Cahill, also a clinic grad, joined the staff of the New York–New Jersey Harbor Baykeeper as part of a program with the Rutgers University Law School Environmental Law Clinic. The UCLA Environmental Litigation Clinic, founded in 1994 by the Santa Monica and San Diego Baykeepers, along with the NRDC and UCLA, is modeled on Pace's clinic and named for Frank Wells. The San Francisco Baykeeper works with litigation clinics at Golden Gate University and UC-Berkeley law schools.

Soon after Long Island Soundkeeper had been established, a prominent national foundation had offered funding to turn the Hudson Riverkeeper into a national organization that would establish chapters throughout the country. The offer was extremely generous but premature. The Hudson Riverkeeper and Long Island Soundkeeper programs emerged out of the needs of their grassroots constituency. We hoped a national organization would emerge in the same fashion, from the bottom up rather than the top down. A national organization would be the offspring, not the parent, of a national community of Keepers.

In 1992, the Keepers created the National Alliance of River, Sound, and Baykeepers, which is headed by John Cronin. The Pace Clinic also serves as counsel. Members of the alliance work together on issues of national interest and license all new Keeper programs. Before allowing a group to use the Keeper trademark for a new program, Riverkeeper and the alliance must be convinced that there is a need for the program; that its work will not duplicate efforts by another organization in the area; that it has sufficient financial support to sustain itself; that its philosophy is consistent with Riverkeeper's philosophy; and that there is a qualified person to fill the job.

The alliance's first major offensive case grew out of a clinic student's research on a topic of historic interest to Riverkeepers since the Storm King days: the battle to eliminate fish kills at power plants. On the Hudson, litigation, publicity wars, and negotiations had continued since the 1960s.

Theoretically, power utilities should be the easiest industry to regulate. Prisoners of their infrastructure, they cannot threaten to move to another state. They can't claim competitive disadvantage; most are virtual monopolies. They can't claim protection of trade secrets; everyone knows how to produce power. They have no manufacturing jobs to send to Mexico or Canada. But power utilities deal in money and influence. Their board members are campaign contributors and power brokers, and the EPA and state environmental agencies have a knee-jerk history of crumbling under their pressure.

The tragedy is that the electric power industry has the resources and technology to solve the fish kills but prefers instead to carry on the fight against environmental regulation power plant by power plant. Utilities lend each other experts, lawyers, and lobbyists, and sponsor training sessions on how to defeat the Clean Water Act requirements. By suing individual plants over the years we effected a few hard-won improvements—we forced the Indian Point nuclear power plants to install $25 million worth of fish-saving equipment and the river's five utilities to fund a research foundation and conduct long-term fishery population studies. Still, power plants on the Hudson killed billions of fish per year, and we were locked in a perpetual fight over their permits. And the Hudson's problems were not unique.

Despite the availability of closed-cycle cooling—which recirculates water harmlessly like a car radiator—and other technologies for limiting fish kills, power plants across the country use sixty trillion gallons of once-through cooling water each year and kill one trillion fish! Larger fish are crushed on the screens that filter debris out of the cooling water while the smaller ones are sucked inside the cooling systems and superheated. Southern California Edison kills fifty-seven tons of fish annually at its Onofre plant on the Pacific. According to one research report by the Martin Marietta Corporation, Public Service Electric and Gas of New Jersey kills 155 billion weakfish and 175 billion bay anchovies every year at its Salem nuclear plant on the Delaware. Both fisheries have since collapsed. Despite declining inland

and coastal fisheries, industry and government allow these piscine slaughterhouses to flourish. Almost every member of our national Keeper alliance could complain of a power plant that was combing the life from its local waterways.

In 1989, a Pace Clinic student named Brendan Kennedy jumped at an opportunity to finally snaffle-bit the power industry by changing national policy. Brendan had been an Airborne Ranger in Vietnam and enrolled in Pace Law School after being fired from his engineering job at Indian Point Power Plant. In 1982, Brendan broke both legs during a recreational parachute drop into a Bronx parking lot at night. Con Ed had fired him after he refused to tell police the name of his pilot. When he applied to the clinic he was among the top students in his class. We enrolled him and put him to work on power plants. (Each spring, Brendan commemorates the case by parachuting into the annual Riverkeeper shad fest.)

Brendan dredged up the long-forgotten and unfortunate history of federal regulation of power plants. The 1972 Clean Water Act required EPA to promulgate regulations that specified how power plants would minimize fish kills. In 1974, sixty power utilities, under the leadership of Edison Electric Institute, an industry trade group, successfully challenged the EPA's regulations. They based their case upon a nit-picking technical error in the way the EPA published the proposed regulations. Instead of republishing with the simple procedural error fixed, EPA inexplicably walked away from the case, leaving a blank page in the federal register and the power companies operating without standards or rules. "EPA's only run at the regulations was pro forma," recalls Brendan. "The second the utilities hoisted the Jolly Roger, the agency turned and ran." The EPA never attempted to promulgate those regulations again. In the absence of federal standards, the states are still required to use the permit process to stem the massacre. However, not a single state has shown the expertise or stomach to challenge this powerful industry. After twenty-four years, not one has put limits on the number of fish power plants are permitted to kill!

Based on Brendan's research, on July 23, 1990, the members of the National Alliance of River, Sound, and Baykeepers formally notified the EPA of their intent to sue the agency for its failure to repromulgate regulations to control fish kills.

The EPA's first response to our suit was to offer to publish "guidelines" to assist state regulators responsible for drafting power plant permits. We told EPA attorneys that guidelines wouldn't do. State regulators needed nothing less than the law behind them in order to stand up to the power utilities. After months of our filing court papers and negotiating with EPA staff and attorneys, the agency agreed to schedule the promulgation of regulations.

The day before the EPA and the Keepers were to sign an agreement to submit to the federal judge, Edison Electric Institute and fifty-eight power utilities filed court papers to halt the agreement. We spent most of the next year fighting the utilities.

In the end, the judge ruled in our favor and entered an order requiring the EPA to begin the regulatory process. But the battle was far from over. Although we beat the utilities in their bid to stop the regulatory process, their lawsuit won them another year of delay. The EPA needs seven years to promulgate any new regulations (this might come as news to those who claim environmental regulations are too easy to promulgate!). The power industry will certainly file legal challenges to any regulation that hits their bottom line, adding years to the process. Meanwhile, the utilities are lobbying a sympathetic Congress to amend the Clean Water Act so that mass killings of fish will no longer be considered an "adverse environmental impact." Nonetheless, the ruling was a wonderful inaugural victory for the national alliance. Most importantly, it proved concerned communities from all over the nation could join forces to fight the dangerous complicity of the power industry.

By 1997, twenty Keeper programs would crisscross the country from Cook Inlet in Alaska to the Chattahoochee River in Georgia, from Casco Bay in Maine to San Diego Bay in California.

Each time a new Keeper program started, the public embraced the idea because people understood that watching after a river, sound, or bay should be the job of someone in the community whose phone number was only as far away as directory assistance or a magnet on the refrigerator door.

The Riverkeeper philosophy is based on the notion that the protection and enjoyment of a community's natural resources requires the daily vigilance of its citizens. The Riverkeeper movement is an environmental "neighborhood watch" program, a citizen's patrol to protect the nation's waters. A Keeper does not work for government. A

Keeper's constituents are not culled from the databases of political contributors who will later call for a political payback or for "hands off" a certain polluter. They are found among the rank-and-file public, the owners of the water body. Keepers symbolize the ancient right of those owners to enforce the law and defend their home waters.

# CHAPTER 5

# King John
# to General Electric

*People have a right to what they produce themselves, but man has another right, declared by the fact of his existence—the right to use of so much of the free gifts of nature as may be necessary to supply all the wants of that existence, and which he may use without interference with the equal rights of anyone else; and to this he has title against all the world.*

HENRY GEORGE,

*Progress & Poverty,* 1874

Guy Hoffman loves to fish. It is not his job but his passion. When he isn't fishing he is a carpenter, deck builder, and home-improvement contractor. In 1993, Guy's business suffered a severe downturn. Most of the American building industry had already been stagnating for years, and the Hudson Valley was no exception.

By late spring, business had slowed to a crawl. Guy had calls out to contractors all over the county offering his services at a cut rate. But he soon learned that he wasn't the only one feeling the pinch. "Sometimes I worried if me and my family were going to get through these times. When I did, I went to the river and realized that no matter how bad things got, there were some things nobody could take away from you." So, late on a sunny June afternoon, Guy took his problems to his favorite fishing spot on a piece of the Hudson called Roa Hook.

Roa Hook is a thrust of land on the river's east bank, a one-minute drive out of the city of Peekskill, two if the red light catches you at the

Annsville Creek Bridge. Here shallow bay waters receive the narrow, deep fjord that cleaves the Hudson Highlands. By the time *The Angler's Guide and Tourist Gazetteer* of 1885 was published, Roa Hook had long been established as one of the favorite fishing spots in New York. Depending on the season, you can catch striped bass, young bluefish, carp, or eel. In the summer, blue crabs scurry in the shallows, while farther off in the deeper water a seven-foot Atlantic sturgeon may break the surface in a slow dive.

Guy rode the back roads to his usual parking place. He didn't lock his car; he never did. He stepped into his boots, collected his fishing gear, and bushwhacked through the dense woods, over a hillock thick with underbrush, across the railroad tracks, and down fifty feet to the exposed tidal flats. He set his pack on a rock, chose his tackle, opened a beer, and stepped into the river to fish. Solitary and peaceful amid the free-flowing waters, Guy set his feet firm in the river's bottom mud and cast his lure out in a long, graceful arc, as he had so many times before. But this afternoon, just as he began to feel the calming effects of the river, Guy was arrested by railroad police, charged with criminal trespass, and taken away for arraignment in local criminal court.

For over one hundred years, fishermen had freely crossed the railroad tracks to access the Hudson River. In the early 1990s, Metro North railroad's private police force began arresting and ticketing fishermen. Since then, nearly one hundred fishermen and duck hunters had called us to report harassment by Metro North police. Many had been menaced with drawn guns. One father, on vacation with his family, had been pulled from his canoe, handcuffed in front of his children, and dragged to a precinct house where he was fingerprinted. Metro North maintained that it was arresting fishermen who crossed the commuter tracks as a public safety precaution. But when challenged to provide safe access to traditional fishing locations, the railroad replied that it was "in the business of running a railroad, not providing public access to the Hudson."

Some fishermen accept the occasional fines as part of the cost of fishing the river—a kind of toll or tariff imposed by the railroads that now own the better portion of both banks from New York to Albany. Guy Hoffman could have retired the whole matter by pleading guilty and paying a fifty-dollar fine.

But the humiliation of being yanked out of the river and handcuffed, on top of his other woes, had pushed Guy over the edge. When he called us for help, his question was simple: "Don't I have a right to stand in the Hudson River?" We believed the answer was equally simple: Yes, a fundamental right. "I want to fight this," Guy told us. "This is my river, too."

Riverkeeper agreed to provide legal representation to Guy since the gravamen of his case was a precise statement of Riverkeeper's mission: "The people own the Hudson and they cannot be evicted." We argued that Guy had an inalienable right to stand in the Hudson River. Since the railroad police had not actually seen Hoffman cross railroad property, and since Hoffman refused to testify as to how he had arrived on that particular piece of river bottom, we quickly convinced the prosecutor that there was no basis for a prosecution. The state dropped all charges. Within days of Guy's victory word spread among fishermen and bait shops in the Hudson Valley that the railroad no longer owned the Hudson River and that fishermen were once again free to fish the near-shore shoals without harassment—so long as they employed the fairly simple precaution of crossing the tracks out of sight of the Metro North Police.

General Electric's crimes against the Hudson raise the same question about who owns the river. General Electric discharged two million pounds of PCBs into the Hudson over thirty years. According to Ogden Reid, who served as DEC commissioner during that period, GE met every effort by the government to moderate its pollution with threats to leave the state. By sparing itself the costs of proper disposal or recycling, the company presumably was able to lower the per unit cost of its transformers enough to undersell its competitors and increase its profit margin.

In 1975, the DEC finally acknowledged that Hudson River fishes contained toxic levels of PCBs and asked the company to stop discharging. General Electric closed the plant in 1982, taking its twelve hundred jobs with it and skipping out on a $280 million cleanup bill that no one in the Hudson Valley could afford. Later that year, the DEC banned most commercial fishing, citing the danger to human health. Hundreds of fishermen permanently lost their jobs in communities as far as 190 miles downstream. The ban is expected to remain in effect for the next sixty years. The DEC closed the upper river to recreational fishing, resulting in the closure of bait shops, motels, and

boat rental operations. River traffic, including a lucrative barge industry, has dropped 75 percent since 1981 because river channels are
clogged with PCB-laden sediment that can't be dredged without causing even graver contamination.

The Hudson has always generated jobs for New Yorkers and provided an economic safety net during the hardest times. In every previous economic downturn in U.S. history, jobless people in New York
City could take a giant striped bass from the river for the family dinner
table. In the Great Depression thousands of unemployed men flocked
to the river and found work fishing. General Electric's pollution
spelled the end of that legacy. But despite the ban, thousands of New
Yorkers, particularly opportunistic poor and minority fishermen who
line the river's bulkheads from the Battery to Croton every warm day,
continue to catch and feed their families PCB-contaminated fish, presumably causing long-term health problems for which society foots
the bill in lost productivity and health-care costs.

Today, PCB levels in the breast milk of women from Oswego to
Albany approach unsafe levels. In fact, everyone who reads this book
has PCB molecules in their body fat and organs from a plant like General Electric's on the Hudson River. Escalating health-care costs are
borne by society at large. But some of the greatest losses are not economic but cultural and human. Parents can no longer take their children to fish on the banks of the river. And an ancient fishery that
enriched the culture and palate of the Hudson Valley is lost to generations of New Yorkers.

Not long ago, commercial fisherman Everett Nack told John, "My
sons love the river just as much as I do. They were looking forward to
making a living off of it. Thanks to GE's PCBs, now that's gone."

New York State law says that the people of New York State own the
waters and the fish in the Hudson. In truth, General Electric now
owns the fish in the Hudson—it liquidated them for cash. In Riverkeeper's view and in the view of the law, General Electric stole something that belonged to the public.

The right of commercial fishermen like Everett Nack and anglers
like Guy Hoffman to use the Hudson and enjoy free access to its fisheries is set forth in New York State's Constitution and statutes, but
actually is based in the oldest body of law upon which our democracy
rests, the Public Trust Doctrine. Appearing in English Common Law

and Roman law before it, that doctrine establishes public ownership of certain natural resources and is one of two ancient legal principles that underlie modern environmental law and virtually all Riverkeeper's work.

According to the Public Trust Doctrine, the public owns common or shared environments—air, waters, dunes, tidelands, underwater lands, fisheries, shellfish beds, parks and commons, and migratory species. (Some public trust analysis also includes sacred sites and historical monuments.) These things "are so particularly the gifts of nature's bounty that they ought to be reserved for the whole of the populace" (Joseph L. Sax, "The Public Trust Doctrine in Natural Resource Law: Effective Judicial Intervention," 68 *Michigan Law Review* 471, 484 [1970]). Government trustees are obligated to maintain the value of these systems for all users—including future generations. Like other rights, public trust rights are said to derive from "natural" or God-given law. They cannot be extinguished.

Roman law, our most ancient legal heritage, held that the most fundamental "natural" law required that the "air, running water, the sea, and consequently the sea shore" could not be owned as private property but were "common to all" Roman citizens (*Justinian Institutes* 2.1.1 [4th ed., J. B. Mayle, trans. 1889]). The Romans vigorously protected public resources of the sea, seashore, estuaries, wetlands, and fisheries from control by private individuals.

Following Rome's collapse, Europe's kings and feudal lords appropriated public trust lands, including forests and streams, and dispensed them without regard to public rights. In the early years of the thirteenth century, Britain's King John fenced in England's forests and streams, erected navigational tolls, and placed weirs in the rivers in order to sell private monopolies to the fisheries. The exclusion of the public from the rivers and fish, and the stifling of commerce that ensued, helped prompt the ratification of the Magna Carta and the citizens' revolt which followed. In 1225 the English barons trounced King John at Runnymede and forced him to sign the Magna Carta that guaranteed the personal liberties of the people of England. Centuries later it served as the blueprint for the Bill of Rights in the U.S. Constitution. Among the rights reaffirmed by the Magna Carta were "liberty of navigation" and a "free fishery" so that, according to Britain's seminal legal authority, Blackstone, "[the rivers that were fenced by the king] were directed to be laid open" (*Blackstone Commentaries,* 33–34, 4th ed., 1876). The Magna Carta ended the sovereign's monopoly of the fishery, ordering the king to permanently remove "[a]ll kydells [weirs], from the Thames and Medway, and throughout all England. . . ." Subsequent court decisions interpreted that document to mean that "the King was trustee" holding public lands and waters "as protector of public and common rights" and "he could not appropriate them to his own use" ("Comment, the Public Trust in Tidal Areas: A Sometime Submerged Traditional Doctrine," 79 *Yale Law Journal* 762, 769 [1970]). Eleventh-century French law provided that "the public highways and byways, running water and springs, meadows and pastures, forests, heaths, and rocks . . . are not to be held by lords . . . nor are they to be maintained . . . in any other way than that their people may always be able to use them" (M. Block, *French Rural History,* 183 [1966]). Thirteenth-century Spanish law likewise ensured the public inalienable rights in forest and shores.

Neither could the King sell public trust assets to a private party. The nineteenth-century legal scholar Schultes described public trust rights as "unalienable." He explained that "things which relate to the public good cannot be given, sold, or transferred by the King to another person" (H. Schultes, *Aquatic Rights,* 10 [1839]). Woolrych, another legal scholar of the period, added that "notwithstanding such a grant, if the public interest be invaded, or the privileges of the people narrowed, the grant, *pro tanto* is void" (J. Angell, *A Treatise on the Right of Property in Tide Waters and in the Soil and Shores Therof,* 33–34 [1st ed. 1826]).

Following the American Revolution, each state became sovereign, inheriting from King George III the trusteeship of public lands and waters and wildlife within its borders. Both the federal government and the individual states recognized the public trust in their statutes and ordinances. For instance, Massachusetts' "Great Pond Ordinance" of 1641 assured public access to all consequential water bodies, and the federal government's Northwest Ordinance of 1787 gave all U.S. citizens unrestrained access to all the tributaries of the St. Lawrence and the Mississippi and proclaimed that those waters and "the carrying places between shall be common highways and forever free. . . ." (Ch. 8, 1 Stat. 50, 52 [1789]).

In 1821 the New Jersey Supreme Court affirmed that American fisheries were owned by the public. In *Arnold v Mundy,* the defendant

Arnold claimed an exclusive right to take oysters in the Hudson Raritan Harbor based on a seventeenth-century grant from King Charles II to the Duke of York. Mundy prevailed in his claim that the Public Trust Doctrine allows no monopoly over fisheries in American waters.

In an 1892 landmark case, the U.S. Supreme Court nullified the Illinois legislature's grant of one thousand acres of Lake Michigan shoreline and underwater land to the Illinois Central Railroad. The court went on to distinguish the nature of a state's title in public trust lands, such as shoreline, from non–public trust lands that the state could legally sell. "It is a title held in trust for the people of the state that they may enjoy the navigation of waters, carry on commerce over them, and have liberty of fishing therein, freed from the obstruction or interference of private parties" (*Illinois C.R. Co. v Illinois,* 146 US 387, 452 [1892]). A later 1913 Supreme Court decision condemned as "inconceivable" the notion that a private party could claim title to navigable waters (*United States v Chandler-Dunbar Water Power Co.,* 229 US 53, 69 [1913]). Thus the judicial branch of our government affirmed that under the Public Trust Doctrine, the waterways and fisheries and other public resources of America are owned by the public, and no one has the right to use them in a way that will diminish their use and enjoyment by others. The state, as trustee, has no authority to enact policies that favor one public user over another.

While public trust today remains a part of the common law of every state, many jurisdictions have ignored all but its navigational mandates since the early twentieth century. During the industrial revolution in the late nineteenth and early twentieth centuries, American courts increasingly exercised their interpretive power to uphold the right of legislators to promote private uses of these lands so long as some public good could be claimed.

As judicial vigilance in the safeguarding of public trust rights waned, some states began acting more like private owners than trustees. Agencies and legislators, motivated at best by blind faith in market forces and at worst by corruption, practically tripped over each other in a scurry to grant public resources to private parties. California and Florida sold tidal lands and wetlands for a fraction of their market value. Railroads appropriated shorelines, thereby excluding fishermen and recreational users; lakes and wetlands were drained to make way for residential developers; and dumps and industries polluted publicly owned water bodies without redress. In these years of wild industrial growth, the Public Trust Doctrine fell into disuse, enforced only against obstacles to navigation and the most egregious transfers of waterfront property to private enterprise.

Although the courts have nowhere repudiated the Public Trust Doctrine, the effect of this evolution was to dramatically reduce the power of individuals with interests in fishing, bathing, recreation, drinking water, or aesthetics to exercise their rights to redress injuries to public trust resources.

A healthy socioeconomic system rewards the efficient use of resources and punishes their inefficient use. With the breakdown of public trust enforcement, our legal system was no longer confronting polluters with the social costs of their activities. Industry had the economic incentive to "cheat" by imposing its costs of doing business onto society. Environmentalists call this process "externalizing." Those industries that absorbed their own costs would fail in the competitive marketplace.

A manufacturer like General Electric has no reason to invest in the safe disposal of toxic by-products if it can dump that waste for free in a public waterway. Any such investment would result in higher costs and therefore a less competitive end product. The market dictates that the company continue to pollute, even in cases where a tiny investment in equipment could spare the enormous social costs of pollution. Since the courts ignored the fishermen, swimmers, water consumers, bait shops, and fish consumers, industry had no reason to heed these interests. Society would continue to make poor choices about resource allocation so long as the law succeeded in silencing the river's diffuse constituencies who bear the burden of the costs.

The General Electric "deal" was one of many that captured the headlines in the 1960s and 1970s and prompted the popular movement to restore our ancient rights. People realized that the PCB contamination occurred because the law did not require government or industry to account for the costs they imposed upon ordinary people. Resourceful parties like General Electric readily obtained government permission to pollute the neighborhoods of less resourceful parties without their permission or consent. In the late 1960s and early 1970s, as factories closed across the Northeast, communities were left to cope with wasted lands, depleted resources, and spectacular cleanup costs left behind by companies like General Electric. The public finally realized that in relinquishing our public trust rights to industry, we simply had not made a good bargain.

Over the years, industries had been required to give only the narrowest accounting of the costs they were imposing on society. This encouraged a short-term "pollution-based prosperity" for which communities eventually began receiving long-term bills. In the early 1960s, U.S. courts and legislatures began to recognize that environmental injury is theft. When one party, for its own enrichment, takes some public trust right that belongs to another—such as clean air, uncontaminated fish, access to waters and fisheries; one's livelihood, health, recreational opportunities; or publicly owned resources—it is as much as theft as if that party had stolen private property. When this theft is committed against the will of the polluted community but with government permission and protection, as in the GE case, it becomes a human rights issue, with troubling implications for our democracy and our judicial system.

GE didn't get a grant from King George III for sole right to the fishery. Any American court would reject a grant stated this way as an illegal monopoly. But by dumping PCBs into the river, GE closed the fisheries and shut down most barge traffic on the Hudson. In a backhanded way, General Electric was able to obtain government-granted fishery and navigation monopolies—just the things that Roman law forbade and that British citizens fought against and died to abolish at the Battle of Runnymede.

Recognizing a major threat to fundamental American values, twenty million Americans appeared on the street on Earth Day 1970 to demand restoration of our lost environmental rights. In response, courts and Congress began to breathe life into the moribund Public Trust Doctrine, raising it up in a new iteration: modern environmental law. The federal statutes were the modern metamorphosis of public trust, a statutory response to a popular rebellion that demanded the resuscitation of the ancient right. The Clean Water Act, the Clean Air Act, the Endangered Species Act, and the National Environmental Policy Act are all best understood as a modern guarantee of the protection of ancient public trust rights in an industrial age.

The second ancient doctrine that underlies modern environmental law is the Law of Nuisance. It evolved as a separate body of law protecting the public trust, private property, and other community values from malefactors attempting to enrich themselves by harming the community. The Law of Nuisance restricts uses of private property that might injure the public.

The history of nuisance law is a sobering reminder to those who like to view environmental regulation as a recent creation of antiproperty radicals. In fact, nuisance law, like modern environmental law, is a conservative doctrine designed to protect property, public health, and democratic values.

In French, "nuisance" means "annoyance" or "harm." Blackstone expressed the Roman law maxim *sic utere tuo ut alienum non laedas* (use your own property but not to injure another) as the foundation of the Law of Nuisance in the late eighteenth century. Ancient British common law flatly forbade an owner from using his property in such a way. A defendant's use of his land that caused injuries to the community at large (air pollution, bad odors, health threats) was treated as a criminal offense known as "public nuisance." The law was treated seriously; in 1307, an Englishman was put to death for violating a clean air law prohibiting the burning of coal in furnaces.

Over the centuries an entire body of public nuisance law accumulated as a compendium of behaviors forbidden by legislatures and courts. Edward II signed the first known clean air act, a smoke pollution control law, as early as 1273. By 1525, London residents were successfully suing city officials to require private property owners to control their swine, whose stench, they claimed, caused a "dreadful terror." Zoning laws were implemented in seventeenth-century London in the form of minimum lot size requirements and building codes. American jurisprudence implicitly recognized aesthetic injury in 1834, when the Federal Circuit Court in Washington, D.C., upheld the indictment of a landowner for beating her cow to death on the grounds that it occurred "in view of a public street." Public gaming houses and brothels were banned as nuisances, as were farm animals in residential neighborhoods, unsafe buildings, and properties that served as breeding grounds for mosquitoes or rodents. Also categorized as offenses were activities ranging from keeping diseased animals to storing explosives, shooting off fireworks, and obstructing a highway or navigable waterway.

From the early dawn of our legal system, courts and legislatures have enjoyed the authority to respond to social change and the ingenuity of society's mischief makers by adding new categories of nuisance. The law had to be flexible in order to cope with changing threats to the social order.

As the U.S. Supreme Court said in 1992, "[C]hanged circumstances or new knowledge may make what was previously permissible no longer so" (*Lucas v South Carolina,* 1.505 US 1003, 1030 [1992]). The end of slavery is an example of such social change, as is illegalization of alcohol by the Thirteenth Amendment. While private owners were once required by government policy to fill wetlands (for mosquito control), those lands are now protected. Pigs, tolerated in a rural setting, may be judged noxious as the surrounding area suburbanizes. Red cedar trees, once judged fashionable, have been banned within a certain radius of an apple orchard in order to prevent the spread of a communicable disease.

Throughout this country's history, liability in nuisance cases was strict. A private party suffering injury did not need to prove negligence on the part of the defendant. As an Ohio court held in 1832, if a defendant's use of his property causes either hurt, annoyance, or damage "in the least degree, the person creating it must be answerable for the consequences" (*Cooper v Hall,* S Ohio 321, 323 [1832]).

While neighbors could be expected to bear small inconveniences, like occasional whiffs of sauces or the construction of unsightly structures on an adjoining property, the threshold for actionable injury was low. When an activity posed a threat to human health or property, the inconvenience or cost to the defendant of ceasing the activity was irrelevant. In an 1869 decision, the Supreme Court of Illinois maintained that smoke from the defendant's flour mill, if shown to enter the plaintiff's house or inconvenience him even one day each year, constituted an actionable nuisance. The remedy was injunction; the nuisance must cease. The mill must close or move.

Despite the harshness of this doctrine, the idea that a property owner had an absolute right to enjoy his land free of air and water pollution or other disturbances was so well settled that in 1875, American legal scholar Horace Gay Wood wrote that "where the right is clear, and the nuisance is established, an injunction will always be granted . . . an injunction may be said to be a matter of right." The injunction remedy was important because it tended to protect not just the interest of the plaintiff but the public resource as well. The plaintiff, usually a wealthy individual who had suffered measurable financial injury, in effect acted as champion for a resource enjoyed by a diffuse group of people unlikely to bring suit to protect their own interests.

Toward the end of the nineteenth century, in a trend that paralleled the erosion of the Public Trust Doctrine, American courts began to relax nuisance standards in favor of the rising new class of industrial entrepreneurs and robber barons. By 1889, the United States had become the globe's greatest industrial power. For the first time, manufactured products exceeded farm income in value. Manufacturing, railroad, and oil and mineral extraction industries moved to the forefront of American power. In response, the courts began constructing impediments for nuisance plaintiffs. "[T]he onward spirit of the age must have its way," a Kentucky court cheerfully proclaimed in 1839, denying an injunction to forty-three homeowners who sought to stop the construction of a railroad through their neighborhood. "The law is made for the times and will be made or modified by them." These times, as it turned out, were made for industrialists.

Persuaded of the general benefits of industrialization, the courts began to edge away from the Blackstonian view of absolute property rights. They began preferring damages over injunction as a remedy for environmental injury. This subtle shift in remedies had a profound impact on public resources. Whereas the injunction favored all resource users by requiring the injurious activity to cease, the less ambitious goal of extracting cash for the plaintiff had no lasting salutary benefit to the resource itself. If a downstream landowner's cows had died from discharges from a paper plant, the landowner received compensation equivalent to the loss of income from his dairy operation. Maybe he went away happy, but the general public who used the river for fishing, swimming, or aesthetic enjoyment received no benefit. Because of the expense of litigation, these individuals, although they may have suffered appreciable damage from the pollution, were unlikely to take legal action.

Another new impediment to injunction was the "balancing test." Instead of automatically granting an injunction upon finding that the defendant's activity constituted a nuisance, the courts would weigh the inconvenience to the defendant and to society against the injury to the plaintiff. This procedural requirement overwhelmingly favored defendants with large investments that could be weighed against the relatively smaller interests of private homeowners and individual citizens.

In 1868, a Pennsylvania court became the first American court to utilize the balancing test when it denied an injunction to a homeowner aggrieved by the great amounts of dust, soot, and noise generated by a neighboring ironworks. The court concluded that it must "consider whether [it] would not do a greater injury by enjoining than would result from refusing" (Reichard's Ap., 57 PA 105, 113 [1868]).

Even rural states were persuaded. A North Carolina court adopted the same reasoning in 1881 in refusing a homeowner's request for an injunction against the construction of a cotton gin on a neighboring parcel: "[I]t would be unwise . . . for the court to . . . prevent . . . substantial and lasting benefits to a community, because of the discomfort [to] a single family. . . ."

Legal commentators reacted with alarm at this attack on the sacredness of property upon which, they believed, a free society and democratic civilization depended. In *Evans v Reading Chemical Fertilizer,* the Supreme Court of Pennsylvania rejected this sort of balancing, holding that when the public interest demanded a "taking" of the plaintiff's property by pollution, then legislative use of eminent domain power was appropriate (160 Pa. 209 [1894]). In other words, when government gave permission to a party to pollute, the government itself should be obligated to fully compensate any injured parties for the infringement on their right to be free of their neighbors' pollution.

These early decisions demonstrate how perversely modern private-property advocates have twisted the ancient assumptions of the law to their advantage. The anti-environmental movement likes to argue that property owners have an inherent "right to pollute" or to fill wetlands even when doing so would destroy a community water supply, flood neighbors' property, or destroy local populations of fish or birds. They say that property owners deserve compensation from the government when these "rights" are restricted. In fact, owners of nuisance activities have never been compensated under common or civil law, since they never owned the right to use their property in a way that is injurious to society. This is true even when a nuisance activity was once judged innocuous or permissible. Thus, neither slaveholders nor liquor stores were compensated when Congress chose to ban slavery or the sale of alcoholic beverages. Sweatshop owners were not compensated when minimum-wage and child-labor laws were enacted, nor were food purveyors when ordered to destroy tainted goods. Property owners whose land encompasses wetlands or coastal zones are not compensated for "losses" caused by laws that restrict development in those areas, since the rights conveyed by ownership of property do not include the right to injure the community.

Without formally rejecting Blackstone's orthodoxy, some courts introduced weasel words to nuisance analysis so as to avoid antidevelopmental injunctions and to spare polluters from damage suits. Courts raised the threshold for actionable injury, forcing citizens to prove that their injury was "specially uncomfortable or inconvenient," or that it damaged their property interests "materially and essentially," or that the annoyance was "substantial." Other courts abandoned the strict liability rule and began forcing the plaintiff to prove the defendant's negligence in order to prevail. American courts also created the "industrialization defense," which shielded polluters from nuisance lawsuits so long as they conducted their business in an area that was heavily industrialized (*Gilbert v Showerman,* 23 Mich. 447 [1871]). These areas could encompass neighboring residential areas and entire cities. In 1871, the Pennsylvania Supreme Court wrote that "the people who live in . . . a city . . . do so of choice, and they voluntarily subject themselves to its peculiarities and its discomforts, for the greater benefit they think they derive from this residence. . . ."

With these weapons, polluters were able to insulate themselves from annoying lawsuits by landowners and the public. The faith of the courts and legislatures in American industry seemed well placed. By the middle of the twentieth century, the United States was the most powerful economy on earth and its military dominated the globe. New weapons harnessing the forces of the universe allowed us to turn back the Nazis and Japanese and hold the Stalinist dictatorship at bay. Railroads and tarmac girthed the nation, invigorating commerce. Our most powerful rivers were yoked for energy. Even agricultural pests that had plagued mankind since its first permanent settlements in the Fertile Crescent retreated before modern chemical pesticides. The gains to all Americans seemed to outweigh the ancient rights that property owners and the public had sacrificed to the promise of progress. However, in the 1960s, at the very moment that American industrial power reached its apex and Americans found themselves with the highest standard of living of any people in history, a concurrence of events exposed the planet's fragility and the waste of public resources. In 1960, strontium 90, a radioactive by-product of atmospheric bomb explosions, was discovered to have proliferated in virtually all milk drinks. Smog events were killing people in American and European cities, sometimes by the thousands. The wading bird population of the Everglades dropped to 10 percent of historic levels because of a Corps of Engineers canal project designed to make South Florida more hospitable to coastal development. DDT drove the eastern peregrine into extinction in 1963 and caused the disappearance of eagles and ospreys from most of the East Coast. The blue whale population dropped below one hundred. Lake Erie was proclaimed nearly dead from pollution. The *Torrey Canyon* tanker oil spill in 1967 dumped hundreds of thousands of tons of crude onto beaches, killing birds and fish and crippling recreational industries. In 1969, the Cuyahoga River in Cleveland burned and a massive oil spill off California's coast blackened Santa Barbara's beaches. Smog-stained skies, toxic-waste dumps, and oil spills provoked public outrage. Newspapers and magazines carried stories of species going extinct and pictures of denuded hillsides as logging companies clear-cut the last ancient redwoods on private land. Many people were struck by the notion that unrestrained industrialization was eroding the quality of life even faster than it was raising standards of living.

The public began reasserting its right to a clean environment, and the legislature and courts responded in a revolutionary series of cases and statutes. The catalyst for the revolution was a 1962 book by Rachel Carson, *Silent Spring,* which prompted Americans to question whether we had relinquished too much power to industry.

Carson was not a wild-eyed reformer intent on bringing the industrial age to a grinding halt. She wasn't even opposed to pesticides per se. She was a careful scientist and brilliant writer whose painstaking research on pesticides proved that the "miraculous" bursts of agricultural productivity had long-term costs undisclosed in the chemical industry's exaggerated puffery. Americans were losing things—their health, many birds and fishes, and the purity of their waterways—that they should value more than modest savings at the grocery store. In other words, the public wasn't getting the benefit of the bargain. *Silent*

*Spring* raised America's indignation not only about the loads of chemicals in our food and the destruction of wildlife but, equally, about the deception dealt us by the very industries that we entrusted with our publicly owned resources. People began demanding that industry provide an honest, comprehensive accounting of the costs of pollution. Public outcries prompted the courts and legislatures to begin looking for ways to reopen the "bargaining" process to citizens with interests in endangered public resources.

It is not surprising that the first critical beachhead in the battle for legal recognition of the right to a clean environment occurred in the Hudson Valley. By the late sixties industry had fled the Hudson Valley and New York State, leaving behind armies of unemployed workers, closed factories, vast cleanup costs, and an overall skepticism toward the claims of industrialists. Proud Hudson Valley communities that had absorbed insult after insult to their river finally bridled at Con Ed's proposal to decapitate Storm King Mountain, a geological monument that was a potent symbol of the region's natural legacy.

When the Federal Court of Appeals in New York City ruled that environmental advocates have standing to sue to protect non-economic interests in public trust resources, it created a special new category, "environmental standing." The judges said that a citizen who lives near, fishes, hikes, swims in, or drinks from a public resource, or who walks by it occasionally and derives some aesthetic pleasure from the view, has an interest in its welfare that gives him or her standing to sue. This new "environmental standing" doctrine overcame the constitutional barrier to citizens' participation in decisions about how private industry utilized or wasted public trust resources.

The court also made history by mandating the first-ever full environmental impact statement. The Federal Power Commission was ordered to include, in its permit application process, a complete accounting of all the costs and benefits of the proposed project including the impacts on the environment and aesthetics, fisheries, and recreation. Such an accounting, the court said, would allow the public to evaluate the need for the project, not just based upon its potential profitability to ratepayers but upon the full array of long-term costs to all citizens.

In 1969, Congress codified the Storm King decision in the most momentous piece of environmental legislation since the Magna Carta.

The National Environmental Policy Act forced federal agencies to "look before they leap"—to assess the full environmental impacts of every major decision, including the social costs, benefits, and alternatives. Prior to committing resources, each agency must give the public opportunity to comment or to demand a hearing on actions that may affect the environment. After considering scientific studies as well as feedback from the public, the agency must publish the findings that justify its decision to proceed with the project. Any member of the public may appeal these findings in federal court. In other words, this statute gives citizens the right to demand a complete and long-term cost-benefit analysis of any decision that may erode the value of their public trust assets.

The Storm King decision and its codification in NEPA were the first giant steps in a democratic social movement to restore control of publicly owned resources to the people. With the help of the courts and Congress, the public was beginning to reclaim its ancient common-law rights.

The extraordinary democratic outpouring at Earth Day 1970 fueled the cascade of environmental legislation from Congress during the next decade. Using the constitutional door opened by Storm King and the political clout won by the movement on Earth Day, Congress created the Environmental Protection Agency (EPA) and passed upwards of forty major environmental statutes. These included:

*The Clean Air Act (1970):* Required the EPA to develop emissions and air-quality standards with which industries and municipalities must comply.

*The Clean Water Act (1972):* Required that by 1985 all the water bodies in the nation be fishable and swimmable and that all discharges of pollutants be eliminated. During the transition period, EPA could issue permits for small amounts of pollutants, according to established guidelines and only following a period of public comment and hearings.

*The Coastal Zone Management Act (1972):* Provided for the development of coastal zone management programs for the protection of estuarine and coastal waters.

*The Endangered Species Act (1973):* Authorized the EPA to develop a list of endangered species and made it illegal for any individual to "harass, harm, pursue, hunt, shoot, wound, kill, trap, capture, or collect" any listed plant or animal.

*The Migratory Bird Treaty Act (1973):* Illegalized the unpermitted killing or taking of migratory birds.

*The Federal Insecticide, Fungicide, and Rodenticide Act (1975):* Required the EPA to test and develop protocols for handling and applying pesticides and made violations of those protocols illegal.

*The Resource Conservation and Recovery Act (1976):* Mandated procedures for the safe disposal of toxic waste and made violations of those protocols illegal.

*The Toxic Substance Control Act (1977):* Provided cradle-to-grave accountability of toxic substances by their manufacturers.

*The Comprehensive Environmental Response, Compensation, and Liability Act (Superfund) (1980):* Ordered the inventorying and cleanup of existing toxic waste sites, with the costs paid by those who profited by the disposal.

The legislative onslaught constituted a revolution in American law, but in fact it was a conservative revolution. While the uninformed observer might regard this assortment of environmental statutes as hastily assembled and incohesive, in reality they form a careful patchwork reconstruction of the common-law rights guaranteed under the ancient nuisance and public trust doctrines.

Today, in the United States, statutes regulating land no longer use the term "public nuisance," but the same principles apply. Modern environmental law merely redefines nuisance with particularity. Instead of terms like "noxious stench," we have numerical air-quality standards. Instead of banning "unpotable water," we have instituted maximum contaminant levels and water quality standards. The London Building Code, a seventeenth-century law that forbade the construction of more than one house per acre, is a precursor to modern zoning laws.

Eleventh-century smoke abatement laws predicted the Clean Air Act. The ancient common-law right to public access to coastal zones and water bodies is revived in the Coastal Zone Management Act. Nuisance laws forbidding storage or spilling of noxious or poisonous materials predated our modern toxic substances legislation. The precise standards of modern environmental law benefited industry as well as common citizens by making nuisance law more predictable.

Taken together, these acts mark a recognition by Congress that these rights were improperly taken from the American people and must be returned. Air, water, land, and wild animals, once seen as "free goods" that industries could destroy at will, have been returned to the people. With provisions allowing greater public scrutiny of the negotiations over government permits, the statutes move toward guaranteeing protection of the public trust and citizens' rights to review the government's performance as public trustees. Some of these laws recognize the final inviolability and inalienability of public trust rights, holding that certain trust assets *cannot* be liquidated—no matter what the cost. For example, endangered species cannot be extinguished, and water cannot be polluted to the point where fish will die.

Beginning in the early 1970s, the federal government and states also passed sunshine laws (or freedom-of-information or right-to-know laws) granting citizens access to government records and community members access to information about toxic materials handled by private companies in their neighborhoods. These laws addressed the need for citizens to know as much as possible about the environmental costs and consequences of any community bargain with industry.

Responding to Storm King's new doctrine of environmental standing, Congress included in most of these statutes a "citizen suit" provision, modeled on the Civil Rights Act of 1965. This important provision, which is the centerpiece of Riverkeeper's legal strategy, gives every citizen with standing the right to step into the shoes of the U.S. Attorney and prosecute violators in federal court whenever government prosecutors fail to enforce compliance with the statute. To facilitate these suits, Congress also provided that the citizens, when successful, could recover their litigation costs from the polluters. Penalties for violating the statutes are severe—up to $25,000 for every day of violation. These extraordinary provisions also allow individuals to sue the government for polluting or for failing to perform a duty under the Clean Water Act—citizen power that is unheard of in any other country on the globe.

The early successes of the Hudson River Fishermen's Association were in large part due to judicial recognition that the Fishermen's feelings of ownership toward the river were not the irrational ravings of marginal quacks but were firmly grounded in ancient "natural" or God-given law. As Bob Boyle reasoned, "We felt we owned the Hudson. For most of us the Hudson was the largest thing we ever hoped to own. We would be simpletons or fools if we allowed someone to take it from us. If someone pulled a truck up to your backyard and unloaded a tanker full of PCBs, you would sue them. What on earth would stop us from protecting our rights in the river with equal vigor?"

The struggle over public rights to natural resources in Western society is inseparable from the struggle for democracy. One of the emblems of a democracy's strength is its ability to withstand the tendency to concentrate society's resources in the hands of a few. Natural resources are the basis of wealth; the struggle to control them is the fire in which democratic institutions are continually tested.

Several years ago Bobby went with Puget Soundkeeper Kenny Moser to the remote Suquamish Indian Reservation on Sinclair Inlet to advise tribal leaders about a lawsuit against nearby Bremerton naval shipyards. As counsel for the National Association of River, Sound and Bay Keepers, Bobby was representing the Puget Soundkeeper in a lawsuit against the navy yard. While walking near the shore, one of the Suquamish chiefs, Georgia George, pointed to the thick mats of mussels and oysters and the sea cucumbers, crabs, and fishes trapped in tidal pools. A nineteenth-century treaty with the federal government gave the Suquamish control of all the fisheries and shellfish of Sinclair Inlet "so long as the tide shall rise and fall." Marveling at the richness of those pools, she recalled what her mother had told her as a girl: "No matter how poor we are in cash and clothes and things, we will always be rich so long as the tide goes out." Now the tribe finds itself facing the unthinkable. Discharges from the nearby Bremerton navy yard have poisoned the shellfish, making them inedible. Even the fruits of the tide have been stolen from them.

A people's inherent wealth lies in nature: fresh air, clean water for drinking and cooking, green places to walk, a beautiful scene, a fishing hole, a place to row a boat or to swim, to pick wild berries, to hunt. No matter how great the disparities in wealth, these are things one always assumed could not be taken away—from anyone.

The Public Trust Doctrine protects some of this "everyman's" wealth by forbidding appropriations of shoreline and bottom land. The nuisance doctrine protects public wealth and quality of life from other invasions, smoke, and erosion. However, the chemical revolution has given those who seek to concentrate wealth new avenues for expropriating the people's assets. Witness how General Electric took ownership of virtually all the fish in the Hudson River.

The "environmental revolution" was only revolutionary in the eyes of those with a vested interest in pollution: the General Electrics and the Metro Norths who had wrongly evicted the public from the public trust. In truth, the "revolution" simply recognized public rights that had always existed. These public rights of individuals like Guy Hoffman and Everett Nack—to be free of nuisances and to have unimpeded access to the river and its fishes—were regarded as "self-evident" by Roman and early British jurisprudence. In 1913, our Supreme Court called it "inconceivable" that public trust could slip into private hands. Nevertheless these rights were subverted over time. The authors of the erosion were powerful and the process was often subtle.

Democracy affirms individual rights to our natural resources. If we are to succeed in safeguarding our environment for future generations, it will be because of a courageous citizenry in whose hands democracy has evolved from a system that merely caters to commerce and industry to one that recognizes and protects the individual's right to good health; safe air, water, and food; and the enrichment of God's creation.

# CHAPTER 6

# Westway and NIMBY:
# Democracy at Work

One of the best examples of how modern American environmental law has empowered community groups to protect themselves from over-bearing government and industry was the successful campaign by Hudson Valley citizens to stop Westway, a $2 billion construction project that would have added 242 riverfront acres to Manhattan's West Side and enriched the city's most powerful developers by billions of dollars.

Westway was the brainchild of the State Urban Development Corporation, which in 1971 proposed building a highway on pilings and filling in the Hudson River to replace the dilapidated West Side Highway. In 1977, New York's Environmental Commissioner Peter Berle denied an air quality permit for Westway because of the dramatic increases in traffic it would precipitate. That decision cost Berle his job, and his replacement, Robert Flacke, dutifully issued the permit. The project also required a landfill permit from the Army Corps of Engineers. To fight its issuance, a group of Westway opponents who believed the highway would destroy air quality and the unique character of lower Manhattan hired Storm King attorney Al Butzel. Led by Marcy Benstock of the city-based Clean Air Campaign, Westway opponents argued this was not a highway project but a pork barrel for developers, and the money ought to be used, instead, to upgrade the city's deteriorating transit system.

Predictably, most of the major real estate and development companies supported the project. It was championed by New York City's powerful construction unions and even the United States Army, whose Corps of Engineers would manage the project's river construction. New York State's Republican senator Alfonse D'Amato and his Democratic colleague Daniel Moynihan, who chaired the powerful Senate Transportation Committee, and two New York governors also supported Westway, as did the editorial boards of all three city newspapers—the *New York Post,* the *Daily News,* and the *New York Times.* The *Times* forced the dismissal of one of the country's most influential reporters, Sydney Schanberg (who had previously risked his life reporting from the killing fields of Cambodia), when he wrote a series of hard-hitting articles questioning Westway's wisdom and criticizing the media for its anemic coverage of the project. Schanberg called Westway "that grand boondoggle on the Hudson that would keep developers and contractors fat for years while starving the forgotten riders of buses and subways." Mayor Edward Koch and President Ronald Reagan, both at the height of their popularity, were strong Westway proponents. When he learned that Westway would destroy the Hudson's striped bass populations, Koch pronounced, "then the striped bass can move to New Jersey." Less candid public officials pretended the bass didn't exist. An environmental impact statement developed by the New York State Department of Transportation and the Army Corps of Engineers declared that the Westway site was "biologically impoverished."

The Hudson River Fishermen's Association became involved with Westway when one of its directors, Peter Silverstein, read the Corps' data on fish populations in the harbor area. Silverstein, the Fishermen's youngest director ever, had joined the group at age thirteen when he was a gifted student at the Bronx High School of Science. "They are lying," Silverstein told Robert Boyle. "There are a lot of fish down there!" Boyle spoke with Al Butzel, and the Fishermen joined the lawsuit.

In the spring of 1981, the Corps issued its fill permit, and Butzel sued on behalf of all the plaintiffs in the Federal District Court.

On the morning that the Hudson River Fishermen's Association flew its expert biostatistician, Dr. Ian Fletcher, to New York City to review the Westway files, the *New York Times* printed a front-page photograph of President Reagan handing Mayor Koch a poster-sized $85 million check to commence construction of Westway. "I had the paper on my lap on the shuttle from Boston," Fletcher recalled. "I looked at that picture and said to myself, 'We don't have a chance.'" Years of fruitless legal challenges had discouraged the neighborhood associations and public transportation advocates who opposed the project. By all accounts, Westway couldn't be stopped.

At Butzel's office, Fletcher pored through dozens of file boxes that the Corps of Engineers, the State Department of Transportation, and their scientific consultants had provided in compliance with Butzel's discovery requests. Among the documents were hundreds of pages of tightly printed numerical formulations comprehensible to only the boldest of statisticians. The numbers described fish collection data from thousands of different points in the Hudson River Harbor. Using this information, the New York State Department of Transportation and the Army Corps of Engineers had projected that Westway construction would harm the habitat for less than .04 percent of the Hudson River's commercially valuable striped bass. But when Fletcher examined the same data, he concluded that 64 percent of the striped bass habitat would be destroyed. He then retraced the Corps' formulations and proved that their consultants had known the true impacts and had deliberately massaged the numbers to mislead the court. Renowned experts in their field, the Corps' consulting firm was confident that no one would be able to retrace their steps among the dense thicket of fractions and decimals to find the proof of their deceit.

During the trial, Federal District Judge Thomas B. Griesa questioned Ian about the concealment. Fletcher was a figure who struck fear in the hearts of industry scientists. A brilliant statistician and oceanographer, he not only published regularly in peer-reviewed journals, but also could translate arcane concepts into English so precise and eloquent that they seemed not just simple but obvious to the layman. Knowledgeable in math, physics, biology, engineering, oceanography, and fluid dynamics, he identified himself as a biostatistician, an expert on fish populations. His varied knowledge uniquely qualified him to predict the precise impacts of pollution, shoreline development, and water withdrawals on aquatic ecosystems. Ian defended the truth above all else and was fearless about testing even his own most cherished assumptions. Ian was the scientist that EPA had called in to untangle the twisted science in the Indian Point case. He'd been terrorizing industry "biostitutes" ever since. When Ian came to testify at a hearing or trial, industry scientists would appear from across the countryside to see their most frightening nemesis at work.

During the Westway hearing, Ian explained how the Corps consul-

tants, after finding that 64 percent of the Hudson's striped bass win-
tered in the Westway construction zone, had created a giant imaginary
grid stretching from Westway across the river to New Jersey. In order
to deceive the court into believing that the fish were distributed homo-
geneously across the Hudson, they then averaged the number of fish
in the grid area and assigned an equal share to each block in the grid,
thus concealing the high concentrations in the Westway area.

Ironically, there was no legal requirement in the National Environmental Policy Act (NEPA) that would have prevented the Corps from
exterminating the river's striped bass population. NEPA only requires
public disclosure of a project's impact; it does not mandate results.
The Corps had lied because it was afraid of public opposition to a project that would threaten the Atlantic Coast striped bass, the sacred cow
that had killed Storm King. After Fletcher's testimony, Judge Griesa
excoriated the testimony of the government's witnesses as perjury and
warned them, "I have sentenced people to prison in securities fraud
cases where the conduct was less blatant than the drafting of [the scientific reports]. I am deadly serious about this. . . ." He accused the
Westway lawyers of also participating in the cover-up. He reluctantly
decided not to hold up the trial to pursue criminal charges against the
government witnesses but urged appropriate prosecutors to do so.

Griesa's scathing admonitions did little to curb the nature of Westway's
promoters. The Corps' district engineer promised a two-year study of
striped bass, but amid extraordinary political pressure, the study was cut
back to four months. With Ian testifying in a second trial before Griesa,
that new study was exposed to have been the product of yet more
fraud and political pressure, conflicts of interest, and the imposition of
silence by high Defense Department officials against the Corps officer
who wanted to tell the truth this time around. In the end, Judge Griesa
ruled that "two failures to justify the Westway landfill and federal funding for Westway under applicable legal standards should bring the matter to an end." His finding was upheld on appeal. And with that,
Westway was killed. Today, as a result, the Hudson's striped bass population is the most abundant on the East Coast of North America.

Critics point to the Westway case to argue that environmental laws
make society inefficient. They mourn the passing of simpler times
when engineers and "disinterested" public officials, like the famed
builder Robert Moses, selected the best site for a highway, toxic dump,

or nuclear power plant and easily steamrolled local interference. They have branded Westway opponents with the new acronym NIMBY—Not in My Backyard—a pejorative meant to demean environmental advocates as selfish and unenlightened. But rather than shun the NIMBY label, community groups should wear it as a badge of honor.

Environmental laws passed since Earth Day 1970 allowed grassroots groups to organize political movements to take back their neighborhoods and block government- and industry-sponsored dams, dumps, incinerators, and highways. The community-based environmentalism that was born at Storm King matured at Love Canal, where housewives and mothers in a lower-middle-class neighborhood in upstate New York organized mass protests to force government officials to relocate community members injured by seepage from a government-sanctioned chemical dump. The movement gathered steam with each new local disaster—Three Mile Island (1979); Times Beach, Missouri (1983); Bhopal (1984); Chernobyl (1986). In the aftermath of Love Canal, community leader Lois Gibbs founded Citizens' Clearinghouse for Hazardous Waste, which has assisted over seventeen hundred community groups in fighting facility siting in their neighborhoods. Keepers who drag polluters into federal court are also saying, "Not in my backyard," using the rights granted them under the Clean Water Act. Critics lament that environmental laws pose unreasonable obstacles to the construction of public works and contend that, for the good of society, such siting decisions should be made by nonpolitical engineers. But it is worth asking whether politics wasn't also a factor in those "efficient" engineering decisions of yore.

It is hard to imagine Robert Moses running a highway through his own neighborhood or engineers siting toxic waste incinerators on Chicago's South Shore instead of its South Side. Without environmental law, the political elite had their own ways of protecting their interests, exercising power through whispers and nudges in government corridors.

Long before there was environmental law, the wealthy and politically connected had their own version of NIMBY. They had always been able to divert undesirable land uses toward poorer neighbors. The environmental statutes—particularly NEPA, the statutory iteration of the Storm King decision, which took effect in January 1970—for the first time put NIMBY power into the hands of the middle class and the poor.

NIMBY arose out of public anger and a general sense of helpless-ness. Across the United States, people watched their communities and quality of life compromised in favor of increased profit margins for waste, energy, and chemical companies and the extractive industries. The Hudson's fishermen were only one of thousands of community groups across America who spent years banging against the doors of government bureaucrats and their industry cronies while their health and welfare were continually threatened.

The battle to stop Westway and other NIMBY struggles in urban slums, in poorer suburbs, and Indian reservations are as much a part of the environmental movement today as are the traditional battles to preserve wilderness and national parks. As Bob Boyle recognized thirty-five years ago, environmentalism is a battle to save neighborhoods. Environmental issues cannot be separated from other quality-of-life issues. PCBs in our fish, polluted drinking water, lead exposure from paint chips, highway auto emissions, ugly suburban sprawl, and dan-gerous fumes from nearby incinerators affect jobs, health, educational competency, and property values. Contaminated fish cause disease and the loss of community jobs. Closed beaches on Long Island Sound leave inner-city families stuck in sweltering New York City apart-ments. Lost recreational opportunities, smog, and filthy streets no doubt contribute to the anger and demoralization of citizens and ulti-mately to crime and domestic violence. In a nation where everyone shares aspirations for a higher living standard, environmental injury is the falling tide that lowers all ships.

Not surprisingly, pollution tends to gravitate to the communities less adept at manipulating the political system. In the case of the Hud-son, the commercial fishermen paid the most direct costs of General Electric's pollution. Without lobbyists in Albany to protect their inter-ests, government and corporations conspired to rob them of their livelihood. Jesus, in the Sermon on the Mount, proclaimed that the meek shall inherit the earth. In the meantime they are inheriting our toxics. Society's wastes are flowing toward communities already debil-itated by social disorganization, lower voter registration, high illiteracy, and staggering unemployment.

The Hudson's North River sewer plant provides a classic example of this process. Outraged over the proposed siting of a river sewage treatment plant at Seventieth Street on Manhattan's affluent Upper

West Side, well-connected residents insisted the plant be built else-where. The plant was soon resited in West Harlem by city officials who believed that the minority community would present the path of least political resistance. Now, the chronic stench of this poorly designed plant has become one more demoralizing obstacle between the people of West Harlem and the revitalization of their community.

Our daily work at Riverkeeper is filled with cases where the poorest communities are asked to bear a disproportionate burden of environ-mental injury. Park access is a public trust commodity that has tradi-tionally been reserved for wealthier classes. Robert Moses designed and built thousands of parks and playgrounds in his thirty years as New York City Parks Commissioner, making New York the greenest major city on earth. Only a handful of significantly inferior parks were built in black neighborhoods. Over the nearly five hundred miles of parkways that he built to carry New Yorkers to dozens of state parks, the beaches of Long Island, and upstate as far as Niagara, Moses ordered his engineers to construct bridges low enough to prevent bus travel in a deliberate effort to keep African Americans from visiting state parks and beaches. For the same reason he forbade subway exten-sions or bus stops near large city parks. This tradition of discrimination continues.

In 1990, we brought a successful suit against Westchester County to reopen half a dozen county parks on the Hudson and Long Island Sound. The county had closed the parks purportedly to meet a budget shortfall. Because of their proximity to the Hudson-Harlem train line, these parks were heavily utilized by residents of the Bronx and Harlem and other New York City minority communities. On any nice day, the bulkheads at Croton Point Park, the county's largest riverside park, were jammed with Hispanic and black fishermen. For many minori-ties, these parks were the only green access to the river. The county chose to keep open its many public golf courses, which catered to a better-heeled clientele even though they represented a far greater drain on county revenues than did its riverside parks. Ironically, Westchester County purchased the Croton Park in 1923 in order to prevent a Harlem businessman from purchasing the land to construct a summer bungalow community. "County Foils Negroes," the local papers crowed approvingly.

In 1991, Riverkeeper was a coplaintiff with the Village of Ossining

NAACP in a successful suit against the Ossining Planning Board to reverse its decision to allow a fivefold expansion of a construction-debris processing facility in the oldest stable African American community in the Hudson Valley. Despite the fact that it had been a residential community for over fifty years, Ossining's Hunter/Hamilton Avenue neighborhood had been rezoned as industrial during the 1960s. The planning board that made this decision explicitly acknowledged the racial motivation behind the rezoning. Members of the once peaceful neighborhood now choke beneath an asphyxiating cloud of hydrocarbon fumes. They wake each night to the roar of revving diesel trucks, and their houses shake as giant earthmovers crush construction debris against a concrete retaining wall twenty-five feet from some homes. Only by suing did we prevent the even greater insults that would have resulted from the expansion of this facility. This was not our first collaboration with the Ossining NAACP. As early as 1965, the Hudson River Fishermen's Association was part of a coalition with the Ossining NAACP that halted the construction of the Hudson River Expressway, designed to come ashore near Hunter/Hamilton Avenue and punch a six-lane hole through the same community.

In 1990, Riverkeeper helped organize minority communities in New York City in a successful campaign to protect New York City's drinking water. We had sued the city to obtain its water distribution maps and discovered that the Croton Reservoir's water, the dirtiest in the system, was being delivered to consumers in the city's poorest neighborhoods—Harlem, the South Bronx, the Lower East Side, and Hell's Kitchen. Over seventy-five sewer plants, many of them dilapidated and dysfunctional, discharge into the Croton, which travels unfiltered to taps in New York City's most desperate slums. During the driest years a glassful of Croton water can contain as much as 2 percent sewage effluent. The minority coalition would play a critical role in laying the political groundwork for the historic 1996 New York City Watershed Agreement.

Similarly, New York State's largest medical waste incinerator, originally proposed for suburban Rockland County, now towers over a densely populated South Bronx neighborhood. It regularly showers emissions that could contain lead, cadmium, mercury, dibenzofurans, and dioxin, substances known to cause cancer and brain damage. New York City plans to construct an additional seven incinerators in low-income neighborhoods, adding seven thousand tons of poisonous gases per year to the air breathed by inner-city residents.

This sort of "environmental discrimination" occurs across the nation. According to a recent EPA report, three out of every four uncontrolled toxic waste dumps are located in black and Hispanic neighborhoods. The nation's largest is in Emelle, Alabama, a town 80 percent black and utterly impoverished. The nation's highest concentration of toxic waste dumps is on Chicago's South Side. California's most polluted zip code is in East Los Angeles. African American neighborhoods host Houston's five landfills and six of its eight incinerators. And half of our country's blacks and Hispanics live in neighborhoods with an uncontrolled toxic waste dump.

Inner-city children in Los Angeles have a 10 to 15 percent reduction in lung functioning compared with children in less smoggy areas. Pollution-related asthma is killing African Americans in unprecedented numbers—five times the rate it kills whites. And in perhaps our greatest health crisis, eight million children annually, principally minority and low-income, are victims of lead poisoning. They live in substandard housing with peeling paint and lead pipes or near highways, incinerators, or toxic waste sites. Forty-four percent of urban black children are at risk of suffering from lead poisoning. Even minuscule exposures will cost them dramatic losses in IQ points.

Minorities in nonurban areas also bear a disproportionate share of the pollution burden. Two million tons of radioactive uranium tailings have been dumped on Native American lands in recent years, and Navajo teenagers have sexual organ cancer at a rate of seventeen times the national average. Three hundred thousand Hispanic farm laborers annually suffer from pesticide-related illness.

American industry annually produces 275 million tons of regulated hazardous waste and 160 million tons of municipal garbage. We either dump it in our rivers and landfills, or we incinerate it. Since World War II, society has learned that many of the waste products of our chemical revolution are not safely or easily disposed of. Landfills contaminate groundwater and streams. Incinerators affect air quality. Industry and power plants emit pollutants that damage air and water quality and reduce local property values. Despite the reassurances of industry scientists, few disposal methods have proven completely safe. After participating in hundreds of siting hearings and following up on the results, grassroots organizer Lois Gibbs has said that, no matter what scientists tell you, "You can't engineer a dump that will defeat the law of gravity or other laws of nature. Today's state-of-the-art dump may be tomorrow's Love Canal."

In recognition of this fact, waste management has evolved into a process of moving our waste products around from place to place until they finally come to rest in communities that lack political and economic clout. Corporations grow wealthy on chemical shortcuts, and consumers get the short-term benefit of cheaper goods. The costs of this short-term pollution-based prosperity are deferred to working-class communities like the Hudson's commercial fishermen and to minority and poor rural communities and Indian reservations. The residents of these neighborhoods are less mobile in their jobs and residences, less apt to have health care benefits, and are more vulnerable because of low rates of literacy and English fluency. They have less access to the legal system and are underrepresented in the decision-making process by which facilities are sited. But many of them are beginning to identify environmental pollution as the biggest problem of all. Yolanda Riviera, executive director of Banana Kelly, the South Bronx's principal community development corporation, recently told us that environmental injury is now the leading cause of death and injury in some South Bronx neighborhoods, exceeding crime and violence.

According to the NAACP's former chief Benjamin Chavis, "Environmental pollution is more than our most potent civil rights issue, it is an issue of survival." In fact, the original civil rights battles in the 1960s were fought not over poll taxes or statutes forbidding mixed marriage but over segregated parks, playgrounds, and swimming pools.

The new compendium of environmental laws has given civil rights groups weapons with which to fight for their equal right to a clean and healthy environment. The NIMBY battles moved quickly and easily from working-class communities like Love Canal and Times Beach, Missouri, to African American and Hispanic ghettos that had long been plagued with landfills, highways, and paper mills but had never before had the legal standing to divert these facilities away from their neighborhoods.

By 1984, there were over 6,300 active citizen NIMBY groups in middle-class and poor neighborhoods across the United States. The NIMBY movement has revitalized and rooted the environmental movement. As NIMBYs become conscious of a shared struggle, interest has evolved into a national movement for environmental justice. One community's solution should not be another community's problem—NIMBY veterans quickly became "NIABYs," "not in anyone's backyard." In 1980, Congress passed Superfund—the first environmental statute driven by the new grassroots environmental justice movement. In June 1994, the poor, mostly African American town of Chester, Pennsylvania, passed an ordinance forbidding the location of other waste treatment facilities within the town. Both California and Nevada have statutes allowing localities to enact zoning laws restricting placement of waste facilities. And on Capitol Hill, the Congressional Black Caucus emerged as the strongest single voting block for environmental issues.

By "plugging the toilet," NIMBY forces industry to move from pollution control to pollution prevention and to consider manufacturing processes that do not produce toxic waste as a by-product. By employing NIMBY tactics neighborhood by neighborhood, block by block, citizens seek to stop or slow the available sites for toxic waste, raising the costs of disposal and thereby encouraging waste producers to rely on the more cost-effective methods of reduction, recycling, and reuse. NIMBYs want to precipitate a crisis that will push the nation into radical new ways of thinking about waste. And it has been working. No new nuclear power plant has been sited since 1978, and every project begun between 1973 and 1978 has been abandoned. So far NIMBYs have repelled twenty-four attempts to site a mega refinery on the East Coast, from Maine to Georgia.

Industry is responding to the message. The National Association of Manufacturers recently cited the NIMBY movement in a report recommending that members reexamine their waste policies. Some industries have already begun reducing waste loads: Cleo, the nation's largest gift-wrap manufacturer, switched from solvent-based to water-based inks. An aggressive program to reduce pollution at its source has saved 3M $435 million. Many firms once known as polluters are now making handsome profits in the environmental cleanup field. Petrochemical and chemical companies have spun off profitable subsidiaries using what they've learned from cleaning up their own messes.

The Hudson River Fishermen's Association led this national trend. Since 1965, the Hudson River Fishermen have helped turn back half a dozen mega projects that would have doomed the river and dozens of smaller ventures that would have damaged it irreparably, including seven nuclear power plants, two major waterfront highways, the Storm King project, and dozens of residential developments, any of which could have gravely injured or destroyed valuable estuarine resources. Dozens of river polluters, including Exxon, General Electric, and the city of New York, have been called to account for their activities. Consolidated Edison alone has had to spend tens of millions of dollars to protect the estuary's fishery. Hudson Valley environmentalists have proved themselves willing to wage war to save the river, appearing at planning boards, zoning boards, and permit hearings; hiring lawyers (or finding them pro bono); and going to court, when necessary.

The Riverkeeper movement, born of the Hudson River Fishermen's Association, has proved that law and science can be used by community members to protect shared resources. The Riverkeeper movement has helped develop and refine the tools that NIMBY groups use all over the country. It has generated a wealth of black-letter environmental case law that we now use to protect ecosystems from one end of this nation to the other. Rather than an episodic battle against a single project that defines most NIMBY groups, the Keepers commit themselves to a sustained effort to protect an entire ecosystem from every threat. Because each Riverkeeper is a permanent institution connected to a local waterway, it enjoys a wider credibility and a connection with long-term community aspirations that gives it special effectiveness in confronting polluters in the courts and the press and before political decision makers.

While the national environmental groups have been vital at guiding legislation through Congress, the most savvy of these groups have come to acknowledge that pollution's victims fighting at the community level are the only ones, ultimately, who will stop pollution. Community-based groups like the Keeper movement bring local knowledge and vitality to the national battle that often tends to dwindle in the dense thickets of regulatory debate over such arcane subjects as risk assessment and numerical water-quality standards. They are the front- line barrier to the erosion that occurs when democratic laws come into conflict with politically powerful commercial interests. With vital site-specific information and tremendous organizing ability, grass-roots groups are critical not just to the success of local litigation but to national policy objectives. Real change, the national groups have had to acknowledge, must come from the bottom up. The legal battles over Westway and Storm King, fought by grassroots groups, both extended the boundaries of environmental law and helped preserve the Hudson. In fact, the Hudson has been saved, sewer plant by sewer plant, wetland by wetland, by the work of citizens at every bend in the river, on every tributary, fighting for every inch of riverfront. People have taken responsibility for the welfare of their little piece of Hudson River in the faith that if we each protect our own backyard, cumulatively we will protect the nation.

Other nations, lacking a NIMBY or Riverkeeper movement, have suffered devastating and unchecked environmental damage. The Soviet Union did not have such movements and instead witnessed the disaster of Chernobyl. The once rich Aral Sea is now a desert and the Sea of Azov is a biological wasteland, both of them destroyed by irrigation and diversion schemes. In the poisoned Moscow suburb of Zhenya, children are born without arms. In the city of Oskemen in Kazakhstan, 60 percent of all children suffer immune system abnormalities or chromosome damage, and as many as 100 percent have lead poisoning from pollution by local smelters and chemical plants. As with other totalitarian states, Poland also lacked a NIMBY movement. Seventy-five percent of the children in Byton, Poland, are chronically sick by the time they are ten years old because of pollution that has precipitated an epidemic of respiratory disease and caused leukemia rates to double in ten years. On a normal day, the air in Byton is six times worse than the air during a smog alert in Los Angeles. The most fortunate residents retreat from Byton's poison air to an ancient salt mine six hundred feet belowground.

Not only communist countries suffer. Similar human and economic disasters are common in Turkey, Thailand, Iraq, Mexico, Congo, and Brazil—and in many other nations that lack the environmental laws or democratic procedures that foster NIMBYism.

Our own country is still paying the price of the pre-NIMBY era. Indian Point power plant, San Francisco Bay, "cancer alley" in Louisiana, the Everglades, selenium poisoning in western wildlife refuges—these are emblems of a failure, caused by weak environmental law and the lack of democratic procedures. A clean, safe environment is dependent on the maintenance of strong democratic institutions that guarantee the public a voice in the disposition of its public trust resources. By the same token, democracy itself is strengthened by environmental advocacy and strong environmental laws.

Ironically, in recent years, critics have labeled federal environmental law as "command and control." They urge that federal environmental laws should be abolished and power returned to the states to regulate their environments as they see fit. In this way, they argue, "community control" will be increased. But we in the Hudson Valley know that it was the federal law which, for the first time, gave communities control over their resources. Those who speak of "states' rights" or "state control" really mean corporate control. There is no clearer example than General Electric's pollution of the Hudson.

The absence of federal law enabled General Electric to strong-arm New York State and the communities of Hudson Falls and Fort Edward into a diabolical bargain in which the company freely polluted the river with PCBs in exchange for a few hundred jobs and a raised tax base. General Electric's bargaining strategy was a template for the myriad deals that took place in hundreds of small and large towns across America prior to the federal environmental laws. Industry tactics played one community against another and encouraged states to "race to bottom" to dismantle and ignore their own environmental and health safeguards in order to recruit industry. Federal environmental laws were intended to end the dark ages of corporate blackmail—to stop powerful corporations like General Electric from whipsawing one community in New Jersey against another in New York, forcing them to ransom their children's health and future for the promise of a few years of pollution-based prosperity.

Furthermore, NIMBY not only returns control of public resources to the community but reduces the levels of alienation that are the gravest threats to our democracy. We have found that grassroots groups participating in environmental battles tend to feel less alienated and more politicized. When communities coalesce to defend themselves from an environmental threat, they often discover in the process their shared values and the tremendous power of their unity.

Richie Garrett's politicization during the Hudson River Fishermen's early years is a poignant example. Within months of discovering his rights under the Refuse Act, this unassuming Ossining grave digger was lecturing to civic groups, sending letters to editors, testifying before Senate committees, bringing lawsuits—in short, participating. The culmination of our Soundkeeper project was in 1990 when Long Island Soundkeeper Terry Backer, a third-generation commercial fisherman, high school dropout, and unregistered voter, successfully ran for the state legislature and was appointed to both the environmental and the appropriations committees.

During our Newburgh cases we watched a disorganized and largely demoralized working-class neighborhood mobilize around the issue of safe drinking water and clean streams. Joe Augustine and two young mothers, Diana Leicht and Doreen Thayer, organized an environmental group, petitioned the town supervisor and his council, and picketed the town office building.

Diana, in particular, was transformed by the process. The wife of a computer programmer, she had been infuriated when town water reaching her home was so dirty it sickened her eight-year-old child, stained her sink, and spoiled her clothing.

A quiet, almost timid woman, she contacted us for help in researching her rights as a water consumer. We soon discovered that her timidity was more the product of her determination to be a good citizen than a fear of criticism or confrontation. When she realized she had a right to clean water and that the law provided her with redress, she began a crusade that helped transform the town of Newburgh.

Diana organized sixty other mothers in her neighborhood into a clean water coalition. Her group held a series of informational meetings with their neighbors and walked door-to-door to tell their story and get petitions signed. They discovered their rights under the Freedom of Information laws, the Safe Drinking Water Act, and the Clean Water Act. They made contact with the media and taught themselves how to place a story. They contacted state health and environmental agencies, and utilized the permit and public hearing processes. They sued the town, went to trial, and won a judgment for damages caused by dirty water. By gathering almost two hundred people at a town board meeting, they forced the board to publicly repudiate its self-serving position and agree to be more responsive to community demands.

The most extraordinary revelation for us while watching the events in Newburgh was that this was the American democratic system working as it should. We were in one of the few countries on earth where a collection of angry mothers from a blue-collar neighborhood, children in tow, can use the law to force the system to respond.

Environmental threats can motivate people across racial and political backgrounds. When Riverkeeper and the Ossining Chapter of the NAACP fought to stop the proposed expansion of the demolition debris transfer station, homeowners from ethnically diverse surrounding communities took turns conducting surveillance of the operation, counting trucks, estimating their contents, photographing violations, and keeping careful records. In the middle of the fight, upstate farmers contacted us for assistance in their own battle against the same developer, who wanted to put a demolition dump in their rural neighborhood. The striking thing about that case was the way that blacks, whites, suburbanites, city dwellers, and farmers pooled resources, collected money, and attended meetings for a common goal.

In the process of resolving local disputes, participants build an increased sense of ownership and control of their own communities and lives. Joining in these environmental battles helps people overcome the pathological apathy and sense of helplessness upon which polluters depend. It coaxes them into a system from which they often are excluded.

The environmental movement has made the United States a more democratic nation. It has spawned freedom-of-information laws, environmental impact assessments, public notice and comment requirements, and permit hearing procedures, which have made government more transparent, accessible, and responsive at the community and individual level. As a result of these laws, neighborhoods have greater control over their destinies than at any time during this century. Douglas Porter, a director of the Urban Land Institute, commented that the environmental movement "has taught everyone how to fight city hall."

Historians and political analysts often credit the durability of U.S. democracy (as compared to the typically short-lived democracies, say, of Latin America) with the strong connections that Americans feel to their government at the community level. The stability is enhanced by laws that give Americans a sense of proprietorship and self-determination. No body of laws has done more to "democratize" our society than the environmental laws passed since 1970. These laws represent a revolutionary disbursement of power to the grassroots. Alone among the citizens of the world, Americans at the community level have real power now to review, improve, and even stop giant projects forced upon them by powerful industries and government. Federal environmental legislation expressly provides for unprecedented levels of public participation and considers citizen involvement to be an important supplemental enforcement tool. Requirements for public hearings and public comment have been strengthened and refined. Community right-to-know laws and state and local laws governing land use generally provide for significant public participation. NEPA and its state analogues require project proponents to answer the public's questions about the long-term impacts of their proposal on the environment, the economy, and community values. NEPA, which has now been adopted in some form by over 125 countries, has become one of the great promoters of democracy around the world through these same mechanisms.

Nonetheless, the United States is no stranger to envrionmental tragedy. We are the world's largest consumer of resources and producer of toxic wastes. Our environmental history is rife with examples of regulatory failure and corporate abuse. Today we use ten times the amount of pesticides that we did when Rachel Carson died. One out of every four community drinking-water systems violates at least one federal health standard. Cancer rates among farmers and their children exposed to pesticides are six times the normal rate, and the bugs are winning—five hundred species are now pesticide resistant.

But there is reason for optimism. As more of us take responsibility for our communities and demand restoration of our public trust rights, the system will continue to expand to provide individuals with means of reclaiming those rights. As excruciatingly slow to respond as our system often is, the checks and balances and the citizen empowerment inherent in our democratic framework provide the best hope for preserving the world's natural resources. In addition to democratizing our society, the opportunities for citizens to directly participate in enforcement and permit-writing is often the only reason that environmental law actually works to protect our environment. Our experience has taught us that without these citizen empowerment provisions, environmental law would have no more weight than ink on paper.

# CHAPTER 7

# Enforcement

In 1981, conservation officers from the New York State Department of Environmental Conservation charged commercial fisherman Jimmy Bleakley with illegally netting fifty-two striped bass out of season. Bleakley claimed he had caught the bass accidentally while fishing legally for sturgeon. Without hesitation the state agency sought the maximum penalty of $250 per fish. With no money for a lawyer and faced with the prospect of having to sell his home to raise the $13,000, Bleakley called John Cronin, who was then working as a commercial fisherman and acting as liaison between the Hudson's commercial fishermen and the state DEC. After a sympathetic local judge levied a token fine of only $250, angry DEC officials retaliated against all the commercial fishermen by banning winter netting for all species on the Hudson.

While John doesn't condone poaching, the irony of Bleakley's arrest was striking enough that he was willing to help. The DEC had arrested Bleakley less than a thousand yards west of the Indian Point power plant, which was illegally killing upwards of one million fish per day. Most were undersized, yet DEC conservation officers had never issued the plant a single ticket.

On the contrary, the DEC had done its best to shield Con Ed from prosecutions, even attempting to suppress incriminating photographs of the massive fish kills at the Indian Point plant in 1965. When Bob Boyle located those photos and published them in *Sports Illustrated,* he created a national scandal and precipitated congressional hearings on the fish kills and the DEC's suppression of evidence. "The reaction in Albany," says Boyle, was not "Let's stop Con Ed from killing the fish," but "Let's find and screw the guy who squealed to Boyle."

Have times changed? Unfortunately not. Many other fish kills at

Indian Point have been reported in the decades since, and Con Ed routinely kills hundreds of thousands of larger fish each year at Indian Point. More than three decades after the Fishermen first discovered and disclosed the Indian Point fish kill, Ken Wich, who encouraged the suppression of the photos, is now the DEC's Director of Fish and Wildlife.

The Clean Water Act and other water protection laws are intended to protect public property and welfare and improve water quality by forcing dischargers to internalize the cost of pollution. However, the regulations by themselves will not accomplish any of these objectives. Only widespread compliance with the law will achieve these goals. While environmental law gives government the authority to stop pollution, it cannot compel government to exercise that authority.

Polluters have little incentive to comply with environmental laws since noncompliance results in economic benefits (the free use of public waterways for waste disposal), while compliance exacts a financial cost (the construction and operation of expensive pollution removal facilities). Unchecked by aggressive enforcement, these pressures will systematically undermine any system of environmental law. James Elder, the former director of the federal Environmental Protection Agency's (EPA) Office of Water Enforcement and Permits, observed that "we have found repeatedly that nothing is self-sustaining in the [Clean Water Act permit] program. If a state's vigilance or EPA's regional vigilance subsides, their noncompliance and point-source contribution [of pollution] increase" (James R. Elder et al., "Regulation of Water Quality," 22 *Envl Law Reporter* 10,029–10,037 [Jan 1992]). Compliance is essential to the success of any environmental regulatory program because it is the only way that society will enjoy the benefits envisioned by legislation. As environmental law professor David Hodas explains in the *Maryland Law Review*,

> effective deterrence requires four elements: (1) significant likelihood that a violation will be detected; (2) swift and sure enforcement response; (3) appropriately severe sanctions; and (4) that each of these factors will be perceived as real [54 *Maryland Law Review* 1552, 1603].

Unfortunately, in the United States none of these factors is consistently present. Enforcement is underfunded, abused, and ignored in nearly every environmental bureaucracy.

Large, well-organized industries often "capture" regulatory agencies through frequent exchanges of personnel between industry and regulator, and through a variety of more subtle processes by which agency personnel become personally and institutionally vested in industry practices that skirt or violate the law. After many years of working together, agency lawyers and engineers develop close relationships and professional bonds with their industry counterparts. Agency personnel from every level of bureaucracy tend to migrate from government to industry at the end of political cycles or when retirement benefits mature, creating an almost irresistible temptation to ingratiate themselves with their future employers.

Even supposedly fervent environmentalists find their characters and ideals wrested from them by the seductive siren song of industry money. Thomas Jorling, a lifelong environmentalist and former EPA deputy administrator, was a member of the NRDC's board of directors until 1987 when he was handpicked by the environmental community to serve as Governor Mario Cuomo's DEC commissioner. After his final NRDC board meeting, Jorling pulled Bobby aside. "I want you to hold my feet to the fire, Bobby," he said. But he tap-danced over to the industry side so quickly that we could never get hold of them. He spent the next seven years doing favors for the industry and the electric utilities. And after years of being soft on paper companies, Jorling left the DEC to become vice president for environmental compliance of International Paper Company, a major polluter of Lake Champlain. Four weeks before his resignation as DEC commissioner, and with his offer from International Paper in hand, Jorling proved himself to his industry masters by drafting a letter to President Clinton opposing the administration's proposal to limit chlorine discharges by the paper companies.

Of the six EPA administrators since 1973, only one has remained in public service. With the exception of Anne Gorsuch, who retired following her scandalous attempts to sabotage the agency from within, the others have gone to work for big polluters. All three directors of the Department of Justice's notoriously ineffective Environmental Enforcement Division have taken jobs representing industry as soon as they left office. The New Jersey Department of Environmental Protection and Energy Commissioner Scott Weiner matriculated to the power utility, PSE&G, in 1994, immediately after his decision to release PSE&G's Salem nuclear power plant from a $2 billion obligation to build cooling towers.

Their career interests aside, state environmental commissioners also feel pressure from the state governors who appointed them and who are anxious to maintain peace with local industries and municipalities. The agency officials who dare to prosecute politically powerful industries are often punished for trying. Hugh Carey's DEC commissioner, Ogden Reid, was canned shortly after prosecuting General Electric, and Governor Carey fired Peter Berle, who opposed Westway.

Most environmental enforcement divisions are scandalously understaffed. For instance, between 1986 and 1994, Judi Ferry, the chief attorney of the Hudson Valley Region for the DEC, shouldered an average of twelve hundred cases at any one time with the help of only two to three junior attorneys. According to Ferry, there was simply no hope of handling even 10 percent of that caseload. Ninety percent of the cases simply "collected," she told us recently. "A case would come in and we would look at it and everyone would say 'that's a great case,' and after that, nothing could be done."

The dearth of attorneys and technical support for the enforcement program affected the entire office. Judi Ferry recalls that "It was so bad and known to be so chronically hopeless that other divisions in the region just stopped referring cases to Legal Affairs. They knew that nothing would ever happen. There were all kinds of pernicious effects. It destroyed morale across the board, because everyone saw that with Legal Affairs paralyzed, the department had no enforcement capability. There was no sense in pursuing violators because there was no chance of follow-up." Even with the 10 percent of the DEC's cases that receive enforcement attention, the enormous caseloads create pressure on the agency to settle quickly, putting them at the mercy of polluters willing to wait for an easy plea bargain.

The absurd caseload also impacts DEC administrative law judges, who are similarly overburdened. They schedule hearings years in advance. One permit case in which we intervened in 1987 is still awaiting trial at the time of publication, almost ten years later.

A high-level official in the DEC's counsel office familiar with the process by which the governor and legislative leadership negotiate their annual budget admitted, somewhat bitterly, that, "I came to the belief that our lack of resources was a deliberately planned state of affairs. The legislature and governor took the credit for passing all these wonderful environmental laws, but they didn't want to hurt their pals who were making campaign contributions, so they never appropriated adequate funds to make the laws real."

Another impediment to enforcement is that direct political interference in cases against powerful defendants is both accepted and anticipated. Legislative interventions unheard of in the prosecution of most crimes are accepted as routine when it comes to environmental crime. One high-level DEC enforcement attorney recently told us that she spends half of her day fielding calls from congressmen and state legislators' offices, making "inquiries" on behalf of defendants.

Political intervention begins with permit writing, the first stage of the enforcement program. Polluters have captured the permit process to frustrate the goals of the Clean Water Act. In enacting the Clean Water Act, Congress intended that "the discharge of pollutants be eliminated by 1985." Congress designed a permit process—the National Pollution Discharge Elimination System—that would require all dischargers to reduce their pollution loads each five-year renewal period until all water pollution was eliminated. However, state and federal permit writers have relented under pressure from polluters so that pollution loads in every state, rather than being eliminated, are actually increasing. At last count, more than 65,000 companies, industries, government agencies, and municipalities still had permits to pollute. Even the interim goal of achieving a national level of water quality to support fishing, swimming, and other recreational activities by July 1983 has long since passed, unrealized. At least one-third of the nation's water bodies fail to meet this standard.

Despite claims by anti-environmental propagandists that environmental bureaucrats are overly rigid, permits to pollute and to destroy publicly owned natural resources are almost laughably easy to obtain. In 1994, the Army Corps of Engineers, which administers dredge and fill permits under the Clean Water Act, issued more than 45,000 wetlands permits and took judicial action in less than thirty cases! Similarly, between 1988 and 1992, federal officials reviewed 34,600 proposed development projects with Endangered Species Act implications and rejected only twenty-three. Statistics show that during the same period, a developer had a greater chance of having an airplane strike something he built than having a project stopped by the Endangered Species Act!

We have witnessed firsthand how municipal polluters often get the greatest deference from permit writers. In 1988 we learned serendipitously that the New York State DEC was about to renew discharge permits for all fourteen of New York City's sewage treatment plants without any hearings, even though public notice was required by law. When we obtained copies of the permits we found that they included no limitations of any kind on the city's 360 overflow pipes that illegally discharge an average of 300 million gallons of raw sewage per day into the Hudson and Long Island Sound. Neither were there limitations on the city's illegal discharges of toxic chemicals or nitrogen. The former discharges had contaminated most living animals in the New York Harbor; the latter were responsible for robbing almost half of Long Island Sound of oxygen, choking its fisheries.

The federal Clean Water Act made it illegal for the state to issue federal permits that neglected to remove the nitrogen and toxics and eliminate overflow pipes. We asked for a hearing to contest the proposed permits. The NRDC, the Sierra Club, ten New York legislators, and several grassroots environmental groups joined us in the request. We felt confident that we would get our hearing because the law was clear and the DEC's regional director for the New York area was Carol Ash, a recent gubernatorial appointee who was a longtime environmental advocate recommended for the post by the New York City environmental community. Ash met with us and heard us out, and without making a commitment, she asked us, in good faith, to temporarily withhold our request for a hearing until she could meet with us one last time to resolve our dispute. She promised that she would come to that meeting with a proposal for bringing the permit into conformance with the Clean Water Act. We obliged her, never expecting a double-cross. The evening before the scheduled meeting on September 26, 1988, Ash's office called each of the environmental parties explaining that she had to "postpone the meeting." The following day Ash's office issued the permits. Outraged, we sued Ash successfully in New York State Supreme Court to have the proposed permits revoked. The court, noting the agency's duplicity, ordered the DEC to hold permit hearings. Ironically, what it couldn't achieve through mendacity, the agency has achieved through delay. Blaming a chronic shortage of administrative law judges, the DEC has managed to put off the hearing for eight years and the permits still have not been completed—meaning of course that the city has continued to operate without limits on toxics, nutrients, or Combined Sewer Overflows (CSO).

As in most other states, things went from bad to worse in New York with the national environmental backlash in 1994 instigated by the 104th Congress. Governor George Pataki, who promised to make the DEC more "business friendly," appointed as his environmental commissioner a veteran oil company executive, Michael Zagata. Zagata promised to rely on "self-policing" by industry instead of enforcement. He ordered dramatic reductions in the number of factory inspections to avoid "interrupting production." He sped issuance of pollution permits by steamrolling public participation requirements, and he ordered inspectors who found environmental crime not to issue tickets until the company was given six months to bring itself into compliance. Zagata cut DEC's legal staff by 25 percent, firing virtually all of the agency's pollution litigators, including Judi Ferry. "They got rid of every attorney that could do enforcement," said Chuck Dworkin, the DEC's principal litigator who was let go when Zagata took the reins. "The regional attorneys that survived the purge were those that did not enforce to start with. After the purge, everyone put their heads down and stopped enforcing. Now the big companies know they can thumb their noses at the regulators."

Within months, environmentalists were calling him Zagata Go. His reign coincided with the government shutdowns and the gutting of the EPA by the 104th Congress, which brought federal environmental enforcement to a screeching halt. Polluters in New York State quickly realized that no one was minding the store.

David Engle, an attorney for Harris Beach & Wilcox, which represents New York corporations and developers, told Bobby, "After Zagata's purges, enforcement literally stopped. Cases suddenly became easy to settle and they settled cheap. The agency had a large case against one of our clients that, with no prompting from us, just disappeared. It struck me as extraordinary. The agency is no longer taken seriously in the regulated community."

Predictably, Zagata quickly endeared himself to the worst polluter in New York State. At the time, General Electric was facing penalties of up to $20 million for a docket of illegal conduct at its Waterford plant. DEC counsel Joseph Kowalczyk labeled the Waterford facility "the second most significant hazardous waste problem in the state." Three months after he took office and against the advice of staff, Zagata had a secret meeting with GE from which the state attorney general was excluded. After the meeting Zagata quietly signed a deal with company lawyers. In exchange for the DEC's dropping charges and all claims for penalties and insulating the company from further lawsuits, General Electric agreed to finance a small environmental education project in Waterford and install a boat ramp in the Hudson, a few minutes from Zagata's Columbia County home. Zagata's new acting director of the division of environmental enforcement, Greg Caito, privately condemned the deal as a "travesty."

Zagata's few apologists explain his GE giveaway as a reaction to threats made by the company during the 1994 meeting. Once again GE had invoked its reliable old workhorse—it would move jobs from the state if it were forced to comply with environmental laws.

Ironically, the GE education project will provide funds to pay a DEC conservation officer to teach fishermen in Waterford about environmental laws. It's the Jimmy Bleakleys of the world that need to know environmental law, since they are the only ones punished for breaking it.

After a year in office, the lack of new enforcement cases allowed a triumphant Zagata to make the Orwellian claim that he had eliminated environmental crime in New York. Since there are no new enforcement actions, Zagata reasoned that "everyone in New York is now in compliance."

Most disturbingly, New York State, where only a few hundred environmental crimes are prosecuted each year while thousands accumulate unattended on agency dockets, may, in fact, have the toughest environmental program of the fifty states.

Most other states have no environmental administrative law judges or regional attorneys to prosecute polluters within state environmental agencies. Their only method of prosecution is to refer cases to the state attorney general's office. In those offices, environmental crime, with the exception of high-profile toxic waste felonies, almost always takes a backseat to murder, rape, mayhem, burglary, and other conventional crimes. Almost no district attorney's office in the country is willing to routinely prosecute the environmental violations, which make up the bulk of environmental crime. Furthermore, the typical attorney general's office does not have the capacity to collect evidence on air or water pollution crimes nor the support staff with the expertise to do air and water sampling.

The political will to prosecute polluters has worsened substantially since the environmental backlash of 1994. The State of Maine's environmental agency initiated a grand total of 50 enforcement actions in the entire state in 1996, down from a high of 239 in 1991. In Louisiana, the number of enforcement actions dropped to its lowest level in nine years.

An EPA report criticized Connecticut governor John Rowland's new "business friendly" initiative that had reduced enforcement actions to their "lowest level in recent years." Water pollution inspections, for example, dropped from 840 in 1993 to 387 in 1995.

Minnesota's environmental protection unit, once one of the country's most aggressive, has virtually ceased operating. In 1994, the Republican governor appointed a twenty-year executive of Reserve Mining Company, the state's most notorious polluter, as commissioner of Minnesota's pollution control agency.

In 1996, the state of Virginia prosecuted only one polluter the entire year (down from an already inadequate thirty in 1989) and collected a grand total of $4,000 in fines! An investigative report ordered by the Virginia State Assembly in December 1996 found that the state's environmental agency was deliberately coddling polluters and imperiling state rivers. The Inspector General's office of the federal Environmental Protection Agency made similar findings about Virginia, Pennsylvania, and several other states. EPA regional administrator Michael McCabe accused these states of conducting "a race to the bottom to attract the dirtiest polluters in order to form an economic base."

Across the nation, state environmental agencies have learned the lesson that Zagata taught the DEC—if you want environmental crime to go away, just stop looking for it. State agencies in recent years have cut back their environmental monitoring programs for air and water. "The effect when there is no monitoring is that pollution drops off the radar screen of society," explains former DEC Chief Counsel Nicholas Robinson. "Environmental agencies have learned that to make the problem go away, simply ignore it."

The unwillingness of environmental agencies to enforce the law against polluters leaves Riverkeeper and other citizen groups with a vital role in environmental compliances: to enforce the law through direct prosecutions of polluters; through participation in the permit process; and by cajoling, shaming, and inspiring local enforcers to do their jobs.

Not only do agencies feel pressure to be lenient toward industrial and municipal polluters, they often assist these polluters in avoiding citizen enforcement. Since Riverkeeper first started using citizen suit provisions in 1984, we have had to battle turf-conscious regional engineers who deliberately sabotage our efforts to prosecute polluters. In 1996, we obtained an internal memorandum from the New York City Department of Environmental Protection, the agency primarily responsible for environmental enforcement in the New York City watershed. The memo, entitled "Employees Who Become Environmental Liabilities—Spotting the Signs of a Problem Employee," was written by engineer Lyn Sadoski, P.E., Chief of Facilities Compliance, the agency's front-line enforcement unit. The extraordinary memo, which mentions Riverkeeper by name, explains to agency supervisors how to uncover and root out employees who might be sharing information about environmental lawbreakers with outside citizen groups like Riverkeeper.

Sadoski first warns her fellow supervisors of the "problem employee" who, she says, "may subject [supervisory] employees to liability for legal violations, and in some cases, criminal charges" by exposing illegal activities at plants they oversee to outside agencies. She goes on to describe employees who might report such crimes as having "an inflated sense of self-righteousness—an attitude that they somehow care more about the environment than their co-workers do," and suggests that "they are likely to inform other regulatory agencies or other outside groups (i.e., NYSDEC, Riverkeeper, Trout Unlimited, etc.) about alleged violations at facilities where they work."

At about the same time, we obtained a letter written by the State Conservation Department's Hudson Valley Regional Engineer Cesar Manfredi that also mentioned Riverkeeper by name and advised DEC officials on methods for undermining citizen suits against polluters.

In fact, it is quite common for agencies to actually rescue favored industries from our lawsuits. Under the Clean Water Act, citizens can file a complaint and bring prosecutions in federal courts only after giving a sixty-day notice to the polluter and the regulatory agency. If the government agencies elect to initiate their own enforcement action within that sixty-day period, the citizen group's suit is preempted and must be aborted. Oftentimes politically connected industries, upon receiving notice letters from citizens, ask the government agencies to bring an enforcement action in order to insulate themselves from a federal lawsuit by citizens whom they consider less manageable. State agencies routinely oblige such requests. The agency then signs its own cozy consent order with the polluter, often allowing the pollution to continue for years. The polluter pays nominal fines at best. This practice is called "over filing" and was routinely used to derail Riverkeeper cases before Judi Ferry stopped the practice in the Hudson Valley region. It is still routine in other regions of the state and across the country.

In 1986, Bobby was co-counsel in half a dozen NRDC lawsuits against the big three auto companies for polluting the River Rouge in Detroit. On the fifty-ninth day of the waiting period—at company request—the Michigan attorney general sued all three corporations, rescuing them with a series of sweetheart consent decrees. In 1988 Bobby and the NRDC brought eleven cases against steel and paper industry polluters on Alabama rivers. The Alabama attorney general preempted each of these suits, at industry request—again, on the fifty-ninth day.

No one has the capacity and the energy to escape prosecution for environmental crime like a government polluter. Today government is the United States' biggest polluter. Federal military bases and other agencies are responsible for sixty-one thousand contaminated sites across the country. Other federal and state institutions that create pollution include prisons, hospitals, mental institutions, public transportation, and highway construction and maintenance facilities. Local governments and municipalities operate sewer plants and landfills that discharge up to 45 billion gallons per day of treated and untreated sewage into our nation's water, making municipal sewage the largest source of water pollution on the East Coast. According to EPA statistics, municipal polluters cause double the amount of water body damage as industrial sources and are twice as likely to violate federal pollution laws.

The Hudson Valley is a microcosm of national pollution trends. The early Hudson River Fishermen's cases were almost exclusively against industries: Anaconda Wire and Cable, Exxon, Mobil Oil, and others. Since 1984, a significant number of our actions have been against government, including the U.S. Army at Stewart air base and

West Point Military Academy for toxic and sewer dumping; the federal Bureau of Prisons for sewage violations; the state highway department for illegal dumping and filling of wetlands; and a dozen or more Hudson Valley cities, towns, and counties for sewer and water violations, including, of course, New York City, our most frequent defendant.

Since the government is the nation's number one polluter and it does not like to prosecute itself, agencies have been virtually forced to cease prosecuting. Although the federal Clean Water Act provides that federal facilities are subject to the same standards and enforcement mechanisms as everyone else, the U.S. Attorney General has adopted the formal policy that EPA should not bring enforcement action against federal facilities. Instead, disputes between the federal EPA and polluting facilities are handled through a labyrinthian dispute resolution procedure. If the dispute cannot be resolved, it is sent to the Office of Management and Budget—an agency not known for its environmental activism.

The only enforcement, then, against the thousands of federal facilities caught violating federal environmental law comes from citizen suits. Unfortunately, the Supreme Court attacked this final line of defense in 1992. In their 1992 decision in *U.S. Department of Energy v Ohio,* the justices indicated that, despite the clear language of the Clean Water Act, Congress did not intend federal facilities, prosecuted under the citizen suit provision, to pay penalties for noncompliance with federal environmental laws. That decision, typical of the Court's anti-environmental judicial activism of recent years, provides the incentive for federal facilities to continue polluting until caught, and then come into compliance as slowly as possible.

Enforcement against government polluters at the state level is no less bedeviled by self-interest. In practice, state enforcement against state polluters does not exist as anything but a rare exception. In 1985, for example, we obtained an internal DEC memorandum to all enforcement chiefs forbidding environmental enforcement action against sister state agencies without express permission from Albany. In 1991, a report by the New York State Legislature found that across New York State, government agencies were by far the most damaging polluters and that enforcement was virtually nonexistent because of official state policies.

Meanwhile, conventional government prosecutors, who have the power to enforce environmental laws even when the environmental agencies do not, have seldom proven to be reliable enforcers.★

While competent and enthusiastic about high-profile environmental cases, these prosecutors seldom have the time—or the heart—for day-by-day environmental enforcement. They simply have difficulty viewing environmental crime as real crime. This explains the obsession among environmental crime divisions with searching for Mafia involvement with toxic waste. Typically, these units spend scarce resources on long undercover investigations or expensive "sting" operations that net a handful of defendants. It's as if they are embarrassed to be enforcing environmental crime and seek Mafia imprimatur to justify their action.

Back in the 1960s, it often took the early Hudson River Fisherman's Association hundreds of phone calls and months of persistent harassment to persuade the U.S. Attorney to take interest in a Refuse Act case. Things haven't improved all that much. In 1992 we sued Orange County, New York, for destroying a fifty-acre wetland to make way for a new county landfill. Predictably, the county denied that the area had ever been a wetland. The best evidence against the prosecution, of course, was interred beneath fifteen feet of fill. We knew the site had been a wetland because of the complaints by local farmers, hunters, and environmentalists who alerted us to the case. But these were biased sources that might not convince a judge.

Since the state wetlands maps of this area were incomplete, we searched through ancient documents at the county historical society and interviewed muskrat trappers and duck hunters in search of witnesses to prove our claim. Then we hit the jackpot. The defendant's own documents, which we obtained through the discovery process, included evidence that proved the area was a wetland. We found requisitions for dozens of massive pontoons that the county contractors had purchased to float Caterpillar tractors across the construction site during the fill operation. Moreover, the contractor's log contained a series of entries describing an episode in which a giant earthmover had actually sunk into the swamp and was lost. A preconstruction memorandum from the

---

★This is significant, since the federal EPA and its state equivalents cannot prosecute cases in courts except when the U.S. Department of Justice or state attorneys general respectively agree to represent them.

county's construction engineer to the county executive informed him that the proposed site was a wetland and that any unpermitted construction would violate federal law. This prior knowledge made the county officials involved and their contractors criminally liable. When we confronted them with these documents during their sworn depositions, the engineers confirmed that they had indeed known the area was wetland prior to construction and had so informed the county officials, who nevertheless ordered them to proceed with construction.

We passed the memo and deposition transcripts to the U.S. Attorney's staff, who met with us along with FBI agents on a half-dozen occasions, often for several hours at a time. We showed the federal agents the Clean Water Act Section 1319(c), which provides that any person who either negligently or knowingly fills a wetland without a federal permit is subject to punishment by up to three years' imprisonment and a $50,000-per-day fine. The federal agents and attorneys received this news with blank stares. "Was there mail or wire fraud?" they asked us. "Was there any incident where county officials or their confederates crossed state lines?" In frustration, we held the environmental statute book close to their faces and read the simple language to them slowly. We were handing them an airtight case. It was, however, beyond their comprehension that an environmental crime, alone, was sufficient to merit enforcement attention. The U.S. Attorney in White Plains sat on our proof for two years until the statute of limitations expired. The case was never prosecuted.

Not only citizen groups are shunned when they refer environmental cases to prosecutors. In 1993, Lieutenant Ronald Gatto, a member of New York City's upstate reservoir police force, discovered Towne Lyne Motel in Cortlandt, New York, deliberately discharging raw sewage into a Croton Reservoir tributary, a feeder stream to the Croton drinking water reservoir. With proof sufficient for a criminal prosecution, Gatto took his case to the Westchester County DA's office, which at that time refused, as a matter of office policy, to prosecute any environmental crimes. In the end, Gatto was forced to prosecute the case himself, which restricted him to the low penalty exposure provided in the civil sections of the statute. The polluter paid a fine of $250—far less than the amount it had saved in hauling fees.

A month later, Gatto, a highly trained police officer, sat in our office shaking his head. "I don't get it. If a kid steals a car or throws a brick

through your window, any DA in this country will prosecute them—
even though their crime only injures a single person. But if you dump
a toxic chemical or disease organisms into the drinking water for nine
and a half million people, no one is interested in the case."

The contrast between the way the DEC handled fish killing by
Jimmy Bleakley and by Con Ed illustrates a sad truth. Without any
hesitation, the DEC asked the judge to impose upon Bleakley the maximum fine, and when the judge balked, the agency vindictively pro-
mulgated a rule punishing all commercial fishermen. Environmental
agencies, prevented by political interference from prosecuting more
powerful interests, respond to public demand for enforcement by
"rounding up the usual suspects," fishermen like Jimmy Bleakley,
sportsmen, and other traditional resource users whose impact on the
resource is generally insignificant.

Statistics confirm this practice. New York State, for example, had
approximately 330 environmental enforcement officers on its payroll
in 1994. Only 30 of these were investigating pollution crimes such as
illegal discharges and hazardous waste or air violations. These officers
respond to complaints, never engaging in pollution patrols. In contrast, 100 forest rangers patrol public and private lands throughout the
state, issuing tickets for illegal camping, messy campsites, or tree cutting. And 200 additional conservation officers target hunters and fishermen for fish and wildlife violations, such as bag exceedances,
undersized fish, violating license requirements, or forestry violations.*

Vermont is more typical. Vermont employs forty-four fish and
wildlife officers but only eight environmental quality officers. Like
New York's environmental investigators, Vermont Environmental
Quality Police respond only to complaints. They are not in the field
actively searching out polluters. South Dakota Game and Fish employs
seventy-two fish and game officers and no environmental quality officers. Montana employs over eighty-seven game wardens and rangers
and, again, no environmental quality officers.

In the few states that employ them, environmental quality police
seldom engage in field activity searching out polluters. Although many

---

*Although conservation officers technically have jurisdiction over pollution as well as
fish and wildlife crimes, only 15 percent of their arrests pertain to environmental-
quality crimes. The other 85 percent are all fish and wildlife or forestry crimes.

states claim to have environmental quality task forces, none of them are on proactive pollution patrol—walking through the woods, creek beds, or city streets searching for illegal pipes or stacks.

Similar disparities characterize federal environmental enforcement. The federal Environmental Protection Agency has no proactive pollution patrol. The United States Fish and Wildlife Service (FWS), on the other hand, employs seventy-five wildlife inspectors who patrol ports for smuggled animals and two hundred special agents who enforce criminal and civil sections of federal wildlife laws. This division actively seeks out illegal hunters in patrols, stakeouts, and stings, thus deliberately choosing the poorest, least powerful, and generally least threatening resource users as enforcement targets. FWS law enforcement has conducted a series of high-profile, badly bungled sting operations that has earned them a reputation as cowboys who can't shoot straight. They usually succeed in temporarily distracting the public's attention from real environmental crime without offending any powerful environmental criminals.

Sometimes the agents have acted more like poachers than government personnel. In its notorious 1988 sting, Operation Falcon, Fish and Wildlife Service agents illegally trapped thirty-six gyrfalcons and six goshawks in Alaska without state or federal trapping permits and illegally transported them into the lower forty-eight. There, they attempted to sell the illegal hawks to falconers, making themselves the largest source of illegal raptors in the United States. They found that there was no U.S. market and virtually all of the birds were sold to foreigners, were given away, or died in federal holding pens. Among the most tragic results of this operation was when federal agents assisted in raiding the last nest of the endangered Anatum's peregrine falcon in Utah and killed the eggs. Federal agents engaged in dozens of illegal searches, and seized one hundred birds as evidence. None were used for this purpose; many died in government custody as their owners pleaded and fought for their return. The operation lasted three years, involved three hundred state and federal agents, and cost millions of dollars. After all was said and done, not a single American was convicted or accused of taking and selling a wild bird.*

---

*In fact, the U.S. FWS Law Enforcement Division made its decisions on its stings against the advice of, or entirely without reference to, any experts on wildlife populations. It is noteworthy that the Fish and Wildlife Service's expert on raptor population,

That was not the first time that a U.S. FWS sting operation crossed the very high threshold that constitutes entrapment. The FWS's "Operation Eagle," conducted from 1981 to 1983, attempted to ensnare what must have seemed the ideal enforcement targets under the agency's formula—poverty-stricken American Indians. The court chided the FWS for directly and aggressively soliciting "unwary and innocent adolescents" with no criminal record and no history of illegal hunting or trafficking, who had never before killed a protected bird but were eventually tempted by the offers of large sums of money that spelled the difference between having and not having heat and food."*

The U.S. FWS employed similar tactics in its eighteen-month Operation Whiteout in 1992, enticing Alaskan Eskimos into killing walruses. In 1988, in Operation Trophy Hunt, Fish and Wildlife Service agents once again found themselves being scolded by a federal judge, who said that they themselves had committed the most serious offenses and accused them of "active criminal behavior" for killing protected wildlife.

The government's fixation on targeting campers, wildlife users, fishermen, sportsmen, and American Indians is part of a broad political accommodation that reacts to environmental pollution not by punishing polluters but by harassing the public that owns and uses the resource.

Similarly, enforcement has often come to mean erecting fences around the resource to exclude the public. Chain-link fences and closed rivers are the knee-jerk bureaucratic solutions to every case of environmental contamination. In 1975, the DEC reacted to the PCB contamination of the Hudson not by forcing General Electric to clean up the river but by closing most of the commercial fisheries and ban-

---

biologist James Ruos, retired because of his disgust at Operation Falcon and the Law Enforcement Division's obsessive harassment of resource users. Law Enforcement never consulted Ruos on the need for Operation Falcon—if they had, he would have told them that from a bird population standpoint, the operation was silly.

*The tragedy was compounded because the FWS agents didn't specify which kind of eagle feathers and carcasses they were soliciting. American Indians normally use golden eagle feathers in traditional ceremonies because the difficulty in procuring this solitary bird attests to the hunter's prowess. Since the FWS did not specify a species, the poachers began shooting, in vast numbers, endangered bald eagles, which are simple to kill in quantity because of their habit of congregating in flocks on riverside snags well within shotgun range.

ning recreational fishing on the upper river. In 1988, the DEC attempted to permanently close the entire striped bass fishery, including recreational angling. A permanent closure left no hope that the fishery would reopen even after PCB levels dropped. We managed to stop the plan only by suing the DEC.

Over half of America's shellfish beds are today closed to the public by government fiat because it is easier to shut down the resource than to force polluters to restore the value they stole. Virtually every state fish and game agency or health department publishes advisories on eating sport fish and wildlife taken in the state. New York State, for example, issues a general advisory recommending that no individual consume more than one meal a week of *any* fish caught in any of the state's inland waters. Over thirty of New York's major water bodies have even stricter advisories. Collectively, the states have issued similar advisories for over thirteen hundred water bodies where fish are contaminated with dangerous levels of chemicals.

At times environmental groups have been enlisted in the campaign to deny nature to the citizenry, supporting laws that unreasonably restrict public access to nature. In New York, for example, overly restrictive laws make it illegal to hold most wild animals, insects, or fish, or even to pick up a wild bird feather. If a schoolteacher or scout leader picks up a cardinal feather and walks across the Connecticut state line, he or she has committed a federal offense. In many western states, it is illegal for a citizen to pick a flower or remove a pine cone from federal lands— lands which are often being systematically destroyed by the legal activities of mineral and cattle and timber interests.

But fish are jeopardized not so much by individual fishermen with hook and line as by giant factory ships that strip-mine the ocean and by industrial and municipal polluters. Developers who fill prairie wetlands and industries that poison coastal nesting and staging areas kill more of the duck population than illegal hunters. Hawks and falcons are threatened far more by the pesticide industry than by falconers or sportsmen. Until 1973, hawks were regarded as vermin species in every state and in every province in Canada. Many states paid bounties for their destruction. Hunting clubs sponsored autumn hawk shoots on migratory ridge lines. Still their numbers were not threatened until DDT.

Instead of protecting important ecosystems, the policy of harassing the public and fencing off nature has the effect of eliminating a resource's most vocal and protective constituencies. It was falconers, for example, who discovered that DDT was exterminating the peregrines, and it was falconers who learned to breed them in captivity and began releasing captive-bred birds to restore wild populations. Duck hunters and hunter groups like Ducks Unlimited have been among the nation's primary political and financial advocates for protecting wetlands. It was a wealthy waterfowl hunter, Paul Tudor Jones, who almost single-handedly financed the 1997 Florida referendum campaign to save the Everglades by imposing a penny-per-pound tax on the sugar barons. Bass Angler's Sportsmen Society (BASS) and its founder, Ray Scott, have emerged among America's leading advocates for clean water. On the Hudson River, the fisheries have been preserved by the vigilance of commercial and recreational fishermen who intervened at Storm King, who discovered and stopped Con Ed's uncontrolled slaughter of millions of fish at Indian Point, and who revealed the Corps of Engineers' treachery at Westway. Our experience is that fishermen often know more about the water than do government scientists.

When a resource is closed, society loses its best advocates. When the upper Hudson was closed to fishing in 1975, the bait shops went with it. Many of the commercial fishermen hung up their nets and eel pots, put their wooden dories on blocks, and retired their ash poles. We quickly began to forget the techniques and the fishing areas that have been faithfully handed down through the generations. When rivers are closed, the fishing associations, networking groups, and clubs that act as repositories of ancient knowledge disappear. The wharves degrade. The next generation turns its back to the river, making its living hanging sheetrock or laying asphalt. We lose part of our culture, our heritage and legacy. We lose touch with the seasons and the tides.

The career of New York watershed police officer Ronald Gatto offers perhaps the best example of how environmental enforcement ought to work. Gatto, a tough Italian weightlifter, is one of twenty-eight police officers employed by New York City's Department of Environmental Protection to patrol and protect the city's upstate reservoirs and the two-thousand-square-mile watershed that feeds them.

The city had statutory authority under the State Public Health Law to control watershed pollution and to arrest violators. However, the DEP's Sources Division saw to it that civil enforcement against polluters was nonexistent. A tight-knit group of DEP engineers, led by George McKeenian, the Sources Division chief, aimed instead to facilitate development around the reservoirs to ingratiate themselves with local politicians and developers.

In addition to police, the city had forty-four inspectors all reporting to the Sources Division. McKeenian and his cronies made sure that the inspectors did not try to interfere with the march of progress and that the police were kept busy arresting unlicensed fishermen and trespassers, and directing traffic. The police, supposedly stationed there to protect the water supply and enforce the regulations, were under firm orders not to arrest polluters. The few who tried were passed over for promotion. Police records revealed that in eighty-four years prior to 1989 not a single polluter was ever arrested in the watershed. Of the 527 lawyers working for New York City Corporate Counsel and the DEP, none was assigned to prosecute polluters.

Gatto was the first to challenge these rules. Born and raised in Yorktown, New York, he fished the Croton Reservoir and its feeder streams almost daily as a boy. He loved the green hills and woodland of the watershed and despised the garbage that accumulated as the area's population nearly doubled from the 1960s to 1980. Gatto joined the watershed police in 1982, straight out of the prestigious New York State Police Academy. He accepted the meager paycheck ($22,000 annual top pay for patrolmen) because he believed he would be protecting the environment. Instead, he recalls, "they had us drive around and chase swimmers."

On two occasions Gatto bucked the system and ticketed polluters. Back at the station, Police Chief Patrick Murphy and Sources Division Chief George McKennian threatened to discipline him and impounded his paperwork, which he never saw again.

The election of David Dinkins as mayor of New York City in November 1990 presented a fresh opportunity for environmentalists. Dinkins had pledged to implement serious environmental enforcement. Gatto took him at his word and immediately began arresting polluters. In December 1990, after a late-night dinner with his wife at a Katonah restaurant owned by a family friend, Gatto smelled sewage. He parked around the corner and waited in the darkness. At closing, he watched from his car as the owner lifted a coffee can concealing a switch, turned on a sump pump, and emptied two thousand gallons of sewage through a storm drain into the Muscoot Reservoir. Gatto arrested his friend, who was later fined $10,000.

Gatto had a special talent for discovering illegal pollution. He could smell a leaking septic tank from a moving vehicle. To the shock of his passengers he once brought his patrol car to a screeching halt on Catherine Street in Yorktown and began sniffing the air like a bloodhound. In a short time he discovered an illegal septic bypass at the Holy Comforter Nursing Home. Gatto felt a personal responsibility to protect the New York City water supply. With his own money he bought dye tablets that he used to find the source of suspicious pipes. He sat next to pipes through the night waiting for intermittent discharges. He busted apartment buildings, liquor stores, car dealers, restaurants, motels, and the Westchester County Airport. He was persistent and resourceful. When the department refused to provide him with dye tablets and photography or testing equipment, Riverkeeper offered to pay for these items. As soon as Gatto's DEP supervisors learned of our offer, they gave him everything he wanted in order to avoid embarrassment.

Gatto executed the first search warrant in the history of the agency and sent the first violator to jail, a Bronx home improvement contractor whom he discovered shoveling construction debris and broken appliances from his truck down a steep embankment onto the shores of the Muscoot Reservoir.

Within one year Gatto made fifty arrests. Despite Dinkins' pledge, the department's entrenched bureaucracy rebelled and continued to stifle Gatto's efforts. Captain Murphy disciplined Gatto repeatedly, and his other superiors continued exerting every effort to stop him from making arrests. On four occasions, the city inspector general investigated him because of scurrilous charges made by anonymous sources. Each time, Gatto was cleared.

Gatto was fearless. He asked us to arrange a public city council hearing at which he could discuss enforcement policies at the DEP. He insisted on going forward even after we warned him that we would not be able to protect his job or his working conditions.

The hearing at the New York City Bar Association offices evolved into a highly publicized event. Gatto and two fellow officers testified that Captain Murphy and others had discouraged enforcement and had even secretly removed bullets from their guns before they went out on patrol. They complained that the police were intentionally given inadequate equipment and training in order to deter enforcement and were directly ordered by their superiors to drop investigations and tear up tickets against polluters. Virtually all New York City news stations and newspapers gave the hearing—and Gatto's testimony in particular—extensive coverage. As a result of the press attention, Murphy was transferred and replaced and Appleton promoted Gatto to Detective Sergeant and second in command of the department.

Nonetheless, the DEP engineers continued to facilitate watershed development. As fast as the Sources Division could write permits, Gatto would issue tickets. When the Sources Division issued permits for clear-cutting 170 acres in a watershed buffer zone, Gatto blocked the bulldozers with his body and threatened to arrest the next chainsaw wielder, permit or not. He radioed DEP Commissioner Al Appleton's office and had the permit revoked.

When Westchester County prosecutors, under pressure from local developers, refused to take Gatto's cases, he went to court and argued them himself. By Dinkins' second year, Gatto had made one hundred arrests and got fines in each, clearly proving that environmental quality crimes are at least as common as poaching. His success belies claims by Fish and Wildlife enforcement officials that environmental quality violations are difficult to find and prosecute.

Gatto made his arrests without any specific education or training, with very little technical support, and with substandard equipment. Just imagine what would happen if the hundreds of fish and wildlife officers currently employed by federal and state governments were each given a short training program based on Gatto's work and then sent back out to the field in search of environmental violations like illegal pipes, dumpers, wetland fillers, polluting factories, mines, paper mills, and sewer plants.

Gatto's experience proves that we need to bring community policing concepts to environmental law. Community policing theory holds that crime and the deterioration of neighborhoods begins when you let people get away with "quality of life" crimes such as scrawling graffiti and blasting loud radios. When law enforcement ignores these little assaults on the social system, society becomes increasingly tolerant of more serious destructive behavior.

It was precisely because of this lack of environmental "community policing" that in Newburgh we found little consciousness among polluters that they were subject to environmental laws and regulations. The most common response we got when we sued an unpermitted discharger was "I didn't know it was wrong." For this very reason, lawlessness was the norm on Quassaic Creek. Arma Textile's President Greg Massini, who had been in the textile business for decades, told the DEC and an incredulous city court judge that he didn't know he needed permits for any of his twenty-four illegal stacks and pipes. Unfortunately, the DEC's habitual lack of enforcement made this and many other claims of ignorance conceivable. The DEC had not made enforcement a priority; therefore the industries and municipalities had not made the environment a priority.

If we are going to protect the environment, we need to start regarding injury to environmental quality the way we do other crimes. When General Electric poisons the rivers and destroys the fishery, it has also destroyed jobs and threatened the public welfare. When someone discharges toxics into a drinking water reservoir and those toxics cause injury to children, he has committed a form of child abuse. When a power plant kills millions of fish it has stolen property from the public. There has been no effort by government to enforce individual property rights in a community-owned resource.

The good news is that until government begins to enforce the laws it created to protect our rights and hires more officers like Ron Gatto, we have the power to protect ourselves. We are all community police. You don't need a badge to do what Ron Gatto does. Each of us has the power to protect the public trust—to walk local streams, to seek out pipes, to prosecute those who destroy wetlands and stream beds.

CHAPTER 8

# Watershed

On September 8, 1994, David Letterman stood on the stage of the Ed Sullivan Theater, before a *Late Show* audience of five million, and cracked a derisive joke about New York City drinking water—until that very moment almost universally considered the finest municipal drinking water in the world. Earlier in the day, based on information provided by Riverkeeper, the *New York Post* reported that one of the city's three reservoir systems, the Croton, had been shut down because of sewage pollution. In a terse response, a spokesman for the city's Department of Environmental Protection (DEP) told the *Post* that the closure was due to the presence not of sewage but of "organic material." Letterman told his audience that the *Post* story "scared the organic material out of me."

Though bittersweet, the moment was nonetheless a victory for us. Since 1988, Riverkeeper had been campaigning to focus public attention on the crisis of the decline in the quality of city water. The issue was particularly urgent because much of the watershed that surrounds the city's nineteen upstate reservoirs is also part of the Hudson's watershed. The most difficult challenge we faced was communicating our concerns directly to the water drinkers. But Letterman's jibe signaled the public, the news media, and politicians that one of the best-kept secrets about life in New York could be hidden no longer.

City officials were infuriated. Letterman had gored their most sacred cow and embarrassed them before a nation of mayors who had come to envy New York City's water. Worse, they knew that more frightening revelations about the decline of the city supply would now be impossible to keep under wraps. In fact, days later, a second *Post* article disclosed that the New York City Department of Environmen-

201

tal Protection had discovered the presence of *Vibrio cholerae* in Croton water. And although that particular cholera strain was ultimately determined to be nonepidemic, even the most jaded among New York City's water officials were unnerved by the detection of this bacteria. After all, it was the cholera epidemic of 1832, which killed one-fifth of the city's population, that had prompted the construction of the Croton Reservoir system in the first place.

Hundreds of tons of human and animal excrement flowed daily through New York City streets in the eighteenth and nineteenth centuries. The only sources of drinking water for New York City's booming population were municipal wells and a collection pond where Foley Square now stands. Located within the bounds of the city itself, they were replenished by the very storm water that carried the foul wastes off the streets.

By the 1830s, the city's supply was woefully inadequate and horribly contaminated. Tainted by the unceasing flow of sewage and flavored by the "earthy salts" of stale urine, the brew was so unsavory that horses from outside the city refused to drink it. The foul water was potent enough to spread cholera and yellow fever epidemics but too meager to prevent uncontrolled fires from consuming a thousand buildings in the heart of the city's business district, including the entire Dutch city of New Amsterdam. An earlier scheme to construct an upstate water system for city residents was derailed when its chief promoter, Aaron Burr, absconded with the funds for a private banking venture (which later became Chase Manhattan Bank). That scandal led to the infamous duel in which Burr killed banker Alexander Hamilton.

Following the 1832 epidemic and fires, federal engineer Colonel DeWitt Clinton first proposed tapping the Croton River. Son of the New York State governor of the same name who shepherded the construction of the Erie Canal, Clinton called for damming of the Croton's east and west branches in the upstate counties of Westchester and Putnam and delivering the water by a gravity-fed system through forty miles of aqueduct to reservoirs at Murray Hill and Forty-second Street in what is now the heart of Manhattan. Sips of delicious Croton River water distributed from barrels outside voting booths persuaded New Yorkers to vote overwhelmingly in favor of Clinton's brainchild.

The New York State Legislature cleared the path for acquisition of the necessary land, despite the protests of Westchester's aristocratic farmers who were dismayed about the infringements on private property and by the prospect of rubbing shoulders with an army of "unruly Hibernians"—the four thousand mostly Irish laborers who were to work under the direction of Erie Canal veteran John B. Jarvis. Once the ambitious project was under way, New York City merchants, appalled by scandalous cost overruns, appealed unsuccessfully to powerful financier John Jacob Astor to use his influence to stop the project. Astor replied, "No price is too high for clean water."

The Croton Aqueduct was completed in 1842. Four water commissioners riding in a subterranean barge arrived on the first wave of Croton water in Manhattan on June 22 after a forty-mile trip through the cavernous aqueduct. On July 4, giant crowds gathered to celebrate an engineering feat already envied by the world. The floodgates opened and water gushed into Murray Hill. By October, the final link was completed, allowing water to fill the Forty-second Street reservoir and burst from various spectacular fountains to heights of three stories. New Yorkers immediately began savoring luxuries unprecedented in two centuries: indoor plumbing, bathtubs, and clean windows. Real estate values doubled in one decade. The Croton Aqueduct was expanded in 1891, and in 1964 the city completed the half-century construction of two even larger systems that tapped the more distant Catskill Mountains and Delaware River. Even as late as the 1980s, New York City water's purity and savory mineral mixture were winning at annual taste tests. It was bottled and sold in other cities and credited with the incomparable taste of New York City pizza and bagels.

The New York City drinking water system became a jewel of the city and the largest single financial asset in the state of New York. It is a masterpiece of ingenuity and design—nineteen reservoirs and controlled lakes deliver 1.5 billion gallons of gravity-propelled water per day from Westchester and Putnam Counties and from the Catskill Mountains. The world's largest pipes, composing the New York City Aqueduct, transport the water from as far as 120 miles away, passing one thousand feet under the Hudson River and down its east side into a series of distribution and balancing reservoirs. The water runs through six thousand miles of conduits and pipes that serve the homes of 9.5 million water consumers in the five boroughs of New York City and communities that lie along the aqueduct's route in Westchester, Ulster, and Orange Counties.

Seven generations of New Yorkers constructed this engineering miracle. The water it delivers is now being destroyed by our generation. Residences, commercial and industrial developments, golf courses, and roads all drain fertilizers, pesticides, automotive fluids, and septic and sewage wastes into the once-pristine drinking water. The perils that plagued the city in the mid–nineteenth century were in the streets for any New Yorker to see. But twentieth-century threats are tucked away in distant upstate hills and valleys, out of view of those who daily drink city water.

We stumbled upon the issue accidentally ourselves. In the spring of 1988 a severe drought caused the reservoirs to drop to 58 percent of their capacity. In response, New York City prepared to activate an emergency pump station in the hamlet of Chelsea on the Hudson sixty miles north of the city that would send 100 million gallons of river water per day to the city's West Branch Reservoir. We successfully sued to stop the pumping and prevent the destruction of the popular West Branch Recreational Fishery by toxic water treatment chemicals. But the experience opened our eyes to the city's cavalier water policies. We decided to thoroughly investigate the entire water supply. After all, half the Catskill supply and all the Croton waters came from dammed Hudson River tributaries. The reservoirs were popular recreational fisheries for anglers, who were the bulk of our members. Even more important, the reservoirs were the most critical natural resource— drinking water to half the state's population.

One would expect the world's most remarkable water system to have the world's strictest water protection rules or most sophisticated water-treatment system. New York City had neither. The water supply was unfiltered. No pollutant removal technology existed between the reservoirs and the water consumer. But an aggressive program of watershed protection can accomplish what even the best technology can't—prevent water pollution before it starts. Recognizing this, the New York State Legislature in 1905 granted the city special authority to implement and enforce regulations to protect its upstate water supply from pollution. But we found that the city's rules, last reviewed in 1954, were better suited to L'il Abner's Dogpatch or Andy Griffith's Mayberry than to the realities of modern living. The laws controlled the placement of outhouses, chicken coops, and manure piles but never anticipated such threats as millions of gallons of raw sewage discharge, pesticide-saturated golf courses, storm runoff, toxic substances, and spills. The maximum fine faced by a polluter was twenty-five dollars.

We discovered, moreover, that in the forty years that the regulations had been in place, not one watershed polluter had been prosecuted. Without a treatment system, without aggressive watershed protection, and without law enforcement, all that stood between water drinkers and threats to their health was the capacity of the enormous water supply to dilute even the worst pollution.

But the giant size of the reservoirs could not protect against the development boom that had occurred in the two-thousand-square-mile watershed. Since World War II, the Croton system's population had increased by 300 percent. Construction, devegetation, and creation of impervious surfaces, such as parking lots, increased erosion. To accommodate developers, the city and state allowed the construction of sewage treatment plants that actually discharged treated sewage directly into the reservoir system. Violations of law and of discharge permits were commonplace and often grotesque. A report of foul-smelling water and disappearing fish in one Croton tributary, Beaver Dam Brook, led us to the Bedford Correctional Facility sewage treatment plant, which, according to its own records, had violated its Clean Water Act permit ten thousand times by discharging raw and partially treated sewage from its prison population into the watershed stream. The Putnam County Hospital, whose treatment plant discharges directly into the Croton Falls Reservoir, was another chronic violator. On one trip there Bobby found that the plant's main line was jammed and that all of the hospital toilets, tubs, and drains were discharging directly into the reservoir. The effluent included chemical disinfectants, pharmaceuticals, and hospital and human wastes.

Ten million gallons of sewage per day were entering the Croton system from various plants. In those neighborhoods supplied by the Croton, the tap water contained as much as 2.5 percent sewage effluent during the driest years. Most Croton water went to the city's poorest neighborhoods, including Harlem, the South Bronx, the Lower East Side, and Hell's Kitchen.

The same kind of development that was ruining the Croton system was poised to threaten the Catskill/Delaware system, which provides 90 percent of the city's supply. Twenty-five sewage treatment plants were constructed in the much larger Catskill/Delaware watershed beginning in the 1950s and continuing through the 1970s. Hubs of population had recently formed around the region's ski resorts and golf courses. Two hundred Delaware County dairy farms used outdated farming practices that endangered the system with contaminated runoff.

But just as the Chelsea pump case suggested, the worst enemy of the water supply was New York City itself. Of the nine sewer plants owned and operated by the city under agreements with local towns dating back to the time of reservoir construction, eight were chronic polluters. The city's giant Tannersville Plant in the Catskills had 2,800 self-reported violations in five years. The 1930s vintage Mahopac waterworks in Westchester County was called "the medieval plant" by city officials because of its archaic design. These plants should have been reservoir system flagships. Instead, their shoddy design, operation, and maintenance assured that New York City, the primary environmental enforcer of the watershed, was unlikely to draw attention to itself by pointing its finger at other violators.

In all, 112 sewage treatment plants discharge into the watershed of New York City's water supply, the only unfiltered supply in the nation to allow such discharges. It is illegal to put human sewage into *filtered* reservoir systems in virtually every other state, including New York neighbors such as Connecticut, Rhode Island, and New Jersey.

We learned that when the Cannonsville Reservoir, located in the Delaware River drainage basin, turned pea green with summer algae due to sewage plant discharges and runoff from dairy farms, the city dumped the tainted water into the upper Delaware River. A few days after the dumping began each summer, citizens of Philadelphia (which draws its water from the Delaware) complained of a cucumber flavor in *their* drinking water. The Muscoot Reservoir in the Croton watershed wore a thick carpet of filamentous algae every year from May through November due to overfertilization from septic systems, sewage plants, and polluted runoff. Often when the city had algae growth problems it chose to dump thousands of pounds of chemical disinfectants into the reservoirs, killing fish by the thousands in order to keep the water potable. The city routinely dosed the Rondout Reservoir with gross amounts of chemicals wildly out of proportion to the algae problem.

We decided to file suit against the city in federal court for its Tannersville plant and for its misuse of chemicals, algicides, and pesticides at Rondout. Our suits had two aims: to reduce the chemical options available to the DEP, thereby forcing the agency to consider watershed protection, and to make the city an example of environmental compliance throughout the watershed. In 1992, we won our court fights. The city was required to reduce its chemical dependence in the Rondout Reservoir and to commit millions of dollars to bring the Tannersville sewage treatment plant into line. But these victories alone could not stir the city's interest in watershed management in the face of an institutional culture wed to chemical and engineering solutions and sympathetic to intensive real estate development. The DEP's proud and confident managing engineers who wielded the power within the agency instinctively rejected ecological solutions. They were builders, not environmental protectors. Decisions about the watershed reflected political expediency above all. When Pepsico threatened to pull its bottling plant out of Staten Island, Mayor Abraham Beame's administration offered the company a waterside location for its world headquarters on the Muscoot Reservoir if Pepsi would agree to keep operating the city facility. Danbury Pharmacal, a regular handler of toxic chemicals, used its influence with state officials to get permission from the city and state to discharge its wastes into the Croton Falls Reservoir. The city could have used its regulatory authority to block permits for such polluting activities. Instead the government leaders acceded to one project after another rather than alienate upstate watershed communities, which, it believed, would seek their revenge when the mayor made his annual trek to Albany at budget time.

In 1989, Congress strengthened the Safe Drinking Water Act with a new provision called the Surface Water Treatment Rule, which threatened to force New York City to spend money and lots of it.

The rule mandated that each of the nation's surface drinking water systems—those that take their water from reservoirs, streams, lakes, or rivers—must construct a water filtration plant. The city immediately agreed to filter the Croton waters, which received most of the watershed's sewage and were undeniably degraded. The oldest and most densely developed part of the city's systems, the Croton provided only 10 percent of the total supply. A Croton system filter plant would cost the city a mere $300 million.

Filtering the Catskill/Delaware system would cost real money—an estimated $8 billion for construction and an additional $300 million *per year* for operation! The liability would cause the city's bond ratings to plummet. Water rates would double. Thousands of rent-controlled housing units in the city's poorest neighborhoods would be promptly abandoned by landlords as escalating water rates devoured marginal profits. Worst of all, after these calamitous expenditures, no New Yorker would be able look at his neighbor and say "Our lives have improved."

In fact, conventional filtration would not remove many of the pollutants and organisms associated with watershed development. Pesticides, road salts, petrochemicals, and trihalomethane (a chlorination by-product that causes thousands of rectal and bladder cancer deaths annually) are unaffected by filtration. Disease-causing organisms and viruses can often outsmart the most sophisticated filtration systems once source water becomes contaminated. In 1993, 450,000 Milwaukee residents were sickened and 100 died when that city's filtration plant allowed cryptosporidial cysts to pass through untreated. In a city the size of New York, a comparable epidemic would kill thousands and sicken millions. Most important, the requirement to filter would leave the city without the obligation, the political will, or the proper financing to protect its watershed.

Fortunately for New York City, Senator Daniel Moynihan had slipped an exemption in the Surface Water Treatment Rule allowing the EPA to waive the filtration requirement for those cities with populations greater than one million that could demonstrate a watershed protection program capable of protecting their supplies indefinitely. The Catskill/Delaware supply was perhaps the only one in the nation that was of high enough quality to qualify for the exemption. But, to qualify, the DEP would have to overhaul its practices and the city would have to spend hundreds of millions of dollars in its watershed. Failing that, the EPA would have no alternative but to order filtration.

The high cost of filtration provided the city with a serious incentive to begin shifting resources to watershed protection. But a crisis is not a useful opportunity for change when no one knows about it. And no one knew about this one. Prior to our involvement, neither the *Times,* the *Post,* nor the *Daily News* had carried a single article about pollution in the watershed or the prospect of a filtration order. Our first job was to put the watershed on the political radar screen.

We assembled our staff, distributed assignments, and plotted strategy. Clinic students compiled permits and discharge records of all 112 reservoir system sewage plants. The records showed that 30 percent regularly violated their permits. We commenced lawsuits against each of them. We raised money to hire a former clinic student, Dave Gordon, to work solely on reservoir issues. In search of evidence regarding degradation of the water supply, Dave filed freedom-of-information requests for all files on the city's watershed history, watershed police records, and records of water quality in the reservoirs and pollution at city-owned facilities. A volunteer real estate assessor, Ginny Brown, determined the cost of purchasing every acre of land in the Catskill/Delaware watershed.

Using all of this information, Bobby and Dave compiled the first comprehensive analysis of pollution in the New York City watershed and exposed government's role in allowing and encouraging its continued destruction. We distributed this report, *The Legend of City Water,* to every state and city official who might be concerned about water. The report would be widely read and cited, and it played an important role in educating the public, press, and political leaders over the next several years.

In August 1989, Bobby wrote a groundbreaking op-ed piece for the *New York Times* on the watershed crisis. He followed with half a dozen more articles in the *Times, Newsday,* and the Westchester Gannett papers. We obtained meetings with the editorial boards of the *New York Times,* the *New York Post, Newsday,* and the *Daily News.* All of them eventually published editorials endorsing a strong watershed protection program. We also cultivated interested reporters at each paper and educated them on the watershed issue.

Two or three times each week, we brought film crews and reporters on pollution tours of the watershed. Bobby had a public television camera crew in tow when he came upon the Putnam Hospital bypass pipe that was discharging untreated hospital sewage, including wadded toilet paper and catheters, into the Croton Reservoir. PBS producers invited city and state officials to view the tape and respond. DEP Commissioner Harvey Shultz refused to appear. His outraged press flak, Tina Casey, telephoned the show as the tape was being shown and on a live feed dismissed Bobby as an attention seeker and blamed pollution on watershed wildlife. "Do you want us to put diapers on the rabbits?" she asked sarcastically.

By the end of the Koch/Dinkins campaign, the watershed was for the first time an issue in a New York City mayoral contest. On his first day on the job, Dinkins' new DEP commissioner, Albert Appleton, promised to make watershed protection the number-one environmental priority of the Dinkins administration.

But the hammer fell before Appleton could make good on his promise. In January 1991, because of New York City's track record of embracing growth in the watershed, the New York State Department of Health—the EPA's federally delegated state agency responsible for administering the Safe Drinking Water Act—ordered New York to construct a filtration plant for the Catskill and Delaware systems. The EPA backed the state 100 percent. We believed that the order to filter was premature and that Appleton should have been given the chance to demonstrate that the city could protect its drinking water. We agreed to help the city lobby for a temporary waiver of the filtration order, to give the city time to show what it could do.

After a year of intensive lobbying, the EPA agreed to suspend the order temporarily while a blue-ribbon panel studied the issue. That following December the panel reported back that because of New York City's historical unwillingness to exercise the political will necessary to protect its water supply from pollution, it indeed should be ordered to filter.

With the panel's recommendation in hand, the EPA argued that allowing the city to escape this mother of unfunded mandates would set a troublesome national precedent as well as pose a real public health threat. The EPA's position was supported by the national environmental community and by Congressman Henry Waxman, the chair of the National Resource Committee and the primary author of the Surface Water Treatment Rule.

We believed that while filtration might be necessary in the future, it should be viewed as a last resort. Otherwise it was wasteful and, ultimately, harmful. New York City's Catskill/Delaware supply, despite the years of neglect, was still purer by every criterion than the nation's best filtered water supplies. In a series of meetings with other members of the local and national environmental community, we acknowledged that in a perfect world the best solution would be filtration *and* watershed protection, but costs and politics made this impossible. We argued that an ample investment in watershed protection would most effectively control dangerous contaminants and would avoid the devastating financial impacts of filtration. The filtration mandate should be used as a gorilla in the closet, forcing the city to focus on watershed protection. Finally, we committed to supporting filtration if the city failed to accomplish watershed protection.

We pleaded with EPA administrator William Reilly for a temporary filtration waiver, and on his last day in office, in January 1993, Reilly made a compromise. He ruled that New York City must plan for filtration, but if the city was able to demonstrate, within one year, that it could develop a program to protect its reservoirs, the order to filter would be reviewed. The city was also ordered to implement a massive testing and sampling program, which would allow the agencies, for the first time, to determine the safety of the city's water supply.

We were pleased with Reilly's decision. Privately, however, we were concerned that the city was just living from exemption to exemption. The old cabal of do-nothing civil engineers within the DEP was using its influence to make sure Appleton's promise of reform spent an eternity in bureaucrat purgatory. The engineers were in everything from enforcement to laboratories and were committed to business as usual. Many of them talked openly of the lucrative job opportunities that would be available to them from private contractors and consultants were the city ordered to filter.

We recognized our weakness. We had been relying on well-intentioned government officials to act sensibly. When the wheels of reform ground to a halt, we had nowhere to turn. We had no broad constituency of water consumers demanding clean water.

Actually, while we had succeeded in reaching and educating top city officials, most city politicians were still either unaware or unconvinced that such a giant financial liability would ever be handed down from Washington. In the autumn of 1993, Philip Michaels, Dinkins' budget director, was shocked when we told him that the city was facing an $8 billion contingent liability that December. Not a single member of the City Council and only one or two assemblymen and state senators seemed even vaguely familiar with the issues. New York City residents were even less informed than their public officials. When we asked New York City high school seniors where their water came from, they typically answered, "the faucet." In most schools where we spoke not a single student was aware of the city's hydraulic connection to upstate New York.

Meanwhile, people in the Catskill watershed were understandably alert and angry. The history of family and community upheavals associated with the creation of the reservoirs remained fresh in their minds. The city had completed construction on the Cannonsville Reservoir only in 1964. Towns had been flooded, churches ruined, property condemned, barns burned by city workers, and cemeteries relocated. Altogether, thirty-two communities were moved and the best bottom land in Delaware County permanently flooded. When the drought of 1988 dropped water levels in the Neversink Reservoir, the bridges, roads, and foundations of the town of Neversink reemerged like a festering wound beneath an old scab. Likewise, the new talk of aggressive regulatory programs, controlled growth, law enforcement, and large-scale property acquisition rekindled bitter memories of how a distant city, with the approval of the state, once took control of their lands. Upstate developers financed an intensive direct-mail campaign that helped fan worry into fear. They delivered the message to every Catskill household that the city was coming back to take over the rest of the property and pay no recompense to local communities. A coalition of watershed towns formed to coordinate opposition.

If city residents did not know where their water came from, every warm body in the Catskills knew where their water went. And they were mobilized into a potent political force opposed to the city's watershed protection plans. We had a lot of work to do. Distracted by the immediate filtration order controversy, we had been spending all of our energy influencing the mayor, the EPA, and a few select government officials. We decided to take our cue from the folks in the Catskills and go directly to the people.

We started with those least likely to think of themselves as environmentalists and most likely to be sued by them—New York's development community. We appealed to Lou Rudin, president of the Association for a Better New York and one of New York City's most influential real estate holders. Socially conscious as well as fiscally and politically astute, Rudin quickly grasped the disastrous sequence of events that a filtration order would precipitate. Rudin set up meetings with New York's top real estate developers, Tom Millstein and Tony Fisher of Fisher Brothers, all of whom agreed to give us political support and funding.

Next, we arranged meetings with other groups and individuals who could influence the mayor—Stanley Hill of the American Federation of State, County, and Municipal employees; the gay and HIV advocacy groups, including ACT-UP and Gay Men's Health Crisis; various housing and health groups; and the local community boards. Our most productive and enthusiastic allies were Dennis Rivera, the powerful chief of Local 1199 of the Health and Hospital Care Workers Union and Mayor Dinkins' campaign manager, and Basil Patterson, the mayor's closest friend. Rivera took a strong interest in the program because it was a health care issue and because he saw filtration as a drain on city resources. He arranged meetings with Hispanic groups and several African American activist groups, including 100 Black Men, 100 Black Women. These groups took particular offense at the fact that the Croton water, the city's worst, was going to the city's poorest neighborhoods. Everyone to whom we spoke was shocked to learn that sewage and other pollutants were tainting the "champagne of drinking water."

Bobby, John, and Dave Gordon hit the hustings, speaking almost daily to civic and environmental groups, high schools, community boards, and political gatherings about the watershed. We decided to organize an event to consolidate the young coalition. We announced a Walk for Water, an eight-mile march around the Croton Reservoir, to educate New Yorkers about the source of their drinking water.

A few years earlier, we had been invited by actors Christopher Reeve and Alec Baldwin to speak before monthly assemblies of the Creative Coalition, a socially active organization of those involved in New York's performing-arts industry. Now we went back to them for assistance. They helped us to recruit several actors and actresses, such as Billy Baldwin, Glenn Close, and Edward James Olmos, and half a dozen soap opera stars to act as spokespeople and whose presence would help attract crowds and publicity for our march. NBC's Al Roker, a Hudson Valley denizen, agreed to broadcast the *Today Show* from the event. The watershed issue began to appear in the tabloids.

As it turned out, June 8 was one of the rainiest days of the year. Still, close to one thousand people showed up from Westchester and New York City to make the eight-mile march in a torrential downpour. Tweed-jacketed environmentalists marched with African American children from Bedford-Stuyvesant, red-bereted Guardian Angels, blue-jacketed union members from New York City, and hundreds of schoolchildren. Press coverage was spectacular before and during the event, and the watershed issue immediately appeared on the agenda for the autumn political race.

In order to maintain the pressure, we began organizing a rally to take place at the South Street Seaport in lower Manhattan, at which we would unveil the largest painted canvas ever created, an image of Lady Liberty standing in pristine water, with the threats of pollution all about, and underscored by a giant caption: "Protect Our Water." A California graphic artist, Mike McNeally, offered to execute the painting free of charge.

Meanwhile, Cynthia Adler of the Creative Coalition had set up a meeting for us with the partners of Kirshenbaum and Bond, the avant-garde advertising firm that had transformed a local fruit drink into a billion-dollar bottled-drink phenomenon called Snapple. The Kaplan Fund, a charitable trust interested in New York City, had given us a much-needed grant of $50,000 to fund our public information campaign. We wanted maximum impact, and Kirshenbaum and Bond were interested in lending their talents for the cause. They asked us to provide them with information and a list of the most egregious facts about pollution in the city's reservoirs. Two weeks later Richard Kirshenbaum invited us to review his proposed campaign.

He unveiled a series of posters designed to shock. The first showed a man's naked torso, from knee to neck. In place of his penis a chrome-plated water tap issued a graphic yellow spray into an eight-ounce glass suspended by a disembodied hand. "Human waste is discharged into 88% of New York City's water supply" warned the giant caption. A second showed an unmistakable stripe of toothpaste atop the bristles of a toilet brush. "Brush your teeth with Fecaldent?" it offered. A third poster depicted ice cubes and a maraschino cherry–bespangled swizzle stick floating in a hospital urine vial; "Sewage is discharged into 16 of the 19 reservoirs that supply NYC with drinking water." The other posters were in a similar vein. They had their desired effect. Even we were shocked.

Kirshenbaum laid out his plan. He told us that he thought he could persuade Gannett Advertising to donate sixty-five bus shelters to display giant prints of the posters. He proposed putting smaller versions on every New York City subway. But the centerpiece of the poster campaign would be snipes. "Snipes" refers to the thousands of posters that magically appear overnight on every available wall space in the city, usually advertising cultural events like plays or concerts or movies. Kirshenbaum proposed to secure the services of a "snipe squad" that would glue sixty-five hundred of the posters on every bare wall in downtown Manhattan between midnight and 4:00 A.M. on the morning we announced the poster campaign from the steps of City Hall. Extra snipes would be hung strategically along the route from the mayor's Gracie Mansion residence to City Hall and along routes most often used by his campaign challengers and other important city officials.

Finally, every member of the New York City Council, state senators and assemblymen, and county government officials in Westchester, Putnam, and the Catskills would be presented with coffee mugs embossed with facts about the water supply. One of them bore the outside score "2% of every cup of Croton water is human sewage." On the inside bottom was a picture of an exposed rear end with the cheery rejoinder "Bottoms up!"

Kirshenbaum closed his presentation and asked for our reaction. When we recovered our composure, we tried to read the expressions on each other's faces. In fact, the campaign was brilliant. The posters suggested a combination of graffiti and collage. They had an intentionally homemade look—even the masking tape that positioned the art appeared in the finished reproduced work.

Kirshenbaum presented the campaign for what it was, a down-and-dirty grassroots campaign that was funded on a shoestring. He believed that the fierce competition for the attention of New York City residents required that we do something bold and different. While the pictures might be considered sensationalistic and in dubious taste, the facts themselves were the most alarming aspect of the campaign. Thanks to the DEP's tradition of secrecy, this would be the first time New Yorkers were told the truth—there is sewage in your drinking water!

In late summer, Dennis Rivera hosted a meeting with Commissioner Appleton and Deputy Mayor Barbara Fife where we staged a courtesy unveiling of the posters. Appleton and Fife were horrified. Although the campaign was not targeted against the mayor, Fife and Appleton felt that people would nevertheless blame it on Dinkins. They feared that during an election year the poster campaign would reinforce a general feeling of dismay about life in New York City.

The following day Mayor Dinkins placed an angry phone call to Bobby. The mayor reminded Bobby of his undeniably strong environmental record and wondered pointedly why environmentalists were trying to sabotage his reelection campaign. For the first time, we had the opportunity to convey the urgency of this issue directly to the mayor. Bobby explained that in December the EPA was going to order New York City to filter its water. Only a unified plan by city government, the environmental and health communities, and local community groups would divert EPA's trajectory. And this unified approach could happen only if Dinkins made an unambiguous commitment to watershed protection immediately. Best of all for Dinkins, the expenditures for watershed protection would be off-budget since they came not from the general fund but from water rates. And water rates would rise only slightly, if at all, if the city invested in the $1 billion watershed protection program we were urging. Filtration, on the other hand, would cause city water rates to double.

The mayor listened carefully, evidently hearing most of the arguments for the first time, and he arranged another meeting with Appleton and Fife. After a series of intense negotiations during September 1993, Appleton and Fife agreed that the city would commit $750 million to a watershed protection program, including $250 million to purchase ninety thousand acres of watershed buffer lands, $280 million to upgrade watershed sewer plants owned by the city, $120 million in "partnership funds" to assist upstate communities in implementing their own environmental programs and to mitigate the adverse economic impacts of regulation, and $200 million to double the size of the police force and add five hundred new technical and enforcement personnel. This time we insisted that the mayor confirm the terms in a written agreement.

In October we went forward with our rally, but now it was a celebration rather than a protest. Thousands of participants crowded the South Street Seaport to cheer New York City's drinking water and our agreement with the Dinkins administration. As the mayor announced the new program to the cheering crowds, the Miss Liberty painting was slowly raised up the side of the New York Telephone Building for all to see; the collage of pollution symbols that had previously hung over her worried brow had been hastily painted over with a giant American flag.

The EPA agreed to give New York City an additional three years' waiver of the filtration mandate (until December 1996) to prove that it could implement its program. The order contained benchmarks and milestones requiring the city to hire technicians and enforcement personnel, purchase lands by certain dates, and embark upon an extensive contaminant monitoring program.

We were finally on our way. Or so we thought.

In January 1994, following a bitter electoral race with David Dinkins, Rudolph Giuliani became the 107th mayor of New York and the third mayor to face the filtration mandate. The environmental community that had supported Dinkins would have difficulty convincing Giuliani that "greens" were a constituency he needed to please.

Without first developing a coherent water policy of its own with which to bargain, the new administration almost immediately entered into a series of private negotiations with the Coalition of Watershed Towns. Despite our repeated requests to participate, all environmentalists and downstate interests were excluded from these meetings, and no comparable meetings were held with downstate water consumers. The Giuliani administration had placed itself in a fatal negotiating position.

Predictably, the city emerged from those meetings with a dramatically watered-down version of the Dinkins administration's proposed regulations. The Giuliani version eliminated all hazardous waste controls, pesticide restrictions, septic controls, and enforcement initiatives.

When the city scheduled a series of hearings on the new proposed regulations as required by the city's municipal code, the hearing schedule addressed the political needs of Catskill politicians but seemed designed to keep New Yorkers in the dark. Seven separate hearings spread in various Catskill communities would be held to accommodate a total of fifty thousand residents. The city targeted one hearing for the big real estate developers in the northern end of the Croton system; there was no hearing planned for the one million southern Westchester water consumers, or for the two hundred thousand residents of the city of Yonkers who survived on city water.

In New York City, a single hearing would be held to serve the city's 8.5 million water consumers. To minimize attendance it was scheduled on a Monday afternoon at City Hall, and the only advertisement for the hearing appeared in the *New York Times'* obscure notification section in print that would make a hummingbird squint. Meanwhile, upstate hearings were advertised on the front pages of local papers across the Catskills and were to be held in the evenings to accommodate working people. At the same time they slammed shut the door to the negotiating room, the new administration revoked the Dinkins administration's open-door policy allowing citizens and public interest groups to inspect sampling and monitoring data from the reservoir and sewer systems. Giuliani fired the DEP's press officers who had developed relationships with the public interest community.

All these developments made us realize we were back at war with the city. But this time we were ready. We had achieved our initial objective—for the first time since the 1830s, the condition of city water was a concern in the media and on the public mind. And from within the DEP, disgruntled employees were feeding us information. The issue of the city water supply was a bomb ready to explode, and the fuse was in our hands. The needed spark came from Bobby's youngest brother Douglas, who had just gone to work as an investigative reporter for the *New York Post*.

The *New York Post* liked sensational stories about life and politics in New York. Sewage in drinking water smelled like a good story, and the *Post* editors gave Doug the go-ahead to find out more. With two weeks remaining before the City Hall hearing, we began funneling tips to him from our friendly DEP moles. The stories appeared in rapid succession. The first grabbed the attention of David Letterman and much of the nation when it exposed the secret closure of the Croton due to the "presence of organic material." With Doug's second story disclosing the DEP's secret discovery of *Vibrio cholerae,* the agency began to emerge for what it was, a politically inbred branch of city government more interested in protecting itself than the public good.

By now our phone was ringing off the hook with DEP informants giving us damaging information about the agency. We learned that the DEP had found cryptosporidial cysts in the water supply for the first time in its history. Ingesting even a single crypto cyst can lead to sickness or death in immunocompromised individuals, including cancer and HIV patients, the elderly, and infants. Douglas wrote a story revealing that the previous November, increases in the organism had coincided with rises in city hospital admissions of patients with cryptosporidiosis, a diarrheal disease. Some had died. DEP officials had opted not to warn the public even though the Centers for Disease

Control in Atlanta and many of the DEP's own laboratory personnel were recommending that water purveyors give boiled water advisories when crypto is known to be present in a water supply.

The *New York Times* and the *Daily News* followed up the *Post*'s story as did radio and television news in what soon became a frenzy of disclosure about the water supply. New Yorkers began, for the first time in memory, to question the potability of the city's famed drinking water. Dozens of other stories criticized Mayor Giuliani for a lackadaisical commitment to water quality and for discarding the tough regulations of the Dinkins administration.

We assigned two volunteers as watershed organizers, Lori Caramanian, a former Pace Clinic law student, and David Markus, a recent college graduate. Lori and Dave wrote and then patiently called every city councilperson, state legislator, and senator, and the leaders of all the coalition groups that had participated in our earlier actions. Riverkeeper mailed a thirteen-page report card on the Giuliani administration to every member of the state legislature. We sent a copy to the mayor demanding answers. We met with alliance partners from the environmental, housing, labor, development, minority, and gay communities and urged each of them to send representatives to appear at the hearing. We enlisted Christopher Reeve and the Creative Coalition, which had adopted the watershed as one of its three priority issues.

On the hearing day, over two hundred people showed up to testify and hundreds more to watch, including business and real estate leaders, as well as labor union leaders, environmental groups, AIDS and HIV advocacy groups, housing groups representing both landlords' and tenants' associations, minority groups, politicians, and private citizens.

A 2:00 P.M. hearing that the DEP expected to last two hours rolled on until 9:00 P.M. Many people who signed on to testify had to leave without speaking. For seven hours water drinkers stood before the standing-room-only crowd in the giant hearing room to lambaste the panel of grim-faced city officials for failing to protect New York's drinking water.

We also convinced reticent EPA officials to weigh in with their expert opinions. At our urging, the EPA's regional administrator, Jeanne Fox, sent the city a lengthy letter criticizing the proposed regulations as inadequate either to avoid the steady degradation of water quality or to avoid a federal order to filter in December 1996.

In the wake of the hearings, city DEP commissioner Marilyn Gelber asked us for a truce. Mayor Giuliani was angered by stories portraying his administration as uncommitted to water-quality protection. We agreed to suspend our public attacks on the condition that the city would redraft its regulations and reform the agency's upstate watershed division by removing or transferring certain officials whom both we and Gelber knew to be antagonistic to watershed protection. Commissioner Gelber accepted our terms.

Our new alliance with the city came at a critical juncture for New York State politics. We knew both 1992 gubernatorial candidates well. George Pataki was our neighbor in Garrison and had represented John as assemblyman and both John and Bobby as state senator. Pataki and his wife, Libby, were regular contributors to Riverkeeper. They had been out in the boat and frequently attended our fund-raisers. During John's years in the Assembly, he knew Pataki and admired his strong environmental record, which reflected the view of his Hudson Valley constituency. Once Pataki ascended to the Senate, however, his constituency changed. He now represented not just the rabidly environmental Hudson River Valley but also the watershed communities of Putnam County. His contributor base included the big developers, their engineers, and lawyers. In April 1993, Senator Pataki cosponsored a bill to limit New York City's authority to regulate against pollution in the watershed. The bill passed in the Republican-controlled Senate and failed in the Democratic Assembly.

During his gubernatorial run against three-term incumbent Mario Cuomo, Pataki promised he would fight new regulations if he was elected governor. Based on his stance against watershed protection (and not *just* because Cuomo's son was married to Bobby's sister), Bobby campaigned aggressively against Pataki. The New York press picked up on the watershed issue since it lent substance to the character of a race that was increasingly being drawn as a contest between New York City versus upstate New York. Bobby's criticisms were headlined in the city papers, and the city press corps demanded responses, not only from Pataki but from his fellow Republican and presumed ally, Mayor Rudolph Giuliani. Giuliani did not rise to defend his party compatriot. Instead, on October 24, Rudolph Giuliani stood on the steps of City Hall and made his shocking cross-party endorsement of Mario Cuomo. During his endorsement speech, Giuliani named the watershed as the principal issue that had driven his extraordinary decision. Within three days Cuomo moved from a ten-point deficit to a twenty-point lead in the polls, and every political leader in New York City knew about the watershed.

Giuliani's timing was off by five days. The boost that Cuomo received from the mayor's endorsement plateaued on Tuesday, November 2, and began to drop by Wednesday. By the weekend, upstate backlash began to build against the governor. By Monday, November 6, the race was too close to call. On election day, Pataki triumphed by just four points.

The election of George Pataki had not been the only political upheaval of late 1994; the Republican sweep of Congress promised a new era of reduced federal mandates. The city, convinced that regulation of the watershed was undesirable in the eyes of the state and that an order to filter was unlikely in a realigned Washington, began backpedaling furiously. In January 1995, the city released its new regulations—which were in most respects as bad as, and in some cases worse than, the previous draft.

These disturbing political developments did not dampen our resolve. We had obtained proof that high-level technicians at the DEP's drinking water laboratories had been ordered to skew lab results in order to conceal contaminated water in the city pipes. Douglas broke the story in the *New York Post,* and it was subsequently picked up by all of the city newspapers and made the front page of the *New York Times.* Hearings ordered by the City Council and the New York State Assembly Environmental Conservation Committee kept the story in the press for two more weeks.

We arranged for Thomas Georgian, the DEP's former laboratory chief, to appear at the first of these hearings. Georgian had quit the DEP in disgust after complaining that laboratory field personnel were routinely ordered to dispose of contaminated samples without registering them. Georgian's calm, authoritative testimony was supported in press interviews by his superior Eva Chen, Chief Laboratory Engineer, who had reluctantly retired for the same reasons after twenty-two years at the DEP.

As Georgian's and Chen's testimony hit the press, the Giuliani administration sought to reassure the public with the mantric refrain that "New Yorkers have the best drinking water on earth." These reassurances lost credibility when another of Douglas' *Post* articles revealed that all nine DEP headquarters buildings supplied the DEP's staff with either bottled or filtered water. Within days Commissioner Gelber fired her deputy commissioner charged with managing the DEP's labs.

In February 1995, the State Department of Health began the process of promulgating the city's proposed regulations into law, scheduling four hearings—the first in New York City and three others in the upstate watersheds. Again, we helped organize a large public turnout. Over two hundred community leaders appeared at the New York City hearing. Pure Water Alliance, a coalition of twenty-eight environmental and community groups formed to fight for strong watershed protection, distributed buttons embossed with the words "Pure Water, No Shit." Connie Hough, who is John's wife and Bobby's assistant at the Pace Clinic, ended her testimony with the plea that she did not want any, "not even a little," sewage in her drinking water. "If," she said, "DEP officials feel so strongly that there should be sewage in their drinking water, they are welcome to add it themselves at home."

Other testimony was more emotional. In a talk that moved many of the hushed crowd to tears, one woman introduced herself as the primary caretaker of her AIDS-afflicted sister. "Whenever I wash her dishes with New York City water," she related, "I wonder what kinds of bacteria I am leaving on her eating utensils."

The Northern Westchester hearing was the most significant. The New York State Department of Health (DOH) had again sited the hearing at Cross River, in the heart of the Westchester and Putnam Counties development community. The three DOH hearing officers fully expected to hear the usual upstate watershed complaints against overreaching city regulations. Instead they encountered a giant standing-room-only crowd of public interest groups and ordinary citizens, demanding stronger regulations and insisting that the DOH require removal of sewage from the drinking water reservoirs and tributaries. Many of the crowd carried placards depicting toilets embossed with the one-word question, "Thirsty?" One student offered the hearing officer a mayonnaise jar containing effluent from a local sewer plant and dared the examiners to drink from it. Of the 298 people signed up to testify, fewer than 10 criticized the regulations as too intrusive. One week later, 650 citizens signed in at the water supply hearing in Yonkers. Before the night was over 100 testified and 250 filed written testimony, all of them demanding strong regulations to protect their community water supply and rejecting the idea of filtration.

We had finally built a popular constituency, strong enough to challenge the antiregulatory front in the watershed. An unavoidable outcome of that success was an increased polarization between upstate and downstate interests. But when both city and local watershed officials accused us of purposely inflaming the conflict in the media, a more vexing consequence developed: They began to commiserate with each other.

In the spring of 1995, Governor Pataki offered to mediate the watershed controversy between New York City and the upstate towns, and both sides agreed, with the stipulation that environmental organizations would not be welcome at the negotiating table.

We were understandably apprehensive that our campaign had driven the key decision makers behind closed doors. But we also understood that we would never get a place at the table if we relented now. Instead we escalated our public attacks on the mayor and governor and filed lawsuits against all parties.

At the same time, we knew that negotiations were the only way that watershed protection would be accomplished. The Safe Drinking Water Act did not mandate the watershed communities to cooperate with the city's plan to avoid filtration. Reaching a viable watershed agreement would require voluntary cooperation by all the stakeholders, including upstate communities and environmental groups.

Under pressure from our lawsuits and the publicity barrage, the government officials ultimately reached the same conclusion. In April, the governor's chief counsel, Michael Finnegan, called John to say that the governor did not believe the watershed issue could be solved without the environmental community. He asked us to meet him in Albany. We put together a team to meet with Finnegan, including ourselves, Chris Meyer of NYPIRG, and Eric Goldstein of the NRDC. One week later we were sitting in the counsel's office. At the outset of the meeting, we expressed our concern that we were being brought in too late in the game. Finnegan explained that it had always been the governor's intention to involve us. But, before Finnegan could add environmentalists and their collection of volatile issues to the mix, he had wanted to diffuse some of the tension between the city and watershed towns.

Hostility between the two constituencies was running so high that when Governor Pataki attended a public meeting in the Catskills about watershed issues, Perry Shelton, leader of the Delaware County contingent, pointed his finger at the governor and warned that any further regulation of the watershed towns would cause the people of his community to "make Oklahoma City look like child's play."

Although upstate New York had put him in office, Pataki decided not to give up the watershed issue. The governor would reap immeasurable political rewards if he healed the generations-old upstate-downstate rift while protecting the water supply of millions of New Yorkers. But this was a high-stakes gamble that could also leave Pataki appearing like an impulsive political novice.

Pataki would later tell Bobby that his decision was motivated by personal inspiration. Christopher Reeve had been one of our closest allies on the watershed issue. He had testified at each public hearing and stood beside us at our press events. He had traveled to Albany to lobby Pataki and the legislature and he'd been instrumental in arranging the participation of Kirshenbaum and Bond in our campaign. Soon after his election, Pataki met Reeve at the annual Christmas tree lighting at Rockefeller Center. Reeve told him that as governor he would be in a position to be a hero on the watershed. All that the issue was lacking, said Reeve, was a politician with courage. According to Pataki, it was Reeve's courage during the early days following his riding accident that inspired Pataki. Pataki told Bobby that it was while watching a television report describing Reeve's own heroic efforts to survive and recover that he had decided to make protection of the New York City water supply his top priority during the first year of his administration.

Finnegan wanted to know what we could contribute toward making the governor's commitment to watershed protection a reality. We believed that the principal obstacles to the agreement were rhetoric and money. The environmental community was in a unique position to provide a bridge between the crucial issues that defined both sides. We were the only credible countervailing force to the populist antiregulatory platform of the upstate towns. At the same time, we were also firmly committed to the city's investing hard cash in the economic future of watershed communities.

A week later, Governor Pataki, in shirt sleeves and jeans, met with a roomful of environmentalists at the Riverkeeper headquarters in Garrison. After introductions, he sat down at the table, turned to the group, and said, "All right, how do we protect the water supply?" We realized that this unprecedented meeting might be the turning point that we had been working toward for seven years.

We outlined our plan for the watershed and explained our prospective role in the negotiations. For an hour Pataki asked and answered questions. Finally he said, "I want you in the negotiations. The state won't stay involved if the environmentalists are not involved as well."

At the first negotiation session we attended, Finnegan distributed a grueling schedule of twenty-eight meetings. The representatives of the parties groaned audibly. By the end, we would have attended over a hundred meetings—many lasting late into the night.

For several months, the participants took every opportunity to emphasize the divisions—upstate versus downstate, rural versus urban, Republican versus Democrat. The Catskill groups in particular were surly and distrustful, delivering endless recitations of the years of misdeeds by city workers in the Catskills and broken promises by city officials, and flinging angry accusations directed at the environmental "interlopers."

Then, in early October, the tone of the negotiations changed dramatically. At a meeting in the Capitol Building in Albany, Bobby made a strong statement supporting Delaware County's demand for economic development money from the city. This was the first time the environmentalists had taken the Catskill community's side in a dispute. Thereafter, they dropped their knee-jerk opposition to our every demand and even began supporting us in some areas. A feeling emerged that we were all part of one community and shared a responsibility to find a solution. The rhetoric diminished and the horse-trading began.

Delaware County came to terms with the city in mid-October and the other Catskill communities quickly followed. In the last week of October, the city ironed out its differences with Westchester and Putnam Counties. The upstate communities agreed to drop nearly a dozen lawsuits that could have delayed the city's regulations and land acquisition program for decades, and to allow new restrictions on development within the watershed. In return, the city would spend $1.5 billion purchasing critical watershed lands (approximately 120,000 acres), building environmental infrastructures (storm sewers, septic systems, stream bank stabilization, and agricultural runoff controls), refitting all sewer plants with state-of-the-art microfiltration and nutrient removal technology, and creating eco-friendly jobs in the watershed. The agreement represented a historic transfer of wealth from city water consumers to fund economic vitality and environmental protection in the Catskill Mountains.

But the environmental groups believed that the city, in its eagerness to settle the issue, had given away too much. The protective buffer zones around the reservoirs were too narrow and were riddled with exemptions. The rules allowed new sewage discharges in some parts of the system, and the controls on road construction were deficient.

An announcement of the agreement was scheduled for November 3. We told the governor and Finnegan that we would not sign the agreement unless our demands were met. We had invested too much time, energy, and money to give in now.

The most problematic items of our bottom-line conditions addressed our concerns that the agreement be enforceable, that we be able to monitor whether the agreement was working to protect water quality, that we have the power to reopen and strengthen the agreement if water quality declined, and that all land acquisitions be permanent so that the city could not later liquidate its buffer lands for cash to construct a filter plant.

All the other parties balked at our demands for a $100 million plus water-quality monitoring fund and for enforcement power (including attorney fees) against any party that violated the agreement. The city snorted at our requests for an independent watershed inspector general to enforce city regulations and for a five-year limit on filtration avoidance with a formal review of the city's performance before the EPA could grant another waiver. The state Department of Health fumed at our demand for continued federal oversight, and the watershed towns threatened to walk out if our demand for a seat on the committee that distributes city funds was included as a condition.

Nevertheless, with less than forty hours to go before the signing, at an evening meeting at Grand Central Station's Oyster Bar, Mike Finnegan promised the two of us that the state would support us on all of these demands and others, so long as we agreed to sign and appear alongside the governor.

By the evening of November 2, Finnegan had obtained agreement on all points but one. The city had refused our clause that would give citizens the right to enforce key provisions of the agreement in court. We said we would not be at the next day's news conference.

Bobby was in Flint, Michigan, giving a speech and John was at a school board meeting in Garrison. During a frantic series of calls on cell and pay phones, we struggled through the day to patch an agreement together. By 9:00 P.M. it had all fallen apart. We told Finnegan we were out, but he asked us to hold on. Finnegan called Giuliani's first deputy mayor, Peter Powers, away from dinner with the mayor at Gracie Mansion to an emergency meeting at the governor's city office at the World Trade Center. The group, including DEP commissioner Gelber and EPA deputy regional administrator Richard Caspe, who was dragged out of his bed, sat around a speaker phone. They called John out of his school board meeting, and we patched in our NYPIRG partner, Chris Meyer, who had been a vital player throughout the prior year of negotiations. John and Chris repeated the demand for enforcement and refused to budge. After finally reaching an agreement in principle well after midnight, we left Chris on the line to negotiate language. He would not reach a final agreement until 3:15 A.M.

At 10:00 A.M. the following day we gathered at a giant news conference announcing the historic agreement at Governor Pataki's office at the World Trade Center. Governor Pataki, Mayor Giuliani, Bobby, Perry Shelton, and EPA Regional Administrator Jeanne Fox all spoke. The final fifteen-hundred-page agreement would take another year to negotiate. There would not be a single word in it that blood hadn't been shed over at the negotiating table.

The watershed agreement does not solve the problem of pollution in the watershed. It does not relieve us of the need to be vigilant and fight the polluters and developers. The battle will continue but the terrain of the battlefield has been altered in favor of those who want to preserve the crucial resource for the future.

# CHAPTER 9

# Barbarians at the Gate

A small picket line at a local congressional office ordinarily does not attract media attention. But when fifty environmentalists, fishermen, and citizens gathered at the Hudson Valley headquarters of Republican congresswoman Sue Kelly on July 17, 1995, the day before there were to be two critical House votes on bills that would gut the Clean Water Act and slash EPA funding, the *New York Times,* Gannett, two weekly newspapers, a cable television station, and two radio stations chose to cover the event. It was the first time in memory that a Hudson Valley congressional representative had been singled out as an enemy of the environment.

During her 1994 campaign, candidate Kelly had portrayed herself as a staunch environmentalist—a prerequisite in a district that had produced environmental leaders such as Hamilton Fish, Jr., Richard Ottinger, and Ogden Reid. She pledged to uphold that tradition and to support increased penalties for polluters and the strengthening of the Clean Water and Clean Air Acts. Her aggressive environmental posture helped win her the primary endorsement of the New York State League of Conservation Voters and the race to replace the popular Republican Congressman Hamilton Fish, Jr. Yet after only seven months in office, Kelly had earned the enmity of both local and national environmentalists for her slavish support of the 104th Congress' program to dismantle twenty-five years of environmental law. She had received an approval rating of only 18 percent from the Washington-based League of Conservation Voters.

At the demonstration, the press wanted to know how an environmental hotbed like the Hudson River Valley had produced such an anti-environmental renegade. John Cronin explained, "To understand Sue Kelly, you need look no farther than her model, Newt Gingrich."

A Sierra Club member from 1984 to 1990, Newt Gingrich started his congressional career with an environmental platform, fighting for a tougher Clean Air Act, and calling acid rain legislation "the next most important issue" after banishing South African apartheid. All the while Gingrich was quietly currying favor with well-heeled polluters back home. He finally abandoned environmentalism in 1990 for the warm embrace of the New Right, its money, and its powerful corporate friends, and began schooling a new generation of Republicans in ideological warfare and fund-raising. Armed with Gingrich's leadership and large infusions of industry cash, they staged a historic takeover of the House and prepared to do industry bidding with a recklessness that was breathtaking.

The environment was the first loyalty test for the members of the realigned House of Representatives, and Sue Kelly had quickly caved to the pressure. Industry money helped make this the most anti-environmental Congress in history. Without once mentioning the word explicitly, Gingrich's Contract with America took aim at the environment with a legislative program that would strip the nation of most of its federal environmental protections.

Gingrich's majority whip, Tom DeLay, was a former pesticide salesman who branded the EPA "the Gestapo of Government." DeLay identified the Endangered Species Act as the second greatest threat to Texas after illegal aliens and called for the lifting of the ban on mirex and DDT, which he labeled "safe as aspirin." Gingrich chose DeLay as the revolution's chief of environmental policy and assigned him the task of drafting and managing the Contract's environmental provisions. DeLay invited a group of 350 lobbyists representing some of America's biggest polluters to collaborate with him in drafting legislation to dismantle federal health, safety, and environmental laws. Their initial barrage was a stealth attack—a series of "supermandates" concealed in the Contract, each designed to eviscerate whole bodies of environmental law without debate.

One of these, the Takings Bill, purported to protect property rights but masked an initiative giving constitutional protection to the right to pollute. It required environmental agencies to use federal tax dollars to pay polluters and landowners to comply with the Clean Water Act, the Endangered Species Act, and federal wetlands laws. Another, the Unfunded Mandates Bill, ostensibly protected states and localities from being bullied by Washington legislators. Actually it erected new procedural hurdles to prevent Congress from creating national environmental standards such as those regulating contaminants in municipal drinking water supplies and reducing fish kills at power plants. An amendment that would have exempted laws that protected children's health was handily defeated.

The worst of DeLay's bills was the so-called Regulatory Reform Bill, which, under the pretense of encouraging smaller government, employed a complex legal mechanism to give polluters veto power over all health and environmental laws, and established new bureaucracy and technical requirements designed to tie federal agencies in knots.

Far from streamlining government, these laws were intended to paralyze it. They were driven by industry money and by the 104th Congress' virulent, mindless antigovernment fever. After every item in Congress' stealth attack against the environment passed the House within the first one hundred days, congressional bomb throwers unveiled their direct assault.

Legislators invited their favorite industry lobbyists to rewrite key environmental statutes, including the Clean Water Act and the Endangered Species Act. Congressman Bud Shuster of Pennsylvania, chairman of the Transportation and Infrastructure Committee, sponsored a reauthorization of the Clean Water Act written by lobbyists for the chemical, food, metal finishing, petroleum, strip mining, and paper industries that was promptly dubbed the Dirty Water Bill. Shuster's bill relaxed restrictions on dumping sewage and toxins into our nation's waters, weakened regulations of fish kills by power plants, removed as much as 80 percent of the nation's wetlands from federal protection, and required that the government pay landowners to protect the rest.

Don Young's Extinction Bill rewrote the Endangered Species Act to allow species to go extinct unless their current economic value exceeded the financial benefit of destroying them. The Superfund rewrite removed the central requirement that polluters pay to clean up after themselves, putting the burden instead upon taxpayers. Legislation by James Hansen of Utah created a Parks Closing Commission that would have put three hundred national parks on the auction block to the highest bidder from the timber, oil, or mineral industry. In April, the Republicans forced

Clinton to sign the Timber Salvage Bill (by attaching it as a rider to leg-islation providing vital relief to the victims of the Oklahoma City bombing and the L.A. riots), reopening the National Forests to 1950s-style clear-cutting. Gingrich's majority leader Dick Armey promised to "close down the Environmental Protection Agency" and slashed the EPA's fiscal year 1996 budget by 34 percent, a cut that would leave the agency structure in place but all its personnel gone or paralyzed.

Big polluters drafted over a hundred bills designed to dramatically weaken or eliminate environmental laws and attached them as riders to the budget bills. The EPA Appropriations Bill became a wish list for corporate polluters, and the Interior Department Appropriations Bill became a natural resources bazaar for western timber, oil, and cattle barons where the public trust was dispensed at bargain-basement prices. The freshmen threatened to shut down the government if Clinton refused to sign them.

Dan Shaefer of Colorado, the chairman of the House Subcommittee on Energy and Power, defended the new drafting method for its efficiency: "We go to industry and we ask industry, 'What is it we can do to make your job easier and to help you in this competitive world we have?' rather than writing legislation and having industry comment on what we write."

The 104th Congress was swinging a sledgehammer at a cornerstone of contemporary American democracy and undermining the most extraordinary body of environmental law in the world. Instead of empowering the citizenry through regulatory reform, the Gingrich revolution sought to remove power from local communities and deliver it to corporate board rooms. Emboldened by the brazen new Congress, states raced to undo environmental protection laws and regulations passed by previous legislatures. In the Hudson Valley, virtually all environmental enforcement ceased as the state regulatory agency reacted to the federal trends. In the midst of the New York City watershed negotiations, we watched the EPA's resolve to protect drinking water collapse as the agency reacted to the battering it was taking in Washington. The EPA became a piñata for upstate development interests, doling out gifts of compromised water quality at every blow. With the rapidity of a California-to–New York red-eye, anti-environmental forces across the nation pulled together a massive legislative agenda virtually overnight.

The juggernaut appeared unstoppable. National environmental groups considered the transformation of the Hudson Valley's most secure pro-environment congressional seat into an anti-environmental vote a harbinger of worse things to come. To many it looked like the age of environmentalism was over. Even our oldest friends in Congress would not take our calls. Newspapers, mesmerized by the social aspects of Newt's revolution, considered the environmental issue an abstraction. Some environmental groups were folding their tents and talking about how we had to abandon health and safety standards for a "free market system" as they watched twenty-five years of legislative work crumble in one hundred days. One national environmental leader called Bobby to announce he was going to quit his job. "They are tough and well funded," he said, "and they're winning."

Gingrich claimed that his vision simply gave voice to the majority of Americans who wanted the federal government off their backs. But the Gingrich vision and the anti-environmental agenda of the 104th Congress had in fact been written by a decades-old coalition of industry attorneys, public relations geniuses, and scientific hacks who had been waiting for this moment in the sun ever since their ignominious defeat at the hands of a mild-mannered but indomitable marine biologist named Rachel Carson.

Without living long enough to hear it proclaimed, Rachel Carson came to be regarded as the mother of the contemporary environmental movement. It is doubtful the modest scientist would have accepted the accolade. But she would have been the first to recognize that the very same interests that had attacked her 1962 book, *Silent Spring,* were the first link in an unbroken chain that led to the architects of the 104th Congress.

With the publication of *Silent Spring,* Carson riveted America's attention on the coming age of environmental horrors. Following World War II the Department of Agriculture and a robust young chemical industry were promoting DDT, the chemical that promised America the unchallenged position as food supplier to the world. With meticulous scholarship, Carson showed Americans how pesticides were exterminating their songbirds, waterfowl, raptors, and game fish, killing their domestic animals with monotonous regularity, and threatening humans with cancer and sterility. She realized that her conclusions would threaten the core financial interests of a powerful $300 million industry with strong governmental allies. Anticipating possible criticism for inaccuracy, she carefully checked and rechecked every fact, assuring that each statement had at least three references. Carson asked sixteen experts to review the text and comment on it prior to publication. She provided fifty-five pages of notes and cited specific authorities throughout the book for the various propositions.

Nonetheless, as soon as the *New Yorker* magazine published the first of a three-part prepublication condensation of *Silent Spring* in June 1962, the chemical industry mounted a deliberate and expensive public relations attack designed to destroy Carson's credibility. The Monsanto Company, a major chemical manufacturer of pesticides and PCBs, threatened to sue Carson and her publishers if the book was released, and implicated her in a communist plot to cripple American agriculture.

Other chemical companies threatened to withhold advertising from garden magazines and weekly supplements should they publish favorable reviews of *Silent Spring*. The industry invested millions in public relations, which paid off in supportive articles from the mainstream press including the *New York Times, Time, Sports Illustrated,* and *Reader's Digest*. The American Medical Association, one of the targets of the industry barrage, criticized Carson's book as "a serious threat to the continued supply of wholesome nutritious food . . ." and urged its members to contact the pesticide industry if their patients had any safety questions.

Despite these attacks, the book was a popular sensation, selling 100,000 copies by December and climbing to the top of the best-seller list where it remained for a record eighty-six weeks. Carson, dying of cancer, largely let the attacks go unanswered, gratified by the public support of many internationally known scientists.

Carson's final dramatic vindication came in a report prepared by President Kennedy's Scientific Advisory Committee, which had spent eight arduous months investigating the facts of *Silent Spring*. The report condemned the USDA and chemical industry scientists and recommended that the government eliminate the use of persistent toxic pesticides. The report endorsed all the principal findings of Carson's book and closed with praise for its author.

By the end of 1963, forty states had introduced pesticide legislation. But Carson's book did not just expose the dangers of toxic chemicals. It questioned the unrestrained control of the national environment by special interests, who were abetted by government allies, and ignited the generation of activists who founded the environmental movement and celebrated the first Earth Day.

The message of Earth Day resounded with the same democratic principles Carson had expressed in her final public appearance seven years earlier when she testified before Congress. With the knowledge of her impending death from cancer, she urged the committee to consider what she termed "a much neglected problem, that of the right of the citizen to be secure in his own home against the intrusion of poisons applied by other persons. I speak not as a lawyer," she said, "but as a biologist and as a human being, but I strongly feel that this is or should be one of the basic human rights."

The notion of environmental protection as a basic human right represented a greater threat to industry than the banning of DDT. For those industries benefiting heavily from environmental subsidies or reliant on pollution, environmental regulation represented a genuine threat to their profit margins. Many of these concluded that the best return on investment was not in retooling their plants, retraining workers, or research and development but by investing it in political clout to thwart the application of environmental laws.

By funneling huge sums of money to compliant politicians, the pesticide industry evaded regulation of its deadly products by having its political foot soldiers insert a "cost-benefit" analysis provision in the federal Insecticide, Fungicide and Rodentide Act (FIFRA). This provision made it next to impossible for the EPA to remove a pesticide from the market. In the thirty-some years since Carson's book was written, only sixteen of six hundred chemical pesticides used on foods have been removed. Today we use ten times the amount of pesticides that we did at the time when Rachel Carson died.

The pesticide industry wasn't alone with the incentive and capacity to manipulate the political process to advantage. Over the coming years, similarly affected industries—lumber, coal, power, tobacco, mineral, oil, and automobile—would pay hundreds of millions of dollars in direct political contributions to industry-friendly candidates, industry lawyers, public relations geniuses, and trade associations to promote their antiregulatory political agenda. These investments played a key role in creating the advent of the 104th Congress.

★　　　★　　　★

235

The techniques used by the pesticide industry in their attempt to discredit Rachel Carson have been refined and widely employed to advance industry's anti-environmental agenda. The pioneer of corporate public relations campaigning has been the tobacco industry. In 1958, the public relations firm Hill and Knowlton helped create the Tobacco Institute, which today is a $20-million-a-year effort that has successfully shielded an industry that kills 10 percent of its customers from regulations that might interfere with corporate profit taking. Other industries also employ PR firms to promote stories portraying environmentalists as hysterical and antihuman or driven by sinister socialist agendas, and to argue that environmental protection will cost jobs and destroy the economy. They create phony think tanks and front organizations and retain crackpot scientists to persuade the public that global threats from overpopulation, ozone layer depletion, pesticides, depleted fisheries, or global warming are illusory.

By 1990, according to *PR Watch,* U.S. businesses were spending an estimated $500 million on hiring the services of anti-environmental PR professionals and "greenwashing" their corporate image. That number doubled to $1 billion by 1995. That year, the top fifteen firms took in $100 million in environmental PR.

Among the most successful greenwash consultants is E. Bruce Harrison who, in 1962, at age thirty, served as the pesticide industry's "manager for environmental information" charged with orchestrating the smear campaign against Rachel Carson and *Silent Spring.* Harrison, now the president of his own company, has written a book on greenwashing: *Going Green: How to Communicate Your Company's Environmental Commitment,* which uses corporatespeak to teach polluters how to use scientific misinformation, emotional appeals, front groups, and mailings; how to recruit doctors and scientists; how to create grassroots groups to serve as "objective" third parties in the battle to defend corporate profit making.

Harrison's company does $6 million worth of annual greenwashing for the likes of Coors, Clorox, R. J. Reynolds, Vista Chemical, Uniroyal and General Motors, Dow Chemical, Union Carbide, Monsanto, Laidlaw Waste Systems, Ford, and AT&T.

Probably the best-known greenwasher is Burson-Marsteller, which took in nearly $18 million in 1993 on its environmental PR projects. Burson-Marsteller (B-M), the world's largest PR firm, made its bones whitewashing Argentina's "dirty war," Ceauşescu's murderous Romanian regime, and South Korea's human rights abuses. Exxon and Union Carbide hired B-M to "greenwash" the *Valdez* spill and the deadly Bhopal chemical explosions, respectively. In 1990 Bobby battled the company in Quebec, where B-M is pushing Hydro-Quebec's efforts to drown the largest wilderness area in eastern North America, and two years later on Clayoquot Sound in British Columbia, where B-M's client, MacMillan Bloedel, is cutting the earth's largest intact coastal temperate rain forest against the wishes of Indian owners. In Clayoquot Sound, B-M has helped to create phony grassroots groups on behalf of the Canadian timber industry to persuade the public that old-growth harvesting is sustainable and that the government should deregulate the industry.

A prime tactic of each of these firms is to discredit environmentalists who oppose the client's interests. In 1994 Bobby gave a speech to Canadian forestry activists and NRDC members in New York City on forest protection in British Columbia. Two public relations officials from B-M's timber industry–funded "grassroots" group attended the speech and then reported a phony version to an industry-friendly reporter. The reporter published the fake statements, critical of Prime Minister Harcourt and the British Columbian people, as if he had attended the speech and provided them to the *Vancouver Sun,* another Burson-Marsteller client. Before he was even aware of the controversy, Bobby had been officially declared persona non grata by the government of British Columbia.

In August 1991, Greenpeace obtained a revealing memo prepared by Ketchum Public Relations for its client, Clorox Corporation, for dealing with new studies showing that the chlorine derivatives in its household products were highly carcinogenic. Among the tactics recommended by Ketchum to counter anticipated criticism from environmentalists and the press were labeling environmentalists as "terrorists" or "irrational," suing "unalterably green journalists" for slander, enlisting the support of unions to defend Clorox in the name of saving jobs, and dispatching teams of "independent" scientists to serve as "ambassadors" to the media and government officials.

Over the past decade, industry has spent hundreds of millions creating phony groups with deceptive names to carry on lobbying and public relations or to pose as scientists or experts in order to persuade Americans that the environmental crisis is a myth. In 1976, public relations firms created the U.S. Council of Energy Awareness, with a $20 million annual budget paid by the nuclear industry, to promote commercial nuclear power.

The deceptively named Citizens for the Environment (CFE) has no citizen membership but gets its support from a long list of corporate sponsors who use the organization to lobby against the Clean Air Act and all other environmental regulations. The Environmental Conservation Organization is a front group for land developers and other businesses opposed to wetlands regulations. The Evergreen Foundation is a timber-industry front group that tries to promote the idea that clear-cut logging is beneficial to the environment. The National Wetlands Coalition, whose logo features a duck rising off a wetland, is a coalition of oil drillers and large real estate companies opposed to wetlands regulations. Citizens for Sensible Control of Acid Rain is a phony grassroots front opposed to *all* controls of acid rain. Created by paid public relations consultants for the oil and electric industry, this group was the biggest-spending political lobby in Washington in 1986.

There are hundreds more of these groups. They pop up wherever there is an environmental controversy. In 1992 Riverkeeper was forced to trademark the "Keeper" name because it became so attractive to polluters organizing phony grassroots groups. For example, the upper Delaware Riverkeeper was organized by real estate developers in the Catskill region with the stated purpose to fight water quality regulations on the upper Delaware. More recently, the notorious polluter Con Edison tried to create a "Bronx Riverkeeper" as a corporate mouthpiece.

Using these front groups, industry bombards Americans with a steady stream of propaganda on radio and television talk shows, editorial pages, and hard-news outlets, while keeping both audiences and news reporters ignorant about the true source of the misinformation. Most Americans are shocked to learn that the famous "America the Beautiful" television ads that ran during the 1970s and 1980s featuring an American Indian shedding a tear over a littered street was a critical element of a stealth campaign to derail Bottle Bill legislation in the United States. "America the Beautiful" is a corporate front group of the aluminum and glass industry that was able to use its nonprofit status to garner over $550 million in free air time at taxpayer expense. The weeping Indian ad was meant to shift the guilt about pollution from the bottling industry to the consumer.

238

Most of these front groups are letterhead organizations with no membership, but in some cases the industries have organized a kind of hybrid grassroots organization that relies on paid professional organizers and a large flow of dollars.

The tobacco industry, which kills 400,000 of its customers annually in America alone, can claim credit for perfecting the use of grassroots front groups. The National Smokers Alliance, created by Burson-Marsteller with millions of Philip Morris dollars, has become the model for corporate grassroots campaigning. The alliance uses full-page newspaper ads, direct telemarketing, paid canvassers, free 800 numbers, and newsletters to bring thousands of smokers into its ranks each week. By 1995, the NSA claimed a membership of three million smokers. The campaign's game is to rile up and mobilize a committed cadre of foot soldiers in a grassroots political operation directed by Burson-Marsteller to produce the illusion of broad public interest and participation opposed to tobacco regulations.

The tobacco industry's success has helped make "AstroTurf organizing" an industry unto itself. Dozens of PR firms specialize in organizing "grassroots" support for the oil, chemical, and extractive industries and for big mall developers. "Company employees usually form the core of any AstroTurf environmental group," James Lindheim, Burson-Marsteller's director of public affairs, told Joyce Nelson of *Chemistry and Industry* magazine in 1989. "Don't forget, the chemical industry has many friends and allies that can be mobilized . . . employees, shareholders, and retirees. Give them the song sheets and let them help industry carry the tune."

Industry fronts adopted the tactics that authentic grassroots groups developed during the 1970s—telephone, fax, and letter-writing campaigns; research reports, public testimony, lobbying, forming political coalitions. They also use advertising, press releases, public testimony, bogus surveys, and public opinion polls, and generally disseminate disinformation to the press and hate-radio jocks. They use telemarketing techniques that, for the right price, can flood a congressional office with thousands of phony "constituent" letters and telegrams in a single day. These groups not only deceive the public and some politicians but also support certain politicians who want to do industry's bidding and need "grassroots support" for political cover.

★          ★          ★

Beginning in the late 1980s, industry money and a cadre of professional grassroots organizers and charismatic leaders from the radical right helped create a hybridized grassroots movement that would help industry take over Congress and make naked anti-environmentalism politically acceptable even in the Hudson Valley.

The new movement found its roots in the American West where stockmen, large farmers, and mining and timber companies have dominated the political landscape for over a century. Western historians call them "boomers." Teddy Roosevelt called them "land grabbers." Today they are known as "welfare cowboys."

The boomers grew fat exploiting subsidized water and grasslands originally made available to their forebears by a federal government eager to encourage western pioneering. They cut timber below cost and dug minerals for free at great loss to U.S. taxpayers.

They made billions each year denuding National Forest lands, turning public lands into desert, sucking salmon streams dry, robbing our nation's mineral wealth and leaving behind thousands of miles of polluted streams and great expanses of wilderness poisoned with deadly mine wastes. The boomers converted their federally subsidized economic success into a political power base that maintained their system of socialism for the rich. The unfortunate workers employed in these destructive industries became the frightened armies of their movement.

In 1976, the Carter administration adopted legislation requiring federal land managers to start granting equal priority to all uses of federal lands including those that compete with grazing and mineral extraction. At the same time, hunters, hikers, and fly fishermen began taking an increased interest in desert land. Their subsidies threatened, boomers declared that these federal land policies amounted to a "war on the West." Wealthy ranchers and miners demanded greater access to public lands for grazing, logging, and mining. The cattlemen and timber companies who started what came to be known as the Sagebrush Rebellion were largely successful because they managed to broaden their constituency with an antiregulatory, antilabor, and anti-environmental rhetoric that had great appeal in certain western communities where hostility to government and dependence on federal subsidies are deeply rooted. They found that with large amounts of money, they could organize this discontent into a political force that would support their continued profit taking.

The first westerner to contribute serious funds was the Colorado brewer Joseph Coors, whose fortune relied heavily on federal natural resources subsidies and pollution-based profits. Coors was one of the largest polluters in Colorado. He cut the initial $250,000 check that opened the right-wing Heritage Foundation, which would help construct the philosophical underpinning of the anti-environmental Wise Use movement. Heritage's function is to produce—at lightning speed—short, concise policy analyses of fast-breaking issues. These simple position papers go out to thousands of news directors and journalists, congressional offices, public officials, and, more recently, talk-radio jocks. Through clever invocations of patriotism, Christianity, and laissez-faire capitalism, Heritage offers pithy philosophical justification for national policies that promote the narrow interests of a wealthy few.

Not surprisingly, Heritage claims to advocate open markets and property rights, but its agenda is more pro-pollution than anything else. The foundation dismisses global warming, acid rain, and other environmental crises as "henny pennyism." In a recent forum, leading conservatives writing in Heritage's *Policy Review* urged their followers to "strangle the environmental movement," which they named "the greatest single threat to the American economy." Heritage's prominence as the leading voice for pollution-based prosperity helped it attract giant donations from the automobile, coal, oil, and chemical companies and right-wing foundations that currently contribute $23 million toward its annual funding.

Just as the Heritage Foundation became an imitation of a think tank, Coors founded the Mountain States Legal Foundation in 1976 to mimic the work of public-interest organizations like the Natural Resources Defense Council, which fought the frontline legal battles for the environmental movement. Funded by major companies such as Phillips Petroleum, Marathon Oil, Amoco, Shell, and Chevron, it filed nuisance suits to block efforts by environmentalist unions and racial minorities that might slow the companies' easy profits.

That alliance between wealthy western extractive industries and a radical right-wing antigovernment element helped Ronald Reagan win the presidency and laid the foundation for building the Wise Use movement. "I am a Sagebrush Rebel," candidate Reagan declared in 1980.

After Reagan's inauguration, the people who had funded the new institutions such as the Heritage Foundation and the Mountain States Legal Foundation found themselves with immeasurable power. Heritage became known as Reagan's "shadow government." Its opus "Mandate for Change" became the blueprint for the Reagan revolution. Joe Coors was one of the most prominent of the right-wing millionaires who now constituted Reagan's "Kitchen Cabinet." Reagan gave them an office in the Executive Office Building directly across from the White House where they set priorities and recruited appointees.

Coors handpicked his Colorado associate Anne Gorsuch Burford to administer the Environmental Protection Agency and her husband, Colorado rancher Chuck Burford, who for years had vowed to destroy the Bureau of Land Management, as head of the BLM. For the post of Secretary of the Interior Coors chose James Watt, president of Mountain States Legal Foundation. Watt was a proponent of "dominion theology," an authoritarian Christian heresy that advocates man's duty to "subdue" nature. His deep faith in laissez-faire capitalism and apocalyptic Christianity led Watt to set about dismantling his department and distributing its assets rather than managing them for future generations. He explained to the Senate Interior and Insular Affairs Committee, "I do not know how many future generations we can count on before the Lord returns." Watt believed that environmentalism was a plot to delay energy development and "weaken America," and dismissed environmentalists as "a left-wing cult which seeks to bring down the type of government I believe in." As secretary, Watt sold off public lands and water and mineral rights at what the General Accounting Office called "fire sale prices."

Similarly, Anne Gorsuch Burford enthusiastically cut the EPA's budget by 60 percent, crippling the agency's ability to enforce the law. She purposely destroyed the Superfund program at its birth, reducing it to a welfare program for industry lawyers. She appointed lobbyists fresh from their hitches with the paper, asbestos, chemical, and oil companies to run each of the principal agency departments. Her chief counsel was an Exxon lawyer; her enforcement chief was from General Motors.

Toward the end of the Reagan era, however, the Sagebrush Rebellion began to collapse under its own internal inconsistencies and unpopularity with the public. Western hunters and fishermen, who had formed the populist base of the rebellion, realized that privatization of federal lands would fence them off from public resources. By 1983, more than a million people had signed a petition demanding Watt's removal. After being forced out of office, he was indicted on twenty-five felony counts. Burford and twenty-three of her cronies were forced to resign from the EPA following a congressional investigation of sweetheart deals with polluters, including Coors. Her first deputy, Rita Lavelle, was jailed.

The indictments and resignations put a temporary damper on the boomers, but they soon recouped in a new iteration, the Wise Use movement, born in August 1988, at a three-day conference at the Nugget Hotel in Reno, Nevada. The meeting's 250 sponsors were a motley assortment of right-wing funders and subsidy-grubbing lobbies: the Reverend Sun Myung Moon's American Freedom Coalition, the NRA, Exxon, Du Pont, Boise Cascade, Louisiana Pacific, the beneficiaries of cheap federal lands (the Farm Bureau, the Cattlemen's Association, the National Association of Wheat Growers, and the Idaho Wool Growers Association), James Watt's Mountain States Legal Foundation, Reed Irvine's Accuracy in Media, as well as fifty off-road vehicle (ORV) clubs funded by Japanese manufacturers.

The conference produced a booklet outlining the twenty-five goals that constituted the Wise Use agenda, including proposals to open all wilderness areas and national parks to mineral and energy production; rewrite the Endangered Species Act to remove "nonadaptive species such as the California condor"; make anyone protesting corporate activities liable for civil damages; allow immediate oil drilling in the Arctic National Wildlife Refuge and immediate clear-cutting of Alaska's Tongass National Forest; maintain all subsidies to mining companies; transfer control of federal water resources to the states; extend pesticide patents; and grant new rights for industries to sue environmentalists who are blocking corporate activities. In other words, Wise Use meant Corporate Use.

The Reno conference's organizer and Wise Use's principal architect was Ron Arnold, a former public relations director for big lumber. Writing in a lumber industry trade journal several years earlier, Arnold had outlined the strategy that would become the heart of the Reno conference. Industry must "destroy the environmental movement by employing the same activist techniques that have been so devastating in environmentalists' hands." Arnold was convinced that by using industry money and new communications technologies, it was possible to create not just an industry front group of the kind the PR firms were building but a genuine movement that would "orchestrate public hearings, to sue in the courts, to lobby in Congress, to pressure administrations and in general, to out Sierra Club the Sierra Club." This could be done by organizing the thousands of people outside and within industry who have a direct economic stake in eliminating environmental protection.

By using its vast financial resources, Arnold urged, industry could control its destiny in the courts and Congress, actually dictating favorable legislation through its grassroots arms "guided by signals from the forestry industry's professional lobbyists."

After the Reno conference, Wise Use proponents began targeting small communities in the East and West with propaganda that made the environmental movement a convenient scapegoat for rural poverty actually caused by the contractions in the timber, ranching, and extraction industries. Again and again, industry-paid organizers distorted complex economic situations into a simple, yet erroneous, ultimatum—jobs versus owls.

Following Reno, hundreds of small Wise Use groups began to pop up across the West. Usually they focused on some local issue—protecting development, lumber, mining, or grazing. While a few had genuine grassroots support, most were industry front groups posing as grassroots movements. Though small in number and dependent on constant funding by industry, these "grassroots" groups had a disproportionate impact because of their access to tremendous industry resources, the right wing's network of think tanks, and sympathetic hate-radio jocks like Bob Grant and Rush Limbaugh. They fought to exempt industry from toxics laws, to open wilderness and national parks to clear-cutting and lumber extractions, and to prevent wetlands from being protected. At the same time, they gave industry and politicians the cover they needed to pretend that there is a real national debate over the objectives of the environmental movement.

In the eastern states where rural communities were less accustomed to giant federal handouts, Wise Use groups funded by developers and mall builders discovered their most potent weapon in "private property rights" or "unconstitutional takings"—the notion that by passing laws to protect the public, government was stealing private property.

The property rights emphasis represented a key strategic shift for the Wise Use movement. It was, according to Tarso Ramos, executive director of the Western States Center, who monitors Wise Use, "a strategy to move beyond the rural West and find issues that would tap into the larger demographic base in suburban America." In the property rights issue, the Wise Use movement found a way to wrap its agenda in the American flag. Wise Use could now characterize its concerns as a "little guys" issue, by focusing on the protection of the "private property rights of small landowners"—building and zoning codes, wetlands laws, and coastal zone and beach erosion statutes.

"As an organizing strategy, takings is a kind of deviant genius," Tarso Ramos said. "It automatically puts environmentalists in the position of defending the federal government and appeals to anyone who has ever had any kind of negative experience with the federal government, which is a hell of a lot of people."

The Wise Use "property rights" strategy found supporters in the Delaware River watershed and the Delaware County section of the New York City watershed. During the New York City watershed negotiations, the watershed towns and their attorneys examined every significant land use issue through this new lens of "property rights." The Builders Institute, a Westchester developer's group, sued to hold up our watershed agreement on the theory that restrictions on pollution represented a "taking" of their property rights. Although such suits were mostly meritless, they had a chilling effect on state and local officials. In December 1994, a popular proposal by Ulster County, New York, residents to declare the Catskill Mountains to be a biosphere reserve suddenly encountered resistance during a hearing conducted by the Ulster County legislature. The proposal was withdrawn when property rights advocates shouted it down as part of a conspiracy to establish a one-world government known as the New World Order.

The most important vector for carrying the Wise Use property rights movement's anti-environmental agenda into a central plank of the new Republican Party's agenda was the so-called Christian Right.

From its inception the Wise Use movement has been closely linked to a handful of powerful right-wing authoritarian Christian leaders who have brought the anti-environmental movement grassroots support and money, and anointed industry self-interest with a kind of moral legitimacy. For instance, the Reverend Sun Myung Moon's Unification Church, which owns the right-wing *Washington Times,* underwrote the costs of the Reno Conference and provided seed money for dozens of Wise Use groups.

But Pat Robertson's Christian Coalition packaged the most effective attack. Robertson's special contribution to right-wing theology was to substitute environmentalists for communists as the new threat to democracy and Christianity. Robertson's cosmology posits a diabolical role for environmentalists. Robertson believes that an international conspiracy by Jewish bankers and environmentalists, which now controls the United Nations, is poised to impose the New World Order.

In his 1991 best-seller, *The New World Order,* he vilifies the federal government as an alien nation waging war on the family and disarming America through gun control laws. Environmentalists are the evil priests of a new paganism that will be the official state religion of the New World Order. These ravings would hardly be worth mentioning had they not played such an important role in fueling the ideological underpinnings of the anti-environmental movement and the zealotry of its followers. His aggressive anti-environmental proselytizing has opened the door for Christian extremists and white supremacists from the fringe who enthusiastically adopted the issue for their own purposes. But Robertson has also helped make anti-environmentalism acceptable within the ranks of the fundamentalist clergy and the mainstream of the Republican Party. The Christian Coalition, with 1.7 million members, now dominates the party in eighteen states and enjoys substantial power in fifteen more. Beginning in 1991, Robertson and the Christian Coalition's executive director, Ralph Reed, put their media and organizational clout at the disposal of the Wise Use agenda. While Robertson made anti-environmentalism a principal theme on his Christian Broadcasting Network talk shows, news hours, and documentaries, Reed gave seminars to corporate PR executives, coaching them to use electronic technologies and phony grassroots organizing to foil environmentalists who interfere with corporate profits.

Robertson's brand of paranoia has always had a place in American politics, from the populist movement to Father Coughlin to the John Birch Society. That paranoid tradition has been able to achieve limited political power based upon the intensity of its proponents—but until

1994, it was never able to achieve the kind of real power that only comes from money. Suddenly the extractive and chemical industries, their profits threatened by new environmental laws, saw the right wing's anti-environmentalism as a key to continued profitability and donated the funds that sent its candidates to Congress.

While industry made itself an expert at distorting the political process, it also distorted truth at its most fundamental level. Although the scientific paragon strives only for truth, individual scientists are often captured by monied interests. On the Hudson River, from Storm King to Westway, we have seen industry money corrupt talented scientists, and "respectable" consulting firms produce the most outlandish conclusions to justify their client's rapacity. Figures don't lie, the saying goes, but liars figure.

It is therefore not surprising that industry uses the same techniques to corrupt science on a grander scale. Using tricks perfected by the tobacco industry in its successful strategy to shield its product from forty years of scientific bad news, industry and its right-wing allies have produced motley collections of creationists, assorted hired guns, and "biostitutes" to persuade the public that there are no environmental crises.

Phony scientific research in the guise of the Council for Tobacco Research has long shielded tobacco products from the legal prohibitions imposed on other deadly and addictive drugs.

In the late 1980s, "cigarette science" became the corporate public relations strategy of other industries interested in raising phony scientific doubts about a health or environmental threat. Polluting industries and right-wing foundations began investing billions of dollars in phony scientific research. They funded a series of right-wing think tanks that cranked out scientific and economic papers designed to persuade Americans that pesticides are harmless and global warming a myth. These papers have claimed that Mount Pinatubo, not chlorofluorocarbons, caused the ozone hole; caribou "love the pipeline"; trees are the principal cause of air pollution; the Northern California forests are filled with "thousands of spotted owls"; cigarettes don't cause cancer; clear-cutting is good forest management; dioxin is harmless; and overpopulation is not a problem.

Employing the tactics devised by the Heritage Foundation, these think tanks gave business and the Far Right the capacity to circumvent the university system that was the traditional source of scientific research. Industry found that "scientists" came cheaper than lobbyists and began stabling them in Washington think tanks where they concentrated less on science and more on reducing corporate self-interest to palatable platitudes.

Instead of laboring on scientific research, these scientists produce two-page ideologically based briefing papers that are usable by the political system. The "science" is often erroneous and oversimplified, but a congressman can read it on his way to the airport and recite it in a speech. Busy journalists are grateful for the slick, easy-to-understand packaging. "At the shallowest level it's a cheap deception of the general public," says scientist Michael Oppenheimer. "You create high-sounding credentials and talk in tones that seem scientifically sensible while all the time you are just fronting for a political agenda."

One pro-nuke think tank, the Committee for a Constructive Tomorrow, was founded in 1985 purportedly "to protect our fragile environment." C-FACT uses tax-deductible industry money to crank out "scientific" papers opposing garbage recycling, energy conservation, federal air and water quality standards, pesticide control, and efforts to protect the ozone layer; it fights to repeal the Endangered Species Act. These skeptical pronouncements are regularly repeated in the Moon-controlled *Washington Times,* in the Christian Coalition publications, and in the mainstream media.

Another oft-quoted source of misinformation is the Marshall Institute, which was the most aggressive promoter of Star Wars during the Reagan era and now publishes half-baked papers challenging ozone depletion and global warming. Marshall's seven-man board includes representatives from Lockheed and the Electric Power Research Institute, a research and lobbying arm of the electric power industry. These and dozens of other phony science groups work alongside PR firms to promote their environmental positions with the press and policy makers.

Among the most versatile sources of industry-sponsored counter-science is Fred Singer, a retired University of Virginia professor who makes his living posing as a neutral scientist while spouting pro-industry pronouncements on topics as diverse as whaling and fuel efficiency in automobiles. Singer's Science and Environmental Policy Project (SEPP) receives funding from the western coal industry, Exxon, Shell,

ARCO, UNOCAL, Sun Oil, and others who profit from the burning of fossil fuels. SEPP's goal is to discredit global warming, ozone depletion, and acid rain as politically motivated fantasies. Singer claims that the peril of global warming is a fiction, or, eventually, that it will benefit the planet by increasing agricultural production. Conversely, he argues that environmental regulations "have catastrophic impacts on the world economy, on jobs, standards of living, and health care."

Singer is often quoted in the mainstream press as an expert on ozone depletion. A June 13, 1994, *Business Week* editorial, based on an interview with Singer, concluded that the chlorofluorocarbon ban resulted from "ozone depletion hysteria" and "speculative theorizing." *Business Week* identified Singer as "the University of Virginia scientist who invented the satellite ozone monitor" and says that Singer "has noted that no global reduction of ozone levels has been detected."

True, Singer was at the forefront of satellite probe technology during the late 1950s, but a computer search of peer-reviewed journals yields not one article by Singer on the ozone controversy in the last quarter of a century. He does not appear at recognized scientific conferences where ozone depletion is discussed. Instead, Singer publishes his work in pamphlets and press releases for public consumption.

While mainstream scientists publish quietly in peer-reviewed scientific journals like *Nature* and *Science,* reaching a tiny number of interested specialists, Mobil Oil pays for Fred Singer to appear on op-ed pages, television programs like *Nightline,* and before Congress.

Another master of the anti-environmental counterscience movement is Panamanian-born writer Rogelio Maduro, an editor of Lyndon LaRouche's periodical *21st Century and Technology,* and coauthor of *The Holes in the Ozone Scare,* also published by LaRouche. LaRouche is a right-wing paranoid who believes the Queen of England runs the world drug trade and that the KGB—in cahoots with Jewish overlords—is using environmentalism to achieve a new world order; only LaRouche possesses the genius to avert this disaster. Rogelio Maduro is LaRouche's staff science advisor. He claims that DDT, PCBs, and CFCs are victims of slander concocted by sinister environmental "catastrophists" bent on depriving the world of refrigeration, malarial control, a reliable food supply, and safe electricity in an effort to reduce world population to facilitate the takeover.

Maduro's bizarre and demonstrably erroneous theory that ancient volcanic eruptions, not man-made chemicals, caused the Antarctic ozone hole has made him a darling of the New Right. His theories have been trumpeted by right-wing gurus like the late Dixy Lee Ray and Rush Limbaugh. Maduro's convoluted fantasies are the basis of the environmental chapters in Rush Limbaugh's national best-seller, *The Way Things Ought to Be.*

Relying on Maduro's ravings, the right wing–dominated Arizona legislature passed a statute in 1995 allowing the manufacture of ozone-depleting chlorofluorocarbons within the state in direct violation of federal laws and the Montreal Protocol, the international agreement to phase out production of ozone-depleting chemicals.

In September 1995, Republican Whip Tom DeLay sponsored a bill that would effectively repeal the Montreal Protocol. A more moderate bill by Representative John Doolittle, a California Republican, would push back the ban from 1997 to the year 2000. Later DeLay, Doolittle, and California Republican Dana Rohrabacher, Chairman of the House Science Committee's Energy and Environment Subcommittee, announced three special hearings on "Scientific Integrity and Public Trust." The ironic purpose of these hearings was to put an end, "once and for all, to faulty science" by environmental advocates.

During one heated exchange about the proposed bill, Indiana Democrat Tim Roemer asked DeLay if he'd read the Executive Summary of the World Meteorological Organization's 1994 assessment of stratospheric ozone science—widely considered the most authoritative examination of the ozone problem. DeLay said he had not read the paper. "My assessment is from reading people like Fred Singer," he trumpeted. John Doolittle also cited Fred Singer, who had earlier testified before the committee that policy makers had been "misled or bamboozled" by "twisted" science on ozone depletion. When Doolittle was asked whether his conclusions were based upon any peer-reviewed research, Doolittle replied with a verbatim quote by Rogelio Maduro in a recent article in LaRouche's *Intellectual Review,* "I do not get caught up in the mumbo-jumbo of peer-reviewed articles."

Thus, mainstream scientific findings about global warming, acid rain, and the ozone hole are attacked by fringe scientists like Singer and Maduro, who are in turn promoted by right-wing hate-radio hosts like Rush Limbaugh or by media hungry for a boxing match, and finally by government officials on the industry payroll. By using scientific "confusionists," the largest corporations on earth, for relatively small amounts of money, can control public perception of the planet. Writing about scientists like Singer in *Harper's* magazine in December 1995, author Ross Gelbspan observed that "Their dissenting opinions are amplified beyond all proportion through the media while the concerns of the dominant majority of the world's scientific establishment are marginalized. By keeping the discussion focused on whether there is a problem in the first place, they have effectively silenced the debate over what to do about it." They have thus succeeded in creating an impression that scientific understanding is on the same level as political opinion: that one opinion is as valued as the next, and since there is no objective truth, there is no more validity in acting to solve environmental problems than there is in not acting. "I can produce as many scientists who say that there's not global warming as they can produce scientists who say there is," says Rush Limbaugh. Through such efforts, the search for truth devolves into the kind of know-nothingism that characterized the 104th Congress.

At the same time that congressional leaders were glorifying aberrant scientists and parroting the industry line that "more study is needed" before taking legislative action on problems like global warming and toxic pesticides, they were using their budget knives to assure that "more study" would not soon occur. The Republican Congress hastily gutted scientific research budgets in a way that will long erode our country's ability to discern the truth. On October 12, 1995, the House approved a $21.5 billion science budget that explicitly prohibited the EPA from conducting *any* research on global warming. Congress also cut funding for non-military science by 33 percent, slashing NASA's Earth Observing System program, vital to comprehensive monitoring of the Earth's climate and biosphere, by $332 million.

It also cut designated funding to the National Institute of Environmental Health Sciences, which funded seventeen programs at sixty universities to study the impacts of toxic chemicals on human health. And, in an era when the richest U.S. fisheries are being depleted or closed, Congress proposed cutting research on fish populations by 60 percent and eliminated the National Oceanic and Atmospheric Administration's vital research program on zebra mussels, an imported European mussel that has already cost billions in damage to U.S. public water systems and natural habitats and is now threatening the New York

City water supply and many others. Congress cut in half its alternative pesticide research program and eliminated the Department of Interior's research divisions including the National Biological Survey, which researches national issues like wildlife migration patterns and wildlife diseases.

Perhaps the most significant cut of all was one that went largely unnoticed by the media or the public. During the last week of September 1995, Congress permanently shut down the Office of Technology Assessment, the research agency founded in 1973 to ensure that congressional decision making was founded on good science. One of Washington's smallest agencies (with a $22 million budget and two hundred employees), it played a pivotal role in many policy debates affecting space programs, the military, medical policy, and the environment. No other organ existed to assist Congress with impartial advice on the many technical and scientific decisions it makes. The message was clear: Congress preferred to get its science from Fred Singer and his press releases. "If you believe in a rational universe, in enlightenment, in knowledge, and in a search for the truth, this Congress is an absolute disaster," one scientist told us.

In 1994, industry's years of investment in political organizations, greenwashing, front groups, think tanks, and phony science paid off by laying the groundwork for the most anti-environmental Congress in the nation's history. We watched, almost helplessly, as twenty-five years of environmental legislation was eviscerated by industry's champions on Capitol Hill. The new Congress avoided debate on the merits of the bills by rushing them out of committee, concealing them as riders on appropriations bills, or making themselves masters of what Ralph Nader called "the fabricated, phony, incomplete anecdote." It was a trick perfected by the Wise Use movement in its effort to "give anti-environmentalism a human face." Ron Arnold and his followers had learned that by invoking anecdotes about the small landowner, logger, or rancher they endowed corporate self-interest with the moral prestige of victimhood. "They came up with an outrageous anecdote invoking a one-in-a-million problem where some farmer goes to jail because he filled a wetland," Oklahoma congressman Mike Synar told Bobby. "Then they exaggerate it. They convince the public through sincere repetition that this is a national problem." Recognizing the power of the parable, Tom DeLay and his antiregulatory point man

Congressman David McIntosh of Indiana bolstered their case for drastic regulatory reform by falsely claiming that OSHA required bricks to be treated as hazardous substances and that the city of Anchorage was required to add fish guts to its sewage effluent because it wasn't "dirty" enough under federal regulations. The anecdotes were repeated indignantly on the floor and recited in television, radio, and newspaper ads. According to an often-repeated story, dentists were required to confiscate baby teeth as hazardous waste. Outraged congressmen warned that government bureaucrats were out to abolish the Tooth Fairy.

The most potentially devastating anti-environmental legislation passed by the House was the Regulatory Reform Bill. Majority Leader Robert Dole, who was pushing his own version in the Senate as his principal initiative for drumming up industry support during primary season, had hired Kyle McSlarrow, a partner in the law firm of Hunton and Williams, as his chief counsel in drafting the bill and ushering it through Orrin Hatch's Judiciary Committee. Hunton and Williams was the principal lobbying firm for the oil, chemical, mineral, and power industries. We frequently faced them in litigation against Mobil Oil and the electric utilities on the Hudson. The House version of Regulatory Reform, which passed on February 7 as part of the Contract with America, gave industry veto power over all future environmental laws. Hunton and Williams' Senate version was even worse. It made current environmental legislation unenforceable and explicitly gave industry immunity from investigation and prosecution for violations of all health and safety laws. The legislative loopholes that Hunton and Williams drafted for their clients were so arcane and complex that Orrin Hatch's Republican committee staffers, charged with managing the bill, were unable to explain the provisions to minority counsel. At the Senate markup, the committee was forced to call in three senior partners from Hunton and Williams to explain the bill to the minority staff. Phil Weich, Senator Kennedy's chief of staff, led a walkout from the session. Beginning on January 6, Hunton and Williams senior partner Turner Smith sent out lobbying solicitations to polluters across America promising a "quiet behind-the-scenes intervention" in drafting special antiregulatory provisions. Georgia Pacific, the nation's largest wood products processor, arranged to insert a special provision designed to kill an ongoing Justice Department prosecution for Clean Air Act violations at twenty-six of its paper plants. The company's counsel told the *New York Times* that putting the exceptions in the legislation "was easier, quicker, and cheaper than litigating."

The bill was worth billions to regulated industry. The oil and chemical industries were salivating over a provision that repealed laws requiring employers to protect workers exposed to toxic material at the workplace. Among the bill's staunchest supporters were tobacco companies, which were fighting new regulations intended to curtail teenage smoking. The Dole bill also pleased meat and poultry industry lobbyists by blocking the Agriculture Department Safety Inspector system designed to keep deadly E-coli bacteria out of the nation's meat supply.*

Under the direction of attorney Kyle McSlarrow, the industry groups mounted a campaign of similar intensity to the one that drove Regulatory Reform through the House in February. The Senate's Democratic leadership seemed to collapse under the barrage of phone calls and industry pressure.

It was clear that the bill would easily pass on a floor vote, but President Clinton had promised to veto and environmentalists thought they might have the forty votes needed to sustain a filibuster if Democratic leadership took on the issue. By midwinter Bobby was making regular trips to Washington, D.C., on behalf of Riverkeeper and the NRDC to lobby political leaders to oppose the environmental rollback in early spring. Minority Leader Tom Daschle told Bobby, "We know this is a bad bill, but that's not what we're hearing from our constituents. If you want us to stand up to it, you've got to get some [constituent] activity going. We can't do anything unless you get out your troops." Our troops, however, were in disarray. We were running in front of the congressional steamrollers and being crushed. Even our most dynamic leadership was in despair. Surveying the damage, NRDC Executive Director John Adams commented, "They are young and mean and powerful, and everything they believe is exactly the opposite of what I believe. It's two different Americas. And they are rolling over us."

---

*Meat contamination sickens five million Americans and kills four thousand each year. Proposed regulations would force stockyards to change slaughtering practices that mix animal fecal matter with consumer foods.

During the first votes on Newt Gingrich's Contract with America only a handful of Democrats remained loyal to environmentalism. Even when the Clean Water Act was gutted, Democratic stalwarts like Barney Frank voted with the Republicans. "Clinton moved to the right," John Adams recalled. "He signed the Timber Salvage and Unfunded Mandates. For a time there was just no sign for hope or rescue."

Our allies became pariahs in the House. Republican Sherry Boehlert, a confirmed environmentalist from New York's Adirondack Region, found himself enduring derisive comments from his radical colleagues as he worked the House floor. Even John Kasich, the most moderate and thoughtful House leader, dismissed Boehlert as irrelevant because of his environmentalism. "Sherry is not one of the accepted Republicans," he told Bobby.

The newspapers and press were, if not cheering Gingrich on, simply ignoring the issue. Environmentalists had been successfully painted as radicals and were generally ready to accept defeat. Some national leaders talked about disposing of our environmental laws and starting from scratch. The national groups had lost touch with their grassroots membership and revenues had been dropping for years.

Meanwhile, Republican after Republican rose to extol the virtues of the Regulatory Reform Bill. When Paul Simon asked for an opportunity to speak against the bill, the Senate leadership told him, "We can't get you floor time." With stalwarts like Simon unable to take the floor, the moderates like Bob Kerrey, Chuck Robb, Jay Rockefeller, and Kent Conrad, whom we counted on to support a filibuster, were wavering. During spring recess in Palm Beach, Teddy Kennedy told Bobby that the bill was a fait accompli.

On May 31, 1995, Pat Robertson's 700 Club sent out a fact sheet to all Capitol Hill Republicans that took note of environmentalists' statements that Congress was dismantling the bulwark of America's environmental laws and answered the charges with the simple quote from Genesis 1:28: "And God blessed them; and God said to them, fill the earth, and subdue it."

At that point, environmentalists were still shell-shocked and only beginning to regroup. Twenty-six national environmental and health groups had organized under the NRDC's John Adams as the Green Group. The new group's secret weapon was Gregg Wetstone, who lost his congressional post as environmental committee counsel during the

January purge and moved to the NRDC where he began putting together coalitions and nailing down a strategy for the counterattack. A group of foundation and individual funders led by Pew charitable trusts had given them $3 million to educate the public about the congressional attack on environmental laws. The environmental coalition started producing fact sheets to counter industry lies and phony science. Bobby joined the Sierra Club, the NRDC, and others in visiting editorial boards and selling them on our issue. Bobby began a whirlwind tour, speaking to over fifty thousand people in eighty cities and towns to inform Americans about the assault on their environmental rights. We strongly believed that were the American people aware of Congress's assault on environmental protection, they would rise up against it.

Bobby continued his regular trips to Washington to meet with Senate and House leaders and White House officials in an effort to help derail the rollback of environmental protections. In each meeting he related the plight of the Hudson's commercial fishermen, who had lost hundreds of jobs from the kind of pollution that would revisit the Hudson Valley if the Regulatory Reform Bill was enacted. In virtually every one of his meetings, it was this story of the fishermen that convinced the senators and congressmen to pause and listen. The Republican House had so successfully used "victim of the system" anecdotes to cast environmentalists as unfeeling bureaucrats and environmental groups as "just another inside-the-Beltway special-interest" that many of the politicians had forgotten that environmental pollution has very real human victims and that environmental laws are meant to protect people. Bobby's affiliation with the fishermen gave him a special standing to demand a response from political leaders. In other words, the fishermen gave environmentalism its human face.

On the local level, Riverkeeper shifted easily to guerrilla warfare, sounding the alarm on our home ground and mounting local campaigns against Sue Kelly. We called her office, sent letters, and denounced her vote at our Spring Shad Fest, an annual convocation of over one thousand Hudson Valley environmentalists and political leaders, which she and Governor Pataki attended. Hudson Valley environmentalists, including Scenic Hudson and Clearwater, also sent a deluge of faxes to local papers and picketed Kelly's offices. Bobby and Westchester County's other congresswoman, Democrat Nita Lowey, held a press conference condemning Kelly's votes. When she voted for

Bud Shuster's Dirty Water Bill, and called her environmental critics "extremists" in a letter to the editor of the *Putnam Courier,* the formidable Hudson Valley environmental community was outraged. Over Memorial Day recess, Sue Kelly rushed back to the district to soothe her angry constituents. At a series of packed meetings across Westchester and Putnam Counties, Kelly tried to explain her vote on the Dirty Water Bill to seething constituents. When we appeared at one of her informal "meetings" and complained about the devastating effect of her votes on fishermen and the water supply, Kelly kicked us out. Our expulsion caused a firestorm of protest and more negative stories in the Hudson Valley press.

The buzz among political insiders was that Kelly's anti-environmental stand would cost her reelection. When Kelly sought to establish an environmental advisory committee, John Cronin, Larry Rockefeller of the NRDC, and Tensie Whelan of the New York State League of Conservation Voters refused to serve and released their rebukes to the local media. The League of Conservation Voters had strongly endorsed Kelly's candidacy the previous autumn. Now Whelan equally strongly denounced the freshman congresswoman, saying, "She has not lived up to her promises."

Kelly got the message. After voting wrong on the first six environmental bills, she voted right on the next ten. Gregg Wetstone saw her on CNN and called us to thank us for turning her around: "Your congresswoman is now a great environmentalist," he said. "It's like she had a brain transplant. She sounded like an NRDC board member." In early October 1995, the *New York Times* ran an article on the remarkable transformation of Sue Kelly. It was our first glimpse of the potential for victory.

We were delighted to find that we weren't alone—all over New England and the Pacific Northwest, local environmentalists had gathered from their disarray to organize, punish, and persuade congressional members over recess. Finally the media began to cover the story. The *New York Times* published a front-page article on March 31, 1995, detailing how industry had been allowed to write the Dole bill. Isolated articles and editorials began to appear in the *Washington Post* and other papers. The *New York Times* and *Washington Post* ran a series of investigative reports and editorials exposing how federal environmental statutes were all being rewritten by regulated industries.

When Dole called for a vote on the Regulatory Reform Bill on July 17, he failed to mobilize the sixty votes necessary to end debate. Seven votes shy, Dole pulled the bill from the floor to give himself time to find a compromise.

The final vote was on Thursday, July 20, 1995. A last-minute change of heart by influential Senator Chuck Robb gave environmentalists forty-two votes, just enough to thwart Republican efforts to end a filibuster. But Robb and Dole were scrambling frantically to engineer a compromise.

Cartoonist Garry Trudeau administered the coup de grâce, devoting the first week of August to a hilarious lampooning of Dole's bill in his Doonesbury cartoon. The cartoon depicted Dole's Senate packed with industry and tobacco lobbyists drafting legislation. By the week's end the strips were being passed around the cloakroom by nervous senators. "The bill is dead, you guys killed it, and Doonesbury is burying it for you," Senator Kennedy reported to Bobby in a call from the Senate cloakroom on August 9.

Beginning with the Doonesbury strips the national press began waking up to the industry takeover on Capitol Hill. The mainstream press raised the specter of an E-coli epidemic. Now Dole's bill was nationally criticized as part of an industry drive to repeal rules protecting Americans from contaminated meat and dirty air and water. The president, sensing a political home run, publicly condemned the bill by saying that it would assure "more tragedies like what happened to Eric Muller," the California boy who died after eating an infested hamburger. Dole's positive numbers dropped six points during the debate as the senator was portrayed in Doonesbury and in op-ed press across the country as leading the charge to dismantle environmental protection and sidetrack rules that would protect Americans from contaminated meat. Our victory over the Dole bill turned the tide in the battle. The press began to scrutinize a legislative process that had been hidden in the smoke-filled corridors. For the first time since November, the public began to understand that its environmental rights were being stolen. Bad press derailed the Dirty Water Bill and the Superfund rewrite as well as Don Young's Extinction Bill.

Western hook-and-bullet types, regarded by Republican congressmen as core adherents of the Wise Use agenda, bridled at the giveaways of public lands and moneys to the welfare robber barons.

Alaskan fishermen flew to Washington to successfully block Senator Frank Murkowski's bill to clear-cut the Tongass National Forest. On October 18, Ron Moody, president of the Southeastern Montana Sportsmen's Association, called on hunters and anglers in Montana to rise up and say "no way" to legislation cosponsored by Montana's Senator Conrad Burns to transfer Bureau of Land Management lands to the states.

By December, Tom DeLay was openly admitting that the Republican leadership had miscalculated in their environmental assault. "I'll be real straight with you," he told the *Wall Street Journal.* "We have lost the debate on the environment. I can count votes."

On October 18, a widely read *Time*/CNN poll showed the American public firmly opposed to the Republican's environmental agenda: 63 percent of Republicans, 67 percent of Independents, and 61 percent of Democrats opposed weakening of environmental laws.

The polling was no surprise to the poll-savvy House leadership. As early as March 1995 Gingrich's pollster, Frank Luntz, had found almost identical numbers. "I've warned my clients that they are not in the mainstream when it comes to the environment," Luntz told Bobby during a candid moment following a debate. "Americans want regulatory reform, but if you mess with their air or water, God help you. They feel that clean air and water are inalienable rights."

On November 2, 1995, in the "environmental vote of the year," the House, in open revolt against Gingrich and DeLay, voted to strip the seventeen anti-environmental riders from the EPA appropriations bill 227–194, with 63 Republicans voting in favor.

The win was a stunning demonstration that environmentalists could once again mobilize the grassroots quickly. The Sierra Club, U.S. PIRG, and the Green Group delivered eighty-five mail sacks to political leaders on Capitol Hill the day before the vote. Altogether they generated one million signatures by Americans demanding back their environmental rights. The defeat, Gingrich's first on a major bill, shocked Republican leadership. One in four Republicans voted against it. A badly shaken John Kasich, an Ohio Republican, told *USA Today* that Republicans needed "a whole reassessment of what we are doing on the environment."

By January, the tide had turned completely. A poll that month by Republican pollster Linda Divall found that 55 percent of Republicans no longer trusted their party to protect the environment. Thirty Republican moderates publicly attacked Gingrich for a year of "missteps" on the environmental issue that they said "hurt the people and the party." It was the first open rebuke of the Speaker from within his own party. President Clinton, an inveterate poll watcher, saved his only harsh words in an otherwise conciliatory State of the Union Address for the Republican attack on the environment. The president recognized the enormous advantage that the Republicans had handed him and claimed environmentalism as a central element of his presidential campaign.

The environmental movement was once again a vibrant grassroots campaign. When the Washington State legislature approved a "takings" bill, environmentalists quickly mobilized to get the initiative on the ballot and then motivated Washington voters to reject it two to one. A week after the State of the Union, Oregon congressman Ron Wyden ratcheted the environmental issue into an election victory for Bob Packwood's abandoned U.S. Senate seat. Wyden, who won by twenty thousand votes credited his victory to his strong environmental stands. The Sierra Club alone turned out fifty thousand voters to the polls.

Contributions and membership subscriptions to the national environmental groups were soaring. By February, eighty-five thousand new members had joined the NRDC, mobilized by anger at the Republicans. For the first time since the 1970s, the nationals were firmly in touch with local people and their concerns.

But even as we were celebrating, the seeds of future battles were germinating. Minutes of a December 12, 1995, strategy session of American Petroleum Institute lobbyists, one of the masterminds of the regulatory strategy, recorded senior staff agreeing that "there will be another Regulatory Reform fight in 1997. Industry will want relief again . . . but this time the industry needs new spokesmen and new strategy."

They blamed the "extremely anti-environmental" radical Republicans for being too open in "seeking a general rollback of environmental regulations" and in their efforts "to abolish EPA." They concluded that industry made a mistake in betting all its money on the radicals. "The Republicans are too easy to shoot down as serving special industry interests when they argue for changes in environmental policy. Corporate welfare is a continuing 'running sore' for the Republicans."

The minutes contain repeated observations that industry itself is a poor spokesperson for industry because it is not trusted.

The memo concludes that industry must develop new spokesmen to lead the regulatory reform battle: a trusted business leader, a New England Republican moderate, a religious leader, or perhaps a local environmental leader who could "bypass the national organizations." Al Moore, the API secretary, observes that new leaders "should say that they are not cutting the EPA budget to harm the environment. They are cutting because EPA is wasting money and catering to special interests like the ethanol lobby," or say that the changes in the regulations are "necessary to maintain effectiveness." They should employ anti-regulatory anecdote. "Industry should humanize stories about people hurt or unemployed by regulation. . . . We need horror stories to say that we cannot afford such a foolish system."

The petroleum institute's stealth strategy was quickly adopted by the chastened-but-not-changed 105th Congress to disguise a new round of anti-environmental mischief.

A March 1997 memo, "Citizens for a Sound Economy," advised lobbyists and the new Congress to push "efficiency" but not "cost-benefit analysis," a phrase that might remind voters of the "traditional relationship that exists between the GOP and business." Recalling the regulatory reform debacle, the right-wing think tank urged that the better pitch is not "reform . . . it is modernizing"; and don't attack "extremist" environmentalists, says the memo, but "be nonthreatening." Anti-environmental legislators were quick to integrate the advice. Speaking to the National Cattlemen's Beef Association on March 20, 1997, Senator Larry Craig of Idaho—a Wise Use icon—warned fellow Republicans against talking about "changing or reforming" environmental regulations because most Americans believe such regulations have improved the country. Craig said he had "adjusted [his] own vocabulary" to employ more palatable terms like "modernizing and improving" when he tries to sell anti-environmentalism to the public.

By May 1997, environmentalists were once again fighting pitched battles in the House and Senate against anti-environmental Republicans seeking to roll back the Endangered Species Act and Superfund and promoting a "Pave the Parks" rider that would have deregulated road construction on all federal land. As of this book's publication, environmentalists are battling a Frankenstein-like regulatory reform bill patched together from the moribund pieces of the Dole/Gingrich bill.

Anti-environmental radicals like Helen Chenoweth and Billy Tauzin mounted a series of ferocious personal attacks on Republican moderates, especially Sherry Boehlert, who crossed them by opposing an insidious slashing of the Endangered Species Act that the Republicans attached to an emergency funding bill for flood victims in the Dakotas and California. Republican Don Young, chair of the House Resource Committee publicly threatened retribution against the moderates and promised to oppose any positive environmental legislation that might reach the House floor. Speaker Gingrich sided with the anti-environmentalists, telling Capitol Hill reporters that he would make moderate Republican Boehlert "irrelevant to GOP environmental policy."

We were discouraged by these reminders that this was a battle that would never end; our enemy would return after each defeat in a new guise.

At the same time we were heartened by our own strength. In early March, when the Cattlemen's Beef Association ran newspaper ads suggesting that cattle grazing helps preserve clean waterways, leaders of the American Fisheries Association, the Bass Anglers Sportsman's Society (BASS), the Izaak Walton League, and Trout Unlimited jointly released a public rebuke asking the cattlemen to "listen to the better angels of their nature" and to "put more effort into good works as opposed to public relations." An industry-funded poll in March 1997 showed the highest percentage of Americans ever—79 percent—believed the environmental laws should be maintained or made stronger. We could count on a solid core of 54 Republican moderates and 172 Democrats on every environmental floor vote. And most importantly, the links between the national groups and the local groups is stronger than ever—and the hunters and fishermen are back where they ought to be, among the strongest supporters of the environmental agenda.

# CHAPTER 10

# The Human Place

Both of us came to our environmentalism as a human issue, John as a former commercial fisherman who watched a livelihood and culture and community being destroyed, Bobby from his family's legacy of public service.

We migrated from restless boyhoods upriver into the Hudson Valley to settle and make our stand. We were drawn to the Hudson River Fishermen's Association and its emphasis on man at work in nature. Amid communities that relied for centuries on the river for its fisheries, commerce, and tourism, injury to the river by polluters was an attack on livelihoods and families and communities measured in lost jobs and income, spoiled beaches, contaminated public lands and water supplies, and the erosion of stunning natural landscapes.

The word "ecology" derives from the Greek *oikos* meaning "household" or place to live. Ecology, for us, is about our homes, our neighborhoods. We believe that the struggle to develop communities that are models for human dignity is the essential struggle of American history.

In a wonderful essay on the western writer Wallace Stegner, Wendell Berry portrays American history as a tension between two conflicting impulses; the first of these is the "Jeffersonian vision of Democratic communities rooted in a settled independent, frugal life on small freeholds." Stegner called the adherents of this vision "stickers" or "nesters."

In contrast was the plunder-and-run tradition of the American boomer that had little to do with building community or democratic institutions and much to do with greed. Stegner, "who was born into the frontier's failed and still failing dream of easy wealth and easy escape," recognized the pull that the boomer vision exerted on his father, who "wanted to make a killing and end up on easy street."

In his novel *The Big Rock Candy Mountain,* Stegner describes the seductive hold of the boomer mentality. "Why remain in one dull plot of earth when heaven was reachable, was touchable, was just over there?"

Stegner recognized both impulses in himself and recognized that the choice between nester and boomer was a moral one. The preference for settlement, Berry observes, means a commitment to caring.

The Riverkeeper movement is about fostering such commitment. The Hudson Valley sports examples of both paradigms; boomers like General Electric that came for a short time to mine our resources and then escaped with their profits, and nesters, the many communities that fought fiercely against such exploitation and succeeded in preserving the river and its rich traditions.

By placing boats on the Hudson and other rivers and equipping them for patrol, Keepers make a statement: we are here to stay. We are investing in our community by providing for its defense. With the help of an armory of legal weapons to punish anyone who attacks our public resources, Keepers engage in the struggle that goes to the soul of our country.

Americans don't share a common culture, history, language, race, or religion. What we do share, what makes us American, is our commitment both to democracy and to our land. Boomers see land as a commodity. The nester vision derives from the dawn of American consciousness and holds that this land is sacred, given to us to build a community and fulfill a special destiny.

Perry Miller, one of America's greatest historians, traced the roots of that consciousness to a moment in 1630 when John Winthrop, the "Moses" of the Great Migration, stood on the deck of the flagship *Arbella* to deliver a lay sermon to his Puritan followers. Winthrop told the Puritans that the immeasurable wealth of the new world to which they were sailing was being given them not to improve their station but to form a better community "both civil and ecclesiastical." God had appointed them for this mission, and "Wee [sic] are entered into a covenant with Him for this work." Winthrop warned his followers against the empty lure of materialism, power, comfort and amenity, personal acquisition and wealth. Their obligation was to use the divine gifts to build a model commonwealth. "For wee must consider that wee shall be as a city upon a hill, the eyes of all people are upon us."

Winthrop's speech gave a sense of mission to our nation and culture and firmly ensconced the idea in the American consciousness that the people of this nation had a duty to fulfill some higher destiny commensurate in magnitude with the gift of the new world.

In the hundred years following Winthrop's sermon, New Englanders were counseled to resist the impulse of "following the lure of real estate into a dispersion that would quickly alter their character," and to keep their attention focused upon their higher purpose—their "errand into the wilderness." That sense of special spiritual mission flowed from New England and inspired the other North American colonies. It would be adopted by each successive wave of immigrants who entered this country and it would dictate how America was viewed in the eyes of the world.

The notion of America's obligation to use its natural bounties to build model communities was a principal theme in American literature in the centuries between Winthrop and Lincoln. A central tenet of American nationalism, it distinguished the American pioneers from the Latin American conquistadors, whose purpose was to mine the landscape and move on. American writers were convinced that Americans, by their ability to tap the primordial vitality of the wilderness, would be blessed not only with unheralded prosperity but with superior culture and morality that would, in turn, benefit all humanity.

But America's march westward was marked by a less noble impulse—a migration driven not by hunger for culture and community and spiritual mission but by a greed for self-enrichment, power, and wealth, an impulse Winthrop had warned would cause the Lord "to break out in wrathe against" our nation.

In *Democracy in America,* written in the late 1830s, Alexis de Tocqueville described this type of frontiersman "march[ing] across these wilds, draining swamps, turning the course of rivers, peopling solitudes and subduing nature. . . . He clutches everything, he holds nothing fast, but soon loosens his grasp to pursue fresh gratifications." For the boomer, nature was not God's creation to be approached respectfully; as Colorado governor William Gilpin, herald of *America's Manifest Destiny,* trumpeted, "Progress *is* God."

James Fenimore Cooper caricatures the boomers in each of his books. He contrasts their exploitive and restless conduct with that of Natty Bumppo, who honors nature and uses it respectfully. Bumppo is the crafty woodsman hero of Cooper's leather-stocking tales, including *Last of the Mohicans*. He embodied all the virtues assumed by nine-teenth-century romantics to be associated with nature—courage, self-reliance, strength, fortitude, honesty, innocence, and self-restraint.

Cooper was not such a romantic simpleton as to portray our national destiny as a choice between pristine wilderness or raped moonscape. Indeed, Cooper does not hold Bumppo up as the only paradigm. Cooper recognized that Bumppo's wilderness was doomed to pass and portrayed also the America he hoped would emerge from the settlement of the wilderness. In *The Pioneers,* Judge Marmaduke Temple is Cooper's idealized American settler. He loves nature and the landscape, and tends his farm with a benevolence, wisdom, and sense of beauty that Cooper hoped would be the product of the inevitable civilization of the American wilderness. Cooper envisioned commu-nities emerging from the American wilderness that would retain the vitality of their primordial beginnings and achieve a national character and level of virtue commensurate with the world we were given.

A generation after Cooper, the nineteenth-century American tran-scendental movement also condemned the roving, ravaging conquis-tador spirit as the darker side of the American character. Writers like Ralph Waldo Emerson and Henry David Thoreau championed a vision of rooted, wholesome, democratic communities that embraced nature as the spiritual parent of all Americans. Thoreau, who we think of as the philosophical progenitor of the Riverkeeper movement, rec-ognized the importance of wilderness to our national character and heritage; he conceived the idea of the national park as a place of spiri-tual renewal. At the same time, he found wilderness enough to occupy all his faculties in a small pond not far from Boston. He adopted Emer-son's notion that a man firmly planted in a single spot will learn more of the world and experience more spiritual growth than can be achieved through the endless stimulation of restless wandering. Thoreau went into the woods not to escape civilization but to make himself more civilized. The self-reliance he cultivated in the forest was not about selfishness, but self-restraint—the cornerstone of commu-nity. Echoing Winthrop's admonition, he called upon his fellow Amer-icans to re-commit to meeting "the expectation of the land."

What Thoreau and other writers did in prose, American artists did in oils. American art's defining schools, the Hudson River School and the Western School of Remington and Russell, portrayed nature's most indomitable landscapes and often captured the historic conflict between romantic nature and boomerism. Hudson River School founder Thomas Cole's most famous series, "The Course of Empire," depicts on five giant canvases the rise of a new American civilization from a vast wilderness forest, presided over in each stage by a lofty stone peak. The first canvas shows primal forests. In the second, pioneers have transformed the wilderness into pastoral landscape. The third depicts the hillside carpeted with magnificent civilization. In the final two canvases the civilization is sacked by barbarians and left a lifeless ruin, mirroring the same apprehension of doom that Cooper foreshadowed in scenes of reckless boomer greed in *The Pioneers,* Melville portrayed in *Moby-Dick* and Faulkner in *The Bear,* and that Fitzgerald personified in the restless, destructive Buchanans in *The Great Gatsby.*

In America's early political as well as literary culture, virtue was thought to reside in the countryside. The leaders of the American Revolution were profoundly influenced by the European enlightenment philosophers of the eighteenth century, who believed that God was all around. His will could be discovered by the open and rational mind through the observation of nature, which would reveal divine truths about the relationship of men to each other and to God, and the proper structure of political institutions. The "natural law" of the enlightenment philosophers provided the intellectual underpinning for America's democratic revolution.

Most of the constitutional framers shared Thomas Jefferson's vision of a nation rooted in the soil. Jefferson believed that the integrity of our democracy would be sustained by stable communities rooted in land-based occupations such as fishing and farming. Among American presidents, Jefferson was typical in his conviction that the study of nature was a civic and political duty. Indeed, the presidents who have spoken to the American people with the most universal resonance have been those most rooted in the soil. Washington, Jefferson, Lincoln, and the Roosevelts—the men who would top almost every historian's list of the nation's most revered presidents—all boasted unusually strong ties to the land. All of them were competent naturalists. Their close connection to the earth gave them a special clarity of vision about the destiny of our nation.

By the end of the nineteenth century, the philosophical battle between boomers and nesters was being fought out in real-life range wars that pitted frugal homesteaders against rapacious cattle barons and their hired guns like Billy the Kid. As usual, the boomers had not only wealth and weapons but a primal biological imperative on their side. Long-term conservation of resources was not a high-priority survival skill rewarded by natural selection. Our biological evolution has hardwired us to destroy the planet. As we approach the millennium, the population explosion and new technologies have brought the human race within striking range of that objective. Now we must either transcend biological instincts and live sustainably or perish. Only spiritual fire can overcome a biological drive.

One sunny afternoon in 1985 we found ourselves seated at a wooden picnic table on a grassy knoll amid the broad hayfields that surround Riverkeeper's Garrison headquarters at the toe of Sugarloaf Mountain. We sipped sodas and ate cold cuts and spoke with our visitor, Thomas Berry, a Catholic priest who has spent many years thinking about the relationship of human spirituality to the environment. At one point we challenged him with the most controversial episode in America's history of environmental advocacy, the two-and-a-half-year construction delay of Tennessee's Tellico Dam for the sake of the endangered snail darter, a two-inch fish without economic significance. Only in the United States has a mega project been halted or delayed on a minnow's behalf. "How could we put a minnow before people?" we asked Berry. "How could we have delayed a project that might have provided jobs and energy? How could our priorities be so skewed?" Berry was silent for a moment as he composed his answer. "Because," he said slowly, "we know somewhere inside ourselves as Americans, that if we lose a single species, we lose part of our ability to sense the divine." This is a notion that we considered individually and discussed between ourselves on many occasions over the next decade.

Berry's notion that creation is a tableau that reveals God's will is not original. Since ancient times nature has been the primary mechanism for talking about God. From the hymn writers, poets, and the pagan philosopher Aesop, to countless myths attending the spiritual beliefs of Native Americans and aboriginal peoples on every continent, to the modern Christian theologians, mankind's spiritual leaders have found "tongues in trees, books in the running brooks, sermons in stone and good in everything." The great religious books preach that of all the tools we use to understand God—be it scriptures, art, music, or literature—the picture we get from nature is the most graphic and complete.

Organized religion is a human effort to establish community around a set of moral precepts. It is no wonder that stewardship is a universal mandate of organized religion. We best praise the divine by being part of this community and by respecting its other members.

Japanese Shintoism linked God to nature and fostered love of wilderness over pastoral nature since it was the essence of the deity, uncontaminated by man. Indian Jainists and Buddhists and Chinese Taoists projected cosmologies in which man is part of a community of all living things. Each of these traditions emphasized compassion toward nature as a divine virtue and portrayed the beasts and birds as man's companions and helpers in our search for the divine. The central tenet of the Hindu religion is respect for all creatures.

The Koran prevails upon believers to behave as *Khulafa' Allah,* God's caliphs toward creation. "The world is green and beautiful," Mohammed tells his followers, "and God has appointed you stewards over it." The Koran warns believers that the way they care for the earth will be among the deeds by which their end is determined at the final judgment.

God's love for His creation is a recurring theme in the Old Testament. While God puts Adam and Eve in the garden as stewards, He retains title to the lands. The Genesis story of Noah's ark can be read as a mandate for biodiversity. God told Noah to bring two of *all* creatures aboard the ark for preservation, not just those that could demonstrate "current economic value."

The Jewish and Christian traditions offer abundant support for Thomas Berry's conviction that each creature says something unique about God, and that the preservation of biodiversity is a spiritual priority.

"God," observed St. Thomas Aquinas, "produced many and diverse creatures so that what was wanting in one as representative of the divine goodness, might by supplied by another . . . hence the whole universe together participates in the divine goodness more perfectly, and represents it better than any single creature whatever."

The Christian tradition begins with the birth of Christ in a manger, surrounded by animals. He discovered His divinity for the first time as

He spent forty days alone in the wilderness, communing with nature, and virtually all of Christ's parables were drawn from nature.

At the same time, an early passage of Genesis has caused much consternation to environmentalists: "Be fruitful and multiply, and replenish the Earth, and subdue it; and have dominion over the fish of the sea, and over the fowl of the air, and over every living thing that moveth on the Earth." Beginning with Francis Bacon and more recently Pat Robertson, James Watt, and other leaders of the anti-environmental movement, advocates of "dominion theology" have invoked this passage to justify the rapacious conduct of corporate polluters. In emphasizing the exploitive strains of Christianity, these right-wing fundamentalists have ignored the overwhelming biblical mandates for stewardship. But later Genesis passages explain that God placed Adam in the Garden to "serve and keep" it and to "till and tend." In other words, God puts man in charge of nature, He doesn't give him a license to destroy it. "Human beings received mastery because they are fit for service as agents of Providence and capable of restraint," Aquinas explains. "Human dominion over nature must be consonant with normal dominion over human appetites." An axiom to the notion of stewardship is the belief that pollution is sin— an abuse of trust in our relationship with God and an injury to the community. A passage from Isaiah foreshadows John Winthrop's warning that God's wrath would visit the nation that treats nature irresponsibly:

> *The Earth mourns and withers*
> *The world pines and fades,*
> *Both heaven and Earth languishes.*
> *The land lies polluted,*
> *Defiled by its inhabitants*
> *Who have transgressed the laws,*
> *Violated the ordinance*
> *And broken the covenant*
> *Therefore a curse consumes the land*
> *And its people burn for their guilt.*

Stewardship is not the equivalent of ownership. "The land shall not be sold forever for the land is mine, where you are but strangers and guests of mine. In all the territory you occupy, the land is to be redeemed" (Leviticus 25:23–24). Early Christians believed God had so clearly intended His bounty for all men that private property, in itself, was sinful.

Aquinas modified this view, arguing that the possession of private property must be subordinated to community needs since God created nature for the common benefit of humanity. "Private property is not decreed by God and exists only by human agreement," says Aquinas. "But private property is justified only so long as its use is 'for the common benefit of all human beings.'" Aquinas believed that a property holder's legal dominion was legitimate only so long as he was acting on behalf of the larger community.

Acknowledging that human beings in possession of private property do not always act responsibly, Aquinas anticipated environmental law when he commended the development of civil laws to assure that landowners behaved for the "common benefit."

Of all Christian philosophers, John Calvin has been castigated by environmentalists as the theologian least friendly toward nature and most inclined to elevate individual achievement over community values. Even Calvin believed that the only justification for exercising dominion over nature or property was for the benefit of the community of man—for the common good. To abuse nature was to sin against God and other humans. In a sermon recently translated by Professor David Little, Calvin said, "Each time we are inclined to ravage or pollute nature in some way, we should remind ourselves that our Lord has placed us to live in this world and He has given us things which He knew would be beneficial to our life. . . . Am I worthy that the Earth should sustain me when I wish to obliterate God's grace for my neighbors as well as myself? Do we deserve to be sustained by nature if we do not let nature follow its own course, obey its own rule?"

In contrast to Pat Robertson's simplistic notion that private property is sacred, and that laws that protect wetlands and endangered species constitute "environmental terrorism," mainstream religious leaders have upheld the more nuanced view that private property is sacred only so long as it serves the community. Though the Christian Right dismisses environmentalists as "pagans who worship trees" and equates the contemplation of nature with pantheism, every mainstream religion, including Christianity, recognizes that men and women may love nature and care for the Earth without making it the object of devotion.

Rather than elevating the human spirit, Robertson's interpretation of Scripture and his mission emphasize the grimmest vision of the human condition. He embraces intolerance, selfishness, pride, arrogance toward creation, and irresponsibility to the community and future generations.

The deviate genius of boomerism has been to persuade the public that it is robbing the public till for the public good. Corporate boomers and charismatic leaders like Ron Arnold, Pat Robertson, James Watt, and Rush Limbaugh distract the public with cleverly constructed lies and the invocation of scapegoats. In order to divert attention from corporate pilfering, they spread the word that the environmental movement is opposed to basic American values: private property, free markets, sound science, community control, democracy, a strong economy, and individualism.

But on close examination, their version of private property rights would sacrifice both private and public property to the right to pollute. They envision a nation in which government entitlements to the poor and elderly are abolished but individuals with political clout can escape the discipline of the free market and garner huge subsidies and the right to pollute—all at public expense.

Their version of "sound science" is the phony pronouncements of corporate shills like Fred Singer. Beyond the obvious irony that has the same government officials calling for "sound science" while slashing scientific funding lies a subtler and more insidious paradox: The very leaders that condemn the trend toward moral relativism are fostering and encouraging the trend toward scientific relativism. This is significant because science is more than a policy tool or a profession. Science, like theology, reveals transcendent truths about a changing world. At their best, scientists are moral individuals whose business is to seek the truth. Over the past two decades, industry and conservative think tanks have invested millions of dollars to corrupt science. They distort the truth about tobacco, pesticides, ozone depletion, dioxin, acid rain, and the fate of the striped bass. In their attempt to undermine the credible basis for public action (by positing that all opinions are politically driven and therefore any one is as true as any other), they also undermine belief in the integrity of the scientific process and its capacity, ultimately, to discern the truth.

Their version of "community control" is really corporate control. They promise to dismantle the federal government and return power to the states where business lobbyists dominate the political landscape and where big business can blackmail localities by threatening to leave if the community tries to protect its citizens' health and welfare. They ignore the federal guarantees of individual and environmental rights that grant communities and citizens control over their destinies.

We believe that, in Teddy Roosevelt's words, "The nation behaves well if it treats the natural resources as assets which it must turn over to the next generation increased, and not impaired, in value." As trustees of the public trust, our generation may live off the interest of the land, but we must preserve the capital value for the next generation. Riverkeepers are emissaries for those future generations, as well as for the vulnerable members of our communities who don't always participate in the political process. It is the poor and working people who are most burdened by environmental injury. They host the toxic dumps and incinerators and sewer plants, work in the factory fumes, pay for bottled water they can't afford, and suffer in stifling city apartments when public beaches are closed. Meanwhile, the wealthy can cut and run— they can enrich themselves by polluting our rivers or felling our ancient timber, and then fly off to some private paradise behind a guarded driveway. The rest of humanity is left with contaminated and denuded landscapes.

The bulk of the everyday citizen's wealth is in nature, unspoiled landscapes, beaches and oceans and rivers to fish and swim, pure water to drink, and air to breathe. Our laws decree that all these things belong to the public. Our fight is against those who would use these things up.

One of the principal characteristics of the Riverkeeper movement is its willingness to use litigation as a tool to protect local communities. On behalf of the disenfranchised, the poor, and the future generations, we elbow our way into the courtrooms or the hidden corridors of Capitol Hill and the state capitols where the public trust commodities are being divided and dispersed by the corporate polluters and their indentured servants who occupy the political offices. Using the law, the press, and the political tools of our democracy, we take our place at the table and demand justice.

No modern development in government has brought power and decision making within closer reach of the common citizen than environmental laws, which provide for permit hearings, community participation in planning and zoning decisions, citizen suit provisions, and right-to-know laws. When government fails to enforce the law against a polluter destroying a community resource, citizens may step into the shoes of the government prosecutor and do it themselves. When government elects to site a toxic dump or incinerator in your community, each citizen has a right to participate in that decision. The government is required to thoroughly explain and justify each decision and to study its costs and benefits so that communities can make informed decisions about allocating their resources and planning their futures.

Although the boomer manifesto claims that we must choose between economic prosperity and environmental protection, our experience on the Hudson has persuaded us that good economic choices are *always* good environmental choices so long as we measure the strength of our economy by how it sustains jobs and the dignity of jobs over generations.

For human dignity to be fostered, a community must be sustainable. Its long-term economic viability is tied to the investment made toward safeguarding its environment. Investments that ensure a clean, healthy environment do not, as the boomers argue, diminish our nation's wealth. We must invest in our environmental infrastructure— clean rivers, clear air, safe foods, proper disposal of toxic wastes and recycling—in the same way that we invest in our transportation and telecommunication infrastructures. If we doubt that such investments are financially sound, we have only to look at those nations that failed to invest in their environments.

In Bangkok, a city of ten million where there is no Clean Air Act, the average child permanently loses seven IQ points by age six because of contaminated air. In the former Soviet Union, unprotected by a stringent nuclear regulatory review process, one-fifth of the state of Byelorussia and fifteen thousand square miles in the Urals are now *permanently uninhabitable* because of nuclear accidents. In Brazil, the mayor and other public officials of the town of Cubatao will not live in the city because of the industrial gases. Of every one thousand babies born in the town, forty are dead and many more are grossly deformed. Almost all are born in a weakened state. Air pollution in Mexico City closes vital state industries for weeks and forces drivers to abandon their automobiles half of all working days. These are all examples of communities shattered and lives impoverished or lost because of the boomer mentality that says that investments in the environment are an unnecessary luxury. They reveal our own future if we dismantle our environmental laws, as the boomers and the congressmen they influence are urging. Already, within our own borders, environmental catastrophes like the PCB contamination of the Hudson testify to the fiscal imprudence of pollution-based prosperity. Oceanographer Sylvia Earl has said that "the economy is a wholly owned subsidiary of the environment." We ignore that relationship at our peril.

The sound-bite platitudes of "property rights" and "free markets" and "states' rights" are repeated by boomers with such mantric regularity that they have become gods unto themselves. While all of them are important elements of our heritage, they are only legitimized in our political, legal, and religious traditions so long as they build communities. Part of the pain of caring and living in a community is exercising restraint and acknowledging that our own claim to possession of the land is not absolute but is limited by our obligations to the community and to future generations. The rights of the individual are important, but individualism alone, without a balancing commitment to community, is a disastrous social formula. Environmentalism is about asserting the power of community, which is the primary source of human dignity in the postindustrial age.

Environmentalists share some of the blame for the rise of anti-environmentalism. By speaking about nature's "rights" and by arguing that environmentalism is defending nature for nature's sake, some environmentalists have fallen into the trap of pitting nature against humanity. Such arguments are easily exploited by the boomers and invariably lose the attention of everyday Americans whose primary concerns are jobs, health care, or social and economic injustice.

The factory workers and commercial fishermen who gathered at the American Legion Hall in Crotonville in 1966 understood that human beings are part of nature and that if we want healthy, wholesome people and communities, we must preserve our connections with the land and water. As Riverkeepers we protect nature, not so much for nature's sake, but for the sake of humanity. Nature enriches us economically, but we have other appetites besides money. These hungers—spiritual, cultural, and aesthetic—must be fed if we want to grow as we are meant to—if we are to fulfill ourselves. When we diminish nature, we impoverish ourselves. We are not fighting to preserve the great northern forests, as Rush Limbaugh would argue, for the sake of the spotted owl. We are preserving those forests because we believe they are more valuable to humanity standing than cut down. And we aren't fighting for the Hudson just for the sake of the sturgeon, striped bass, and shad, but because we believe that we and our children will have richer lives in a world where these fish thrive, where fishermen on the river wait for the tides and repair their nets, where their families and others can eat their catch. In such a world, our children can connect themselves to 350 years of New York State history and feel that they are part of something larger than themselves—a community. We want them to have clean drinking water, safe fish to eat, and a safe river upon which to play, and we want the river to be integrated into the lives of the Hudson Valley community. We don't want our children to face a world where humans have lost touch with the seasons or the tides and those things that connect us to our American culture, to God, and to the ten thousand generations of human beings who lived before laptops. We can, and do, protect the environment for ourselves. We should engage the debate on behalf of humanity as a whole.

As Seneca Chief Oren Lyons once told Bobby, "It's vanity to say we are protecting nature for the sake of the planet. The planet is four billion years old. Its crust is forty miles thick. It has survived freezing and warming and volcanoes and earthquakes. Nature will survive without us. But what will we be without nature?"

If the environmental movement is to be a force in American politics, it must have relevancy in the daily lives of the majority of Americans, who will never visit Yellowstone. We must engage not only in the important battles over distant wilderness but in the local issues that affect people's livelihoods and health. The national environmental legislation, so critical to the success of our movement, is at its most effective when it empowers people in their daily lives, when it focuses on making communities better, safer places to live and raise children.

Since Earth Day 1970 the power of the environmental movement has rested in people. The movement's early successes at grassroots organizing won environmentalists a place at the bargaining table and by the 1980s the power centers of the movement had moved to large offices inside the Beltway. The battlegrounds were hearing rooms within the regulatory agencies and on Capitol Hill. The shift in focus away from grassroots organizing and the arcane and technical nature of the debate caused a gradual erosion of the movement's power base. It lost touch with the people who gave environmentalism its human face and with the powerful human stories that had driven the movement— DDT, Love Canal, and Times Beach, Missouri. Meanwhile the boomers were cultivating a cast of regulatory victims to "give anti-environmentalism a human face," like the alleged farmer who threw sand in a ditch and was jailed for filling a wetland, like the logger who lost his job because of a spotted owl. They portrayed environmentalists as insensitive ideologues or affluent elitists who put trees ahead of people. Many of our natural constituents—hunters, fishermen, and farmers—turned their backs on the environmental agenda. Some even joined the Wise Use movement.

We were able to avoid the worst of those pitfalls in the Hudson Valley. Riverkeeper was born of a grassroots movement fueled by people power and never lost touch with its power base. Riverkeeper's long relationship with the NRDC testifies to its board's abiding conviction that it is critical for the national environmental groups to exert national leadership and to work the power centers in Washington, D.C. But the movement will wither if local environmental leaders fail to make those national battles relevant at the community level. Tip O'Neill's proverb "All politics is local" applies to environmental politics as well.

During the 1980s, Riverkeeper and the Hudson's other environmental groups made concerted, systematic efforts to maintain contact with local people. Leaders of the commercial and recreational fishing communities sit on our board and give direction to our work. We took on the causes of the fishermen, representing them in permit actions against GE and the DEC and the railroads. We visited their homes and made sure to take our student attorneys out on the fishing boats during shad season to remind them that as hard as they fought for the river, their clients were human beings. We continually emphasized the central tenet of the Riverkeeper movement—the idea that all members of a community are the owners of its resources and that injury to those resources is an act of theft against each member. Our role as Riverkeepers is to redress that theft on behalf of communities and to bring the perpetrators to justice. As commercial fishermen in the Gulf states and elsewhere signed on to the Wise Use agenda, Hudson Valley rivermen remained committed to the environmentalist camp. But we didn't help just the commercial fishermen and anglers. We represented grassroots groups across the Hudson Valley, and we have been rewarded by strong support from each of these communities. When we asked for support at a public hearing about New York City's water supply, more than a thousand citizens showed up to deliver testimony.

Since contact with nature helps individuals and communities to flourish, the Keepers fight to reunite Americans with their lands and waters. Pollution is robbing us of our connection with nature. The Hudson is now the only major estuary in the East with all spawning stocks of its historical fish species. Virtually all of the nation's other great fisheries are in danger of collapse. But despite the Hudson's abundance, most of its fish are no longer available to the public thanks to General Electric. Railroads and industrial pollution have stolen our shores. The twenty-six-acre site at Hastings-on-Hudson is just one example of hundreds of thousands of waterfront acres across America now being fenced off as brownfields and toxic waste sites.

Some people regard wilderness preservation as the central focus of the environmental movement. Indeed, the availability of wilderness for spiritual sustenance and renewal is important to every people and to Americans in particular. Since we lacked the thousands of years of culture that defined that national character of the European and Asian peoples, American leaders have always looked to wilderness as the source of our national virtues and values.

Nevertheless, as Bob Boyle pointed out as early as 1964, we can't satisfy our need for nature by preserving distant islands of wilderness that relatively few Americans will ever visit. Placing so much emphasis on wilderness protection raises the perilous axiom that man can put nature in a place and live outside it. "If we preserve some places," the rationale might be, "it's okay to destroy others. Civilization has its place and nature's is elsewhere." Riverkeeper's philosophy is that for communities to flourish and human dignity to endure, nature must be much closer at hand. Regular contact with the land and water plays a vital role in reviving our senses and defining our sense of common purpose.

In a well-intended effort to protect nature from increasing human pressure, environmentalists have occasionally supported passage of laws that embody the "look but don't touch" philosophy that we consider harmful and counterproductive. It is, for example, illegal in New York to pick up a blue jay feather, for a child to catch a frog, gather minnows for an aquarium, or care for a baby crow that has fallen from its nest. It is a violation of federal law to pick pine cones in the Black Hills, or dinosaur bones on the Badlands where they break from the ground after each rain and rot within a few months of exposure. Well-meaning environmentalists wrote many of these laws. It's time to reexamine them.

Today we are losing touch with the earth and our place on it; the human place. And as we lose touch with our nation's indigenous flora and fauna, the rivers and streams that created our history and culture, and the occupations of fishing and farming that were our principal industries, we lose touch with our identity as a people, our sense of mission and our sense of nationhood. We become a rootless people who can find meaning only in the accumulation of more goods. Community disintegration, rootlessness, selfishness, and the associated epidemics of racism, sexism, and violence, are all by-products of our loss of a sense of place.

At its best, our American heritage celebrates our attachment to the land, air, and waters of home—be it plain, savanna, estuary, port, flyway for geese, or byway for pigeons. That heritage, profound and immutable, is reflected in our religions, our arts, our culture, and our vocabulary, but most especially in our rich democratic tradition from which descends our right to protect our lives, our homes, and our communities. Our work in the Hudson Valley, in the courts, and in the Riverkeeper movements around the country is about every American's right to that heritage, that tradition, and that protection.

# Appendix

## Directory of Riverkeeper Programs

**National Alliance of Waterway Keepers**
Headquarters:
25 Wing & Wing
Garrison, NY 10524-0130
Mailing address:
Pace Environmental Litigation Clinic
78 N. Broadway
White Plains, NY 10603
Tel: 914-422-4410
E-mail: kmadonna@keeper.org
Web page: http://www.keeper.org

**Cape Fear Riverkeeper**
617 Surry Street
Wilmington, NC 28401
Tel: 910-762-5606
Hotline: 800-380-3485
Fax: 910-772-9381
E-mail: cfrw@wilmington.net

**Casco Baykeeper**
2 Fort Road
South Portland, ME 04106
Tel: 207-799-8574
Fax: 207-799-7224
E-mail: keeper@cascobay.org

**Catawba Riverkeeper**
Catawba River Foundation, Inc.
P.O. Box 35008
Charlotte, NC 28235-5008
Tel: 704-376-5888 or 87-RIVERKEEPER
Fax: 704-376-5888 or 803-789-7007
E-mail: fmclauri@charweb.org
Web page: http://www.catawbariverkeeper.org

**Cook Inlet Keeper**
P.O. Box 3269
Homer, AK 99603
Tel: 907-235-4068
Fax: 907-235-4069
E-mail: keeper@xyz.net
Web page: http://www.xyz.net/~keeper

**Delaware Riverkeeper**
P.O. Box 326
Washington Crossing, PA 18977-0326
Tel: 215-369-1188
Hotline: 800-8-DELAWARE
Fax: 215-369-1181
E-mail: drn@delawareriverkeeper.org
Web page: http://www.delawareriverkeeper.org

**Hackensack Riverkeeper**
1000 River Road T090C
Teaneck, NJ 07666
Tel.: 201-692-8440
Hotline: 877-CPTBILL
Fax: 201-692-8449

**Hudson Riverkeeper**
Castle Rock Field Station
Route 9D
Garrison, NY 10524-0130
Tel.: 914-424-4149
Hotline: 800-21-RIVER
Fax: 914-424-4150
E-mail: info@riverkeeper.org
Web page: http://www.riverkeeper.org

**Long Island Soundkeeper**
P.O. Box 4058
East Norwalk, CT 06855
Tel.: 203-854-5330
Hotline: 800-933-SOUND
Fax: 203-866-1318
E-mail: likeeper@netgenie.com
Web page: http://www.soundkeeper.org

**Narragansett Baykeeper**
434 Smith Street
Providence, RI 02908-3770
Tel.: 401-272-3540
Fax: 401-273-7153
E-mail: narraganbay@keeper.org
Web page: http://www.savethebay.org

**Neuse Riverkeeper**
Neuse Station
427 Boros Road
New Bern, NC 28560
Tel.: 252-447-8999
Fax: 252-447-6464
E-mail: neuseriver@keeper.org
Web page: http://www.neuseriver.org

**New York/New Jersey Baykeeper**
American Littoral Society
Sandy Hook
Highlands, NJ 07732
Tel.: 732-291-0176
Hotline: 800-8-BAYKPR
Fax: 732-872-8041
E-mail: nynjbay@keeper.org
Web page: http://www.nynjbaykeeper.org

**Peconic Baykeeper**
Save the Peconic Bays
2560 Paradise Shore Road
Southold, NY 11971
Tel.: 516-765-4145
Fax: 516-765-4024
E-mail: baykeeper@savethepeconicbays.org

**Petaluma Riverkeeper**
521 Walnut Street
Petaluma, CA 94952
Tel: 707-763-7756
Hotline: 800-KEEP-BAY

**Puget Soundkeeper**
1415 West Dravus Street
Seattle, WA 98119
Tel.: 206-286-1309
Fax: 206-286-1082
E-mail: pskeeper@halcyon.com
Web page: http://www.halcyon.com/pskeeper

**Sacramento/San Joaquin Delta Keeper**
3536 Rainier
Stockton, CA 95204
Tel.: 209-464-5090
Fax: 209-464-5174
E-mail: deltakeep@aol.com

**San Diego Baykeeper**
1450 Harbor Island Drive, Suite 205
San Diego, CA 92101
Tel.: 619-299-4484
Fax: 619-299-4485
E-mail: sdbaykeepr@aol.com
Web page: http://www.geocities.com/~baykeeper

**San Francisco BayKeeper**
Presidio Building 1004
P.O. Box 29921
San Francisco, CA 94129-0921
Tel.: 415-561-2299
Hotline: 800-KEEP-BAY
Fax: 415-561-2290
E-mail: baykeeper@aol.com

**Santa Monica Baykeeper**
P.O. Box 10096
Marina del Rey, CA 90295
Tel.: 310-305-9645
Hotline: 800-HELP-BAY
Fax: 310-305-7985
E-mail: baykeeper@earthlink.net

**Tualatin Riverkeeper**
16340 SW Beef Bend Road
Sherwood, OR 97140
Tel.: 503-590-5813
Fax: 503-590-6702
E-mail: bwegener@orednet.org
Web page: http://www.tualatinriverkeepers.org

**Upper Chattahoochee Riverkeeper**
1900 Emory Street
Suite 450
Atlanta, GA 30318
Tel.: 404-352-9828
Fax: 404-352-8676
E-mail: rivrkeep@mindspring.com
Web page: http://www.chattahoochee.org

**Willamette Riverkeeper**
408 SW Second Avenue, Suite 210
Portland, OR 97211-0606
Tel.: 503-223-6418
E-mail: info@willamette-riverkeeper.org

# Index

285